Church of Lies

Church of Lies

Flora Jessop
and
Paul T. Brown

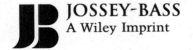

JOSSEY-BASS
A Wiley Imprint

Published by Jossey-Bass
A Wiley Imprint
989 Market Street, San Francisco, CA 94103-1741

ISBN 978-0-7879-9462-4

Printed in the United States of America

Contents

Part Three: Outlaw

Part Four: No More Pain

This book is dedicated to all abuse victims and survivors.
Freedom, love, and family were things twisted and rotten,
but courage, strength, and dreams of safety carried us to a
new life. Hold your heads high, know you are worth being loved,
and let the world see your tears while you look them in the eye.
God is not vengeful and vindictive. Believe in a just and
loving God. Escape the fear and shame of abuse.
Only by breaking the cycle can we finally be free.

To those who abuse: the sin is yours, the crime is yours,
and the shame is yours. To those who protect the perpetrators:
blaming the victims only masks the evil within, making you as
guilty as those who abuse. Stand up for the innocent or
go down with the rest.

Acknowledgments

This book is not about blame. This book is about the things that happened to a child with no way to protect herself and no one to help. I know many good people who live polygamy, but I know none who live polygamy and are happy. I also come from the inside where the protection of the predators is the norm and shunning, shaming, and abusing the victims is common. This abuse of the victims continues today against those who have broken away, only wanting to be free and loved without the conditions imposed by the doctrines of polygamy.

This book is true and is about my experiences growing up in the Fundamentalist Church of Jesus Christ of Latter Day Saints (FLDS). I never wanted conflict; I only ever wanted to be free. For those born into the FLDS, freedom comes at a very high price, staying comes even higher.

If you are God's chosen people, does it never cause you to wonder why He would require you to throw away the families you are supposed to be fighting to spend eternity with? If you spend eternity with those you are with now, can you imagine the agony eternity will be? Break the cycle, and take your minds away from the poison that has become your mantra, where children are sacrificed to deviants and crimes are glorified as the sacred rights of the priesthood. Remember what love feels like. Blind obedience to evil is still evil.

I have many people to offer acknowledgment to for many different kinds of contributions to the writing of this book:

To my brothers and sisters who are still members of the FLDS—I love you all. I know some of you are angry, but I believe your anger comes more from what you are told to think rather than the truth of what I do. I hope someday you all have the freedom of thought to understand that God never asks His children to shun family because they choose a different path. God brought us all into this world as innocent children, and it is the cycle of abuse we were raised in that destroyed the family we were. I hope someday the cycle ends so we can be a family again.

To Mom—you gave me life, and I will always fight to give you yours. I hope someday you will recognize that *all* of your children need and love you. I hope God gives you the strength to find your way to your grandchildren who need you too. We all love and miss you Mom.

To Ruby—a promise was made, and that promise I strive to keep. Freedom is never a lost dream. I love ya, Sis.

To my brother Joe—I got to know you while you were in a coma, and God answered my prayers to pull you through. You are an amazing man, and I am so proud of your integrity and honor. You have broken the cycle. The amazing gift your children give me allows me to keep sight of why I fight for those of our family who remain inside. I will always fight to preserve the innocence of all the children.

To my brother Patrick, who fought for America's freedom while denied the freedom to see his own mother—never let the past catch up, and never let the future come too fast.

To my brother Robert, who has the strength of many and the humor of one—you have the ability to make the sun shine wherever you go.

To my brother Ryan, who was like my own babe—you started out like us all but have found promise in family. Hope to see you soon.

To my brother Lyman (Mom's seventeenth child)—you have the pain and sorrow of a twisted legacy to overcome but you have those who came before to help ease the suffering. Keep your head up, and know that we all suffered as you have. You have the gift of your brothers who understand what you feel but will never let it overwhelm you.

To all my brothers—I thank you for accepting what I do even though you don't always agree. The concept of acceptance and family were foreign to our world until we each took steps to change our thinking. How sad that we grew up together but only got to "know" each other after we left. Let's go to the lake.

To Phillip Jessop—thank you for loving me enough to set me free.

To Dad, Joe C. Jessop—thank you for your part in God's education of me. Without the knowledge you gave me of what a child suffers from the ultimate betrayal of love and trust, I would not know how to help the children I fight for.

To Brent Jeffs, Carolyn Jessop, Kathy Jo Nicholson, Debbie Palmer, Elissa Wall, and Les Zitting—for having the strength to step into the light and the courage to expose the lies behind the mask. Though the sacrifice is bitter, the rewards are the freedom to choose and discover the true meaning of family and friendship. I also acknowledge all those who even though not mentioned by name here have had the courage to step outside the box and grab happiness.

To Ronald and Jenny Larson—thank you for providing a sanctuary amid the chaos. You taught me how to laugh at the world instead of letting it make me cry. Without your support and humor, it would be a dark world indeed.

To Richard Mahoney, who cared more about the children in Colorado City than the political machine—because of your help and the sacrifice you made, the abuse within polygamy was exposed. You brought it onto the table, where ignorance and collusion would never again be accepted or tolerated. You are a true child advocate and hero. God bless you.

To Donnell Diepstraten, Ila Ferguson, Elaine Anderson, and Patsy Lambert—you showed me more friendship and honor than I ever thought was possible between women.

To Don and Drew Hamrick—for raising an amazing family and allowing me the honor of sharing your lives. I miss you, Don, and I've got some new toys to show ya.

To Terri and David Routh—for taking a chance on a sixteen-year-old who was nothing but a child. Thank you for giving me the stability of a real home, the acceptance of a real family, and the guidance of a real mom. You gave me the security and rules needed but never judged me when I made mistakes (of which there were lots).

To Terry Sexton—you gave me the most precious gift of all, my daughter Shauna.

To Kris Sexton—you were a child when we met and you gave me the unconditional love only children are capable of. I was honored, blessed, and humbled by the time I spent with you. You were an amazing child, became an amazing man, and will always be Shauna's amazing brother. I love you.

To Chris and Pridgette Turner—you taught me that racism is for the ignorant and introduced me into a world of acceptance and love.

To Joni and Carl Holm—thank you for sticking it out when the going got rough. You are amazing and my love for you is immense. You provided shelter to many, and because of your knowledge and understanding, there are many who have been given a gift beyond measure by your acceptance with love.

To Candice Miracle and Ron P., who provided a home and security for two girls with battered spirits—you gave those girls a great start on their road to freedom.

To Travis and Julie Fuller, who finally got the chance to have a daughter to love—I will forever regret the heartache you suffered when the system failed both you and a child you loved as your own. You gave all you had to a child worth fighting for. Thank you.

To Jan Brown, who has taken the time to understand our world and provide sanity, love, patience, and understanding for those you hold dear—I admire your strength and dedication to those you try so very hard to protect and support.

To Kathy Jo Nicholson and Brian, who have lost so much and felt such overwhelming pain because of it—I hope you both find peace, and while we shall never forget Johnny, you must learn to live with his light not the shadows of his memory. Never stop fighting for those you love.

To Mohave County Supervisor Buster Johnson—for having the guts to stand firm and for watching my back. You have given more of your time, talents, and self than I will ever be able to repay. You are truly one of a kind.

To Sam Brower—for his ability to track 'em down and hang 'em high.

To Jane Irvine with the Arizona attorney general's office—you have been true and honest and I thank you for that.

To Washington County attorney, Brock Belnap—for having the courage to fight and the integrity to protect the victim.

To Jim Ashurst, Jay Beswick, Rowenna Erickson, Doug White, Dennis and Carol DeFrain, Doris Redlin, Grace and Terry Longacre, Mary Carol O'Malley, KaDee Ignatin, Nancy Mereska, Robert Coody, and all the rest who have given so much to help others.

To David Lujan, Donnalee Sarda, Maureen Williams, and Ginger Wooden at Defenders of Children—without the support and services you offer I would have been lost. You have taught me so much about advocacy, truth, and ability. You believed in the victims first and won my gratitude forever.

To Joel Brand, an attorney worth more than words can say—your dedication to children is amazing and your drive for justice has given renewed life to so many.

To Representative David Lujan, former Senator Linda Binder, and the late Senator Marilyn Jarrett of Arizona—you had the guts to stand for what's right and worked hard to establish better protection for the children.

To Mike Watkiss, the best reporter I know—you have had the integrity and honor to recognize the abuse and spend thirty years exposing the truth. Without your determination and dedication to children everywhere, the victims would have no way of getting the help they need to escape. By telling their stories, you bring into the light the abuses and without your shining a light on the stagnant quagmire of social agencies, justice would still be only a dream. Thanks too to your wonderful family, who has shared you with polygamy without complaint.

To Pastor Larry—for showing me that church was not always hellfire and brimstone.

To Linda Walker—for being my friend and adviser.

To Aunt Betsy Sandy—for teaching me how to raise my children with patience and love.

To Carol, my mother-in-law, who taught me God did not equal Evil—before your love and gentle guidance, I was lost on an ocean of anger and hate. Thank you for the time you spent helping me to understand and find a loving and forgiving God that I am proud to believe in. Thank you also for your wonderful son, who is my heart.

To Shauna and Megan, my two amazing girls who taught me more about love, life, friendships, childhood, family, and fun than I ever knew was there—through you I was able to experience the things I missed, and will be able to experience many more good times. You have both become such beautiful young women, and I am so proud of you both. Continue to be free, stand tall, and always look them in the eye.

To my husband, Tim, the man God gave me so I could overcome the past and strive for a better future—we have had fourteen wonderful years together and I wouldn't trade them for anything. You have held me up when the pain and fear for the helpless overwhelms me. When shattered lives rip me to shreds, your love holds me together and your strength helps me grasp what is important and release what is not. You are my husband, my heart, my courage, my rock, my friend. I love you always and I thank God for you.

To my coauthor, Paul Brown—for his faith, support, and friendship. It's been a pleasure working with you.

Of course to my agent, Craig Wiley—thank you for your enthusiasm for this project.

To the folks at Jossey-Bass—for their first-rate work.

Church of Lies

Introduction

My Name Is Flora Jessop

My name is Flora Jessop. I've been called an apostate, vigilante, and crazy bitch, and maybe I am. But some people call me a hero, and I'd like to think they're right too. If I am a hero, maybe it's because I just didn't know what else to do. Or maybe it's because every time I can play a part in saving a child or a woman from a life of servitude and degradation, I'm saving a little piece of me, too.

I was born in Pligville. That's what some of us there called the society of polygamous families living in the side-by-side border towns of Colorado City, Arizona, and Hildale, Utah—all members of the Fundamentalist Church of Jesus Christ of Latter Day Saints, FLDS, the cult that would later be led by the notorious Warren Jeffs.

I was one of twenty-eight children born to my dad and his three wives. Indoctrinated to believe that the outside world was evil and that I resided among the righteous, I was destined to marry a man chosen for me by the FLDS leader, the Prophet. I would then live in harmony with my sister-wives, bear many children, and obey and serve my husband in this life and throughout eternity.

But my innocence didn't last long. While still a child, I understood that the church of the righteous was nothing but a church of lies.

When I was eight years old, my father sexually molested me for the first time, raping me when I was twelve. I tried to kill myself. Being beaten, molested, taunted, and abused by family members alleging they only wanted to save my soul became a daily routine. I ran from this abuse more than once in my early teens—even attempting to cross the desert on foot. My family hunted me down. I thought government agencies would provide safety for me if I reported my father. Instead, the police and social services staff colluded with the FLDS to return me to my family, and I ended up back inside polygamy, right where I had started.

When I was fourteen I ran away with the help of an underground railroad and wound up living in Las Vegas. I was in a nice woman's home but alone most of the time, and when I got scared, I called my Uncle Fred Jessop to come and get me. Instead of taking me home to my mom, however, he and his first wife, my Aunt Lydia, locked me up in a small room for over a year to teach me to obey without questioning. Shunned, isolated, and alone, I thought they would never let me go. Suddenly, when I was sixteen, the Prophet arranged a marriage for me to one of my first cousins, Phillip. Dad gave me a choice: marry Phillip or be sent to a mental institution for more confinement. So marriage it was. Once again I plotted my escape. After only three weeks I convinced Phillip to drive me to Las Vegas to start a new life. Finally, I was free!

With almost no understanding of the outside world, few social skills, and only a correspondence course GED to serve as a high school diploma, I made every mistake imaginable, darting from one bad situation to another. Convinced that I was already condemned to hell, I partied harder. Before long, the cocaine and bad company wasted me. Then, at my lowest point, I looked at my sunken eyes in the mirror and a miracle happened. I realized that I didn't have to die to go to hell: I'd been born there. *But I didn't have to stay there*. I stopped beating myself up. I cleaned up. But I continued to be a magnet for abusive men.

I hooked up with a man with a young son. I loved that boy dearly. Soon I found myself pregnant with this man's child and with the birth of my baby daughter, I experienced feelings of joy and happiness unlike anything I had ever known. Dancing in a topless bar gave me enough money to support myself and my baby, but the work began to grind me down.

Then I met a different kind of man, good and true, and eventually married him. In the quiet of a happy life, a strange thing happened—I started to feel the fury that had been building up inside for all those years. When I heard that my youngest sister, Ruby, had tried to break away from an arranged marriage at age fourteen, I tried and failed to save her. And then all hell broke loose.

I understood that there were others beside myself who needed help—thousands of children and women were suffering in polygamy, just as I had. Condemned to a life of ignorance, brainwashing, and brutality; treated like property; producing as many as sixteen children; dying prematurely, all used up . . . I was so damn mad, I decided I would spend the rest of my life saving every last one of them. Rescuing a teenager from polygamy is like taking someone straight from hell and delivering her to heaven. So far, I've saved a few.

But I'm far from done with my journey.

Part One

Pligville

*I'm telling you things that you will have to answer for because in learning these truths, if you don't live by them, it will be to your eternal sorrow. **All disease and sickness is guided by evil spirits.** If you're keeping sweet, you have brought your good friends from the spirit world. If you aren't—if you are naughty and doing wrong, you have brought evil spirits into this building. Now that you have been baptized, you either have good spirits or evil. They are real.*

In your family, there may be brothers, sisters, even mothers—and sometimes fathers, who are evil. The righteous live with righteous in the spirit world. Here, you can hide your sins, lie, do bad and say you're good. When you die, you won't live with the faithful. If you've done certain evils, you'll go and live among people who have done those evils. The righteous and faithful are organized in the family and are in perfect harmony. Death doesn't separate family unless you are rebellious. If wicked, you won't live with the faithful in a family.

—FLDS Priesthood History for 5th–8th Grade Students, taught by Warren Jeffs, Alta Academy[1]

1

The End of Innocence

As I walked through the heavy wooden door into the baptismal building, most of the light disappeared. Outside, it was a warm June day. But inside the stone building, everything was cold and wet: the walls, the floor, the tiny dressing room, barely lit by a single lightbulb. I stared at the ceremonial clothes hanging on the damp wall and felt a deep chill. I was eight years old and scared to death.

I traded my long cotton skirt for one of the thin, white polyester dresses and walked reluctantly to the edge of the large pool in the center of the building—the baptismal font. I stared into the dingy water and cringed. One step at a time, I walked down into the four feet of cold water. My white dress started to rise up in the water like a parachute, but I did as I was told: I held my right wrist with my left hand and my nose with my right index finger and thumb.

An FLDS priest stood in the pool with me. He put his hand on my head. In a loud, deep voice, he said, "Flora Mae Jessop, having been commissioned of Jesus Christ, I baptize you in the name of the Father, and the Son, and of the Holy Ghost. Amen." Then he dunked me under the water completely for a few seconds, and yanked me up, triumphant. I struggled to catch my breath and saw that the wet dress was clinging to my body. You could see right through it. Shamed and embarrassed, I walked out of the pool and took my place on the side, shivering, as I waited for the other eight-year-olds to be baptized. I felt like a human sacrifice.

Finally, we had all been baptized. The priest pronounced a special blessing on us. We were all saints now, he said, no longer children. We were full members of the community in the eyes of God, accountable to the priesthood for everything we did. Then he handed each of us our first "sacred garment"—a one-piece, white union suit that would cover us from wrists to ankles. It was designed to keep us modest and pure.

"Flora," said the priest, "you must wear your Garment of the Holy Priesthood throughout your life. If you are true and faithful to the covenants, it will be a shield that will protect you against evil." He looked at me hard. "And if you are ever caught not wearing the garment, you will be damned to hell!"

The garment buttoned up the front and had a flap I could unbutton when I used the bathroom. My dresses and skirts had to cover it completely at all times, from my shoulders to well below my knees, with sleeves that went to my wrists, even in summer. I had to wear up to eight pairs of nylon panty hose at once, making my legs look thick and bulky, like a rag doll's legs.

The dunking was bad enough, but for me the garment was a death sentence. I knew from watching my mom and my aunts that women usually wore the garment for a week before it was washed. By the end of the week, it generally had stains under the arms and smelled to high heaven. A lot of women were so afraid of letting their body lose contact with the garment that they would actually shower with it on. They'd take off one arm and one leg of the dirty garment, get in the shower, wash and dry that side of their body, put the arm and leg of a clean garment on the clean side of their body, and then start all over again on the other side. I thought my garment was the ugliest thing I'd ever seen, and I hated it on sight.

I looked around at my fellow eight-year-old saints, boys and girls until just a moment ago. The boys, I knew, would be given the priesthood when they turned twelve. After that their mothers would have to be submissive to them. All women must bow to a man of the priesthood, no matter his age. As for the girls, we were marching toward an early marriage to a man we would have no say in choosing. As I stood there in the cold, newly baptized and wholly miserable, I didn't think things could get much worse. But they did, and fast. For me and many other children in Pligville, baptism marked not only the end of childhood but the end of innocence.

I was born in Colorado City, Arizona, on June 12, 1969. For the rest of America the years following the Summer of Love were a time of freedom and protest against the establishment. Young people were making love, not war, and oppressed groups—African Americans, Hispanics, women—were all marching for liberation. But back home where I lived, we were well protected from these "evils" of the outside world. Way out in the desert, between the northern rim of the Grand Canyon and Zion National Park, the twin towns of Colorado City, Arizona, and Hildale, Utah, stand on two sides of a dry wash called Short Creek. They were built on top of the bones of the Native Americans who had lived there for thousands of years before us.

Nearly 10,000 strong, most of us related to each other in a hopelessly tangled family tree, we were still living in a dark pocket of the nineteenth century. With only one road in and the same road out, we were left pretty much to ourselves. Hundreds of miles and many hours away from Las Vegas, the nearest big city, we had our own society and our own rules. And chief among those rules was that only the men had a direct line to God.

According to FLDS tradition and law, God had instructed the men to take many wives and father many children. In return, the men got everything they needed on earth and the promise of glory everlasting. And the wives? They got to do their husband's bidding all of their lives on earth. It was their privilege to bear children year after year and raise them to be obedient members of church. When they grew too old to have more children, they would move aside to make room for their more fertile—and younger—sister-wives. But that was OK! Because when they died, they'd get their reward: they were going to serve their husbands in the afterlife. For eternity.

When I was a little girl, Prophet Leroy Johnson—we called him Uncle Roy—led our commune. Everyone loved Uncle Roy. Along with some other members of the priesthood—including my father's half brother, Uncle Fred—he ran the place. God told Uncle Roy what to do, and he told the rest of us. And he expected total obedience.

In the same way, women were expected to give total obedience to their husbands, and children to their fathers. Husbands and fathers may not have been as exalted as the Prophet, but we all knew that God spoke through them. At least that's what we were taught to believe, and what I did believe. But a few days after my baptism, something changed all that forever.

That day I felt a little wicked—I'd already started cutting down the arms and legs of my sacred garment, and that day I'd decided I wouldn't wear it at all. Who would even know? I wandered down to the barn to see my favorite pony. My dad raised horses, goats, and pigs, and I loved the horses. Maybe I'd go for a ride in the orchard. I expected to be alone, so I was surprised to see my father in there, repairing a piece of equipment. I stopped short in the doorway, keeping my distance.

Even though he was my father, I'd never felt comfortable around him. His temper would flare for no reason, and I'd seen him beat my brothers—one older, one younger—without mercy. Now as he worked he puckered his lips in and out, over and over, a nervous habit. His loose-fitting dentures clicked in his mouth. For as long as I could remember, Dad had worn a complete set of false teeth. He thought it was fun to terrorize the babies and younger kids by pushing his teeth out of his mouth and wiggling them back and forth.

Physically, life had been hard on my dad. He was a small man, only about five feet six and 150 pounds. His hearing had been damaged in an explosion at a construction site, and you had to talk loud to make him hear you. He'd broken his back in another worksite accident. My dad was only thirty-six when I was eight, but he looked much older.

"Hey, Flora." He looked up at me and stopped working. He leaned against a stall door, smiling. He was dressed as he always was, in a western shirt, polyester pants, and cowboy boots, with a shabby straw cowboy hat covering his short black hair. "Come on over here."

I walked over to him, and stood there, silent. He just looked at me.

"You are special, Flora," he said, "my special girl." What was he talking about? He was never nice to me. When I was in public with him, I always wanted to be someone else, because he was nice to people he wasn't related to. Why was he being so nice to me now?

"Come here, a little closer." He looked down at me. I know now that he was a small man and not all that strong. But I was tiny for an eight-year-old, and I thought he was as big as God and just as powerful. He reached out for me and put his hand underneath my dress. I froze. He'd know I wasn't wearing my undergarment! But he didn't seem to care about that.

Still smiling at me, he pulled down my panties. My heart was beating like crazy. I wanted to run home, to my mother, but I couldn't move. What was he doing?

"Sit down and open your legs," he said. Obediently, I dropped down to the filthy barn floor and opened my legs, the lips of my vagina spread wide open. I could feel the sudden rush of cold air on my warm skin, and bits of straw tickling my legs. I couldn't imagine why he would ask me to do this. But he was my dad—the priest of our home. What he did was commanded by God, so he must have a reason. Anyway, I knew what could happen if I didn't do what he asked.

At first my dad just stared at me where I was naked. I couldn't even breathe. I was terrified that someone would walk in and see us. But I wasn't even sure if we were doing something wrong. Then he put his rough, dirty hand on my vagina, unbuttoning his own pants and yanking them down. This skinny tube thing fell out and began to rise up. I'd never seen a man's naked body before, not my father's or brother's or anyone else's. My face felt hot and my mind was racing. I didn't know what was happening.

His penis was getting big now, red and hard. He grabbed it with his other hand and started rubbing it up and down while at the same time sticking his fingers deeper inside my vagina. I sat perfectly still, numb with shock, fear, humiliation, and confusion as he jerked harder and harder, grunting. I thought it would never end. Then some white, gooey stuff spurted out of his penis, and he went slack, moaning.

Without a word, he stood up and fastened his pants.

"Button up," he said, no longer interested. "Get out of here. Now." He went back to work.

I left that barn in a hurry. I was still eight years old, but I would never be a child again.

My dad's abuse soon became a regular part of my life whenever he was home. He worked as an electrician for an FLDS business in Salt Lake City, and would sometimes be gone for two weeks at a time. He'd come home for the weekend then leave on Monday. But on that weekend, on every weekend, he made my life hell.

It was amazing how much abuse my dad could fit into two days. He'd call me into his office and close the door, ready to go. Sometimes he told me to suck his penis. Other times he wanted to ejaculate on my chest or have me bring him to climax with my hand. Weekend after weekend, he made me do everything but have intercourse.

Dad took my soul and twisted it. I had been taught at Sunday school and at home that the only two people in the whole wide world who will do you no harm are the Prophet and your father: they would never do anything to prevent you from getting into heaven. So how could what my father was doing be bad? The confusion I felt overwhelmed me.

We children in polygamy were taught at an early age that sex is bad and your body is evil. We were never supposed to touch our own body or even look at it. To look at my sister's body was forbidden, and even to *think* about looking at my brother's body was forbidden. This had been hammered into me for as long as I could remember. So taking my clothes off and getting naked with my father was not only extremely humiliating, it was damning. I assumed now that I'd go straight to hell.

I thought, *He's my dad; it's just our secret. I'm special to him.* But I knew that what we were doing was wrong. Deep down I sensed the evil of it. My unshakable belief that my dad would not harm me together with my deep sense that the opposite was true—and the FLDS mantra that "perfect obedience produces perfect faith"—kept me on the verge of emotional and psychological hysteria for years.

I wanted to tell somebody what was happening, but I couldn't. I loved my mom, but I knew she could never defend me against him. Even at eight years old, I was made sick by her continual submission to his demands.

When I was growing up, it seemed that Mom was always pregnant and struggling to manage babies in diapers. For a while she gave birth to a baby just about every year—seventeen children. I was the fourth. But she only got to keep ten of us. Dad took seven of the girls away from her as soon as they were born and gave them to my Uncle Fred to raise as his own. But I'll get to that later.

Mom was a small woman—she carried a shade over a hundred pounds on her five-foot, three-inch frame. Like Dad, she wore a full set of false teeth that never seemed to fit just right. And like Dad, she had had a hard life that made her look a great deal older than she was.

From a distance she could have been any FLDS woman. She wore her long, dark hair pinned up in a wave in the front, parted on the side, and woven into a bun in the back. Her traditional, homemade, pioneer-style dresses were frayed and worn. She was always pale—as was typical of polygamous wives, who worked so hard in the house from morning to night that they rarely saw sunshine. Mom's fingers were always so swollen from pregnancy and hard work that she could never remove the only piece of jewelry she owned—her wedding band. Except for her glasses, which she always wore, an outsider would think she looked like she'd stepped right out of the nineteenth century. Her life surely was rooted in another time.

Women's liberation has never come to Colorado City. FLDS women are commanded to be demure and dutiful and to keep a low profile. In this regard, my mom was perfect. Around Dad, Mom was silent and subdued. She spent most of her energy trying to shield us kids from Dad's temper tantrums. When he was out of the house, she was soft-spoken and laughed a lot with us kids. But she couldn't hide her deep, underlying sadness, even from her own children. My mother lived a life devoid of hope.

I would often catch Mom crying silently to herself. She spent much of her time staring into space, a distant, hollow look in her eyes. But she never complained. She never spoke against my dad. She never said a word about the seven daughters who had been taken from her.

Mom had three strikes against her right from the start: she was brought into polygamy as a young girl, she was uneducated, and she just naturally wanted to please people. She played the part of the obedient polygamous wife as well as she could; but even in her thirties, when I was growing up, she was emotionally a child. Polygamous women are not allowed to grow up. How can they, when so often they're married off by the time they're fourteen?

Sometimes I'd come home from school to find my mother sitting on the floor coloring with crayons—and not just with the kids. She often colored by herself or with her sister. They would color like two first-graders. Once I saw the two of them fighting over a crayon. It was heartbreaking. It would take me many years to understand the depth of her pain and the complexity of her imprisonment.

So I knew I couldn't tell my mom about Dad. What good would it do? Besides, the church's motto—"Keep Sweet, No Matter What"—was enough to keep me in line. "Keep sweet" doesn't mean the same thing in the FLDS as it does in the outside world—be kind, charming, considerate. It means that no matter what happens, keep smiling and keep your mouth shut. We were taught that keeping sweet was for our own protection—because no matter how bad things were at home, the outside world was evil incarnate. Hell, people from the outside world were always out to get us. I knew it for a fact. I'd learned it firsthand, on a hot summer day a couple of years earlier.

That day Dad was working out of town and we kids were playing around the house. We were relaxed, having fun. Then the phone rang.

"Hello?" Mom didn't say another word after that, she just listened, but I could see her jaw trembling. She was breathing hard. I got scared. I couldn't imagine what was wrong.

Mom slammed the phone down and ran to the window in a panic. I looked out the window with her and saw two strangers walking toward our house. I had no idea who they were. All I knew was that my mother was upset, and I started to panic too.

"Get down and don't move!" She threw me to the floor. "Kids! Get down here now!" Mom tore through the house, gathering all of us kids, huddling with us on the living room floor. She closed the curtains, locked the doors, and ordered us to start praying for protection from the wicked, evil people who were coming to kill us. I couldn't imagine what was happening.

"Don't make a sound!" Mom said in an urgent whisper. "Pray hard for God's protection." We hugged each other, terrified, praying frantically.

Then we heard a knock at the door. They were coming to get us! We hunkered down lower to the floor, shaking from fear, Mom too.

"Mom, what's wrong?" We'd never seen her so upset.

"Quiet, children," Mom whispered. "They're going to kill us if they find us!" I was so scared I thought I was going to throw up.

They knocked again. We held our breath. Eventually they moved on. Mom told us the coast was clear, and we tried to get on with our day. But I was shaken to the core. That memory is as vivid today as the day it happened.

Years later I realized the people at the door weren't vicious killers, just Jehovah's Witnesses looking for converts. But the consequence of their brief visit was lasting terror. Any time outsiders would find their way into our community, everybody would run inside and lock the doors, hiding from the evil ones and praying for salvation. Parents used this intense fear to control their children, the same way they'd been taught as children.

The brainwashing began in Sunday school. Over and over we were regaled with the gory details of the state government's 1953 raid on Short Creek, Arizona—Short Creek was the original name of Colorado City, our home. We heard the story over and over, from those who'd been there and those who hadn't.

The Church of Jesus Christ of Latter-day Saints—the Mormon Church, or LDS—had outlawed the practice of polygamy back in 1890. But that didn't stop people from "living the Principle"— the so-called holiness of plural marriage. Mormon fundamentalist polygamists had broken from the LDS and had been living in Short Creek for a long time. In 1935, they were excommunicated. They formed their own sect, the Fundamentalist Church of Jesus Christ of Latter Day Saints, or FLDS, and dug in.

The Short Creek community was a thorn in the side of the state and federal governments for more than one reason. The men had multiple wives, which was against the law. They didn't pay property taxes, which was also against the law. And welfare payments to their many children—a practice the FLDS calls "bleeding the Beast"—were a drain on the system. Clearly, these practices needed to be stopped. So on July 26, 1953, Arizona governor Howard Pyle ordered a massive police raid on the polygamists of Short Creek. It should have been an easy win for the government, but it wasn't.

Authorities arrested 122 polygamists, and 263 children were placed in foster care. The newspapers had a field day. Photographs showed sobbing children being taken from their mothers, while their fathers were arrested and hustled off to jail. Much like the raids involving the Branch Davidians in Waco, Texas, and Randy Weaver and his family at Ruby Ridge, Idaho, years later, the Short Creek raid was a public relations nightmare.

In the end not much happened: twenty-three men each received one year's probation. But the hoopla surrounding the raid ultimately resulted in public outrage toward the government and a more tolerant attitude toward polygamy that has continued to this present day. Since then mainstream law enforcement has been unwilling to enforce antipolygamy rules and legislation. A raid that should have put an end to polygamy essentially gave the practice a free pass.

In church and Sunday school in Colorado City, the story of the raid was presented as a cautionary tale: the outside world hated us, wanted to destroy us, and would rip us from our parents' arms. This conspiracy scenario was the basis of our study. We were taught, "If you don't keep sweet, you'll be taken over by the evil outsiders."

"Keep Sweet" is the sacred song of the church, preached with relentless passion. It covers a multitude of sins. It means be modest and pure; obey your parents; obey your husband. But to me and thousands of other abused kids, keep sweet meant keep silent as your father is molesting you. Say nothing as your mom or dad beats you with their fists, a belt, a steel pipe. Do as you're told when, as a young teenager, you're ripped away from the boy you love and ordered to marry a man in his seventies. Smile sweetly through your pain because there is nothing you can do about it. Surrender your emotions to the Principle without question. Accept it or go straight to hell.

I remember those mandatory Sunday church services with dread and loathing. The front row chairs, reserved for the priesthood brethren, faced the congregation. The rest of us worshippers sat facing the priesthood men. People would be called on, without notice, to take the stage and give their testimony—usually about the virtues of plural marriage and the importance of keeping sweet. These hollow, rehearsed statements were said to elevate one's good grace with the priesthood and reinforce the Principle with the congregation.

We all sat there in church for three hours every Sunday listening to the priesthood rant, rave, scream, and pound the pulpit, telling us what little demons we were and how we were all going to hell. They would single out individuals—they'd say that they didn't like the color or the style of dress some women were wearing or that someone's hairstyle was unacceptable. Then they would expand the criticism to the rest of us.

"God finds you *all* disgusting," they would say. "Keep sweet no matter what!"

It was hard to escape the teachings. One Sunday night each month, for two hours, we children attended in-depth theology classes. We were assigned pages from printed literature to memorize beforehand, and in class we had to stand up and recite it all. Other Sunday nights were set aside for "family night." The families would get together and read stories and recount parables as told by older people who had been in the raid of '53. Their tales of terror and brutality at the hands of the authorities instilled fear and distrust of the system and the outside world.

The only thing I liked about Sundays was that they gave my father fewer opportunities to molest me. As long as I was around other people, I was safe from his grasp.

But it wasn't just me whom Dad was after. He was an equal opportunity abuser, and my brother Theral, his oldest son, was one of his favorite targets. Ten years my senior, Theral was a very shy, goofy-looking kid who was always getting picked on in school. Worse, as far as Dad was concerned, he used to pee his pants. This made Dad so damn mad. He would hold on to Theral's arm and drag him around the yard, kicking his butt the whole time, just to get him to stop. But his solutions had pretty much the opposite effect on Theral.

One day when I was really little, Dad had finally enough. He grabbed Theral and said, "I am going to teach you not to pee your pants once and for all!" Then he dragged him out of the house. When Dad came back about an hour later, my brother wasn't with him. I sat up all night long waiting for my brother to come home. I was really scared. But my brother was more scared. Dad had taken him up on Canaan Mountain, the mountain that towered over Colorado City, and left him there all night to teach him a lesson.

We kids all knew you *never* went up on the mountain after dark if you valued your life and your soul. We were taught early on that the craggy red mountains surrounding the community were haunted with evil spirits—the Gadianton robbers. According to the Book of Mormon, the Gadiantons were criminals who'd had their souls taken away in ancient times. Now, our parents told us, they rode the mountain at night on their ghostly horses. If they caught you, they would steal your soul. If they got it, you would be doomed to wander the world as a Gadianton robber for eternity—until you could steal somebody else's soul. We were terrified. The one rule we kids obeyed was to never go up in the mountains at night.

My brother didn't come home that night, but the next morning my dad went out early. He came back with Theral, white as a sheet. When we ran to greet him, he cowered away from us. My heart went out to him. I could imagine what he'd been through. Every sound would have terrorized him. But he knew if he got up to move, he'd be a target. If he ran home, Dad would drag him back. Knowing my brother, he probably just curled himself into a little ball and cried all night.

For about a week after his night on the mountain, Theral shook like he had palsy. He continued to be very jumpy for all the years when I saw him regularly, and as far as I know, has never ever been the same as he was before that night.

Sometimes I thought I'd drown in all the tension and anger and craziness in our house. I just had to get out and be alone. I spent hours just sitting high on the limbs of a cottonwood tree, staring at the sky, or sitting on the rocky red cliffs overlooking Colorado City. I daydreamed about running away and disappearing into the mountains, living in a hole-in-the-wall cave where no one could ever find me. But instead of escaping my problems, I soon learned on those days by myself that the children in my family were not the only ones being abused in our community.

One Saturday afternoon, after my chores were done, I slipped out and headed up Big Rock, our name for the small mountain near our house. From Big Rock, I walked along the mountain ridge. Then I stopped at an overlook and looked down into people's yards.

One house belonged to a man I'll call Mark Bailey.* He had several wives and quite a few young sons. They were very cute boys, and I liked them quite a bit—especially Ricky,* who was my age. From my perch, I could see five or six of the brothers, just hanging around the yard talking. Suddenly, Mr. Bailey threw open the backdoor and stormed into the yard with a leather belt dangling from his fist. He ran straight for Ricky and started beating him with the belt all over his body, screaming at him the entire time. The other boys ran into the house to get away. Mr. Bailey was so out of control, chains could not have restrained him.

---

* Mark Bailey and Ricky are not their real names.

I couldn't do anything but sit there, tears rolling down my face, as I watched Ricky suffer a beating that could have killed him. Trying to protect himself from his father's relentless blows, Ricky curled up into a fetal position and covered his head with both hands. There was nothing I could do to save him. It made me sick to my stomach watching, knowing the pain Ricky's father was inflicting. The beating went on for what seemed like two or three minutes. Finally, Mr. Bailey stopped, yelling, "Just do it again and see what happens!" Ricky lay on the ground for a long time.

I wish I could say that this was unusual, but it wasn't. Over the years of my childhood, I saw more scenes like this than I want to remember. After a while, it seemed normal that parents would do this to their kids. But looking back, I can see that most of the families I knew lived in terrible violence and chaos. It's no wonder they so often spun out of control.

When I came back to the house from these time-outs, it was the same old thing. I couldn't tell my mom what my dad was doing to me. I was too ashamed, and I figured it was nothing special. A lot of kids were being abused by their parents in one way or another. Anyway, I knew it wouldn't do any good. My mom was an adult, but Dad treated her almost as badly as he treated us kids. I didn't want her to leave us, but I couldn't see why she stayed. When I asked Mom why she took what he dished out without protesting, she just shook her head and shrugged.

"That's just the way it is," she said. "You don't understand. That's just the way it is."

She was right. I didn't understand. And it made even less sense to me the next year, when Dad took a second wife: Mom's little sister Elizabeth.

2

Home Sweet Home

The FLDS believes that in order for a man to reach the celestial kingdom, he must have three wives. If he has the prerequisite three wives, he gets to become a god. Many men in the FLDS had five, ten, fifteen wives; Warren Jeffs has more than seventy. After over a decade of marriage to just one woman, Dad was way behind in this regard. But when I was nine, he made Elizabeth his second wife and brought her home to live.

Mom was devastated, but she kept sweet about it. In order for a woman to reach the celestial kingdom, it doesn't matter if she lives a life as pure as the Virgin Mary's. It doesn't matter how good she is in this life or how kind. The only thing that matters is her complete obedience to her husband in this life. Because in the next life, when she dies and stands at the gates of the celestial kingdom, if he does not want her there she can't get in. So Mom moved aside without a word and made room in our home for her pretty, sixteen-year-old sister.

Elizabeth was an inch or two taller than Dad, with an attractive, curvy figure. She knew she was pretty—as a young teen, she'd had all the boys drooling over her. She was constantly getting into trouble, but her good looks always bailed her out.

Dad showed his preference for his young wife from the start. Right away, he added on a private space for Elizabeth. He drove an old Army truck-trailer right up to the back of the house, and built a short walkway between the house and the van. Elizabeth's new "bedroom" was just big enough to hold a double bed and dresser. The walls, ceiling, and floor were all carpeted. Small windows on both sides provided the only ventilation. With its heavy, commercial-type door, I thought it looked more like a vault than a bedroom. But even with the heavy padding, it wasn't soundproof.

One morning shortly after Elizabeth and Dad married, Mom was in the kitchen cooking breakfast. All of us kids were underfoot, hungry and watching as Mom stirred gravy in the skillet. Suddenly, we heard "sex sounds" coming from the trailer. Dad made those same sounds when he molested me. My face got hot. Mom didn't say a word. She just lowered her head, continuing to stir the gravy. Tears rushed down her cheeks. My brothers and sisters looked at each other and giggled.

Mom was still silent as we set the table, but I saw the pain in her face. It made me so angry. I wanted to kill my father for his cruelty to her.

We had just started eating when Elizabeth and Dad strolled into the kitchen. Elizabeth looked like she had been crying—her eyes were puffy and her nose was red. But now she was grinning. I wanted to slap that grin right off her face. Dad was feeling his oats and smiling. He began roughhousing with some of the kids. Then he walked over to my mom, hugged her, and kissed her on the cheek.

Mom stood perfectly still. It was surreal. I felt as though I was somewhere else. I thought, *How dare you touch my mother? You are so slimy.*

From the day my dad married Elizabeth, he never spent another night with my mom. He would go to Mom's bedroom, have sex with her, and—quite often—get her pregnant. Then he would climb out of bed and go back down to Elizabeth's room for the night. I lay in bed in my room, just across the hall, and listened to Mom cry herself to sleep every night.

I agonized over what Mom was going through. Dad treated her like dirt. I wanted so much to rescue her, to get her away from this life. And after a while I almost hated my mom for letting Dad treat her this way. I wondered, *Why don't you fight back? Why don't you demand respect?* But she just never did.

Dad spent nearly all of his time with Elizabeth, even time that rightly belonged to my mother. On Mom's birthday, he would ignore her and take Elizabeth to dinner at one of the family-style restaurants in St. George, the nearest larger town. On his and Mom's wedding anniversary, he left Mom at home and took Elizabeth out instead. This mental and emotional abuse never let up. My mother withered inside.

Dad took Elizabeth on all his trips out of town. They'd return with candy and toys for the children Elizabeth had started to have—eventually, she'd give birth to eight, four boys and four girls—but nothing for any of Mom's kids. By this time, I wasn't surprised by my dad's cruelty. But it was tough watching my younger siblings sit silently, watching their half brothers and half sisters get suckers, ice cream, and cookies while they got nothing. Once my dad pounded my little brother for daring to take a piece of candy that one of Elizabeth's kids offered him.

It seemed as if Elizabeth got everything. Dad fixed up a sewing room just for her. She got the new car; Mom had to drive the junker. Dad even replaced Mom's name on their bank accounts with Elizabeth's name. Mom had to buy all the food, propane, and clothes for her kids out of the meager $250 bimonthly check she got from her job working at the compound school. Elizabeth and Dad's money went to care for their kids.

I loved my mom a lot. But sadly, because she was always so depressed and beaten down, she had little positive influence on my life when I was growing up. She did not have the time or energy to give me the one-on-one attention every child desires and needs.

Fortunately, I did have one adult in my life I could talk to. My Grandma Bertha, Mom's mother, was the most important person in my childhood. She was always glad to see me, and made a big fuss about it. She made me feel important and loved. I visited her as often as I could.

Grandma's house was pretty close to ours, across the yard and through a field. Our house on Utah Avenue was surrounded by a huge yard—you could have driven an eighteen-wheeler around the yard if there weren't so much junk scattered around. On the west side of the house was a huge orchard of apple, apricot, and peach trees that led to the horse-tack shed.

I'd climb the horse fences and run west across the big dirt field to Grandma's backyard. A quick knock on her backdoor and I was in, running through the house to find her.

Grandma was on daily kidney dialysis, and she often asked me to read to her while she was on the machine. She loved the novels of Louis L'Amour, and seemed to hang on every word as I read tales of the heroes and villains of the early West. L'Amour's books, of course, were forbidden by the FLDS, like millions of other books. But like many outwardly obedient wives, Grandma knew just where to hide the banned books from prying eyes. It felt naughty and exciting to pull out those books and read them, then bury them deep in Grandma's closet again so no one could find them.

Before Grandma got sick, she would come to our house whenever her sister, whom we called Aunt Mickey, came to visit from St. Louis. Aunt Mickey was different from anyone else I'd ever met. For one thing, she smoked, which is absolutely prohibited by the FLDS. If my father was out of town, Mom and her sisters Lillian and Mary would sit around the kitchen table with Grandma and Aunt Mickey and play cards—another no-no. I had no idea what game they were playing, but I loved to sit and watch them. The smell of the smoke Aunt Mickey took in and blew out of her mouth fascinated me. The stale cigarette smell lingered in the furniture fabric long after Aunt Mickey left, helping mask the stench of our small, overcrowded house.

My parents' house was a wreck—Dad's never-ending construction project. It had started out as a little four-room shanty on one floor, with a small living room, a kitchen, one bedroom, and one bathroom. For the first few years of my childhood, all of us kids slept on the floor in the living room. Mom and Dad slept in the only bedroom. Then the building started.

First, Dad built a big basement on the west side of the house. This was a large, open room that was supposed to be a playroom, with a bathroom and a laundry room. Then he added a floor over the basement and started building five bedrooms. Even though the interiors were never finished, they got used. With babies being born all the time, there was no choice.

Dad built two of the five bedrooms on the north side of the house. One was my mother's and the other was mine—just for me—with a bathroom between them. I had a sink and mirror in my bedroom too, so I wouldn't tie up the bathroom. My little brother, Joe Jr., had the bedroom next to mine along the west wall. Theral had the back corner bedroom on the south end of the west wall. My dad turned the last bedroom into his office.

The only finished rooms were the four on the lower level of the original house. The rest, including my bedroom, had exposed two-by-fours and electrical wiring. Building materials were scattered all over the hallways. We had to step through a hazard course of wallboard and hardware to get around. Even the rooms that did have drywall were either unfinished or unpainted. The floors were raw plywood. The last thing Dad started was an addition that jutted over the top of the original house. It was supposed to be a room for a mother and nursery rooms for her newborns, but it was never finished either.

To be fair, most homes in our neighborhood were like ours—in a state of perpetual construction. The less affluent families were caught in a real Catch-22 situation. The men had no choice but to keep adding on rooms for their new wives and the children they bore on a regular basis. The catch was that they didn't actually hold the titles to their own houses. The titles were held by the church-operated United Effort Plan (UEP), a multimillion-dollar trust run by the Prophet and his council that owned everything in town. So if the men wanted to add on, they had to pay for it themselves. The houses ended where their money ran out.

All these unfinished rooms created an environment that was perfectly suited to the general emotional chaos we lived in and created on a daily basis. Like us, most families had kitchen equipment that was old and broken down. Most light fixtures were simply single-bulb porcelain sockets dangling from a cloth-covered electrical wire. Twenty or thirty kids living in a house means lots of food spills and lots of rubbish lying around. All of this combined with a patchwork of electrical wiring created a nightmare of fire hazards and health hazards.

And dozens of kids also means plenty of laundry. It's impossible to stay ahead of all the dirty laundry a house full of people can produce unless you do a load every day. But when I was growing up, we did laundry only once a week, so it really piled up. Worse, we used those old-fashioned wringer washing machines and hung the clothes out to dry on clotheslines. My braids got caught in the wringer of the washing machine many times when I had laundry chores.

But the bathrooms were the worst. The porcelain covering the cast-iron fixtures was chipped and worn through to the black metal. The damp, musty smell of mold and mildew growing on the Formica tub enclosures permeated the small rooms. Paint was often peeling from ceilings.

And the smell . . . oh, the smell! The combined odors of so many bodies, rotting garbage, and dirty diapers would slam me in the face as soon as I walked into my house or the houses of my friends and relatives. Polygamous families commonly have seven to ten children in diapers in one household, and we couldn't afford disposable diapers. So pails filled with dirty cloth diapers waiting to be washed were commonly found in the laundry room and in bathrooms all over the house.

It usually falls to the teenage girls in the house to wash the diapers. This means that unwashed diapers might sit in the pails for days until the girls are finally forced to do their nauseating duty. When my cousin Crystal was caught neglecting the dirty diapers, I witnessed a particularly horrible instance of abuse that I will never forget.

She and I were in her room at her house one day, reading her mother's secret stash of magazines. I had snuck in, so no one knew I was there, and we were hiding underneath a pile of dirty clothes with a flashlight. We knew that reading these magazines could really get us into trouble and that added to our excitement. But these "evil" magazines weren't *Playboy* or *Penthouse*; we were obsessed with the innocent articles about romance, marriage, and family in the pages of the *Ladies' Home Journal*, *Redbook*, and *Good Housekeeping*. For us, these forbidden tales were sweeter than candy. We could sit for hours reading stories about life in the outside world, where each husband had one wife and small, well-fed families lived in clean houses. As I read, I would think, *This is what my life is going to be like when I get married. This is what it is going to be like for me.*

We were being so wicked! Our hearts would race every time somebody would walk down the stairs, afraid we would be caught. We stayed under the clothing piles, escaping detection for several hours. But then someone started yelling for Crystal.

"Crystal! Get out here right now!" It was Vanessa,* one of Crystal's father's wives. (In the complicated world of polygamy, Vanessa was also Crystal's father's stepdaughter.) Vanessa barged into the room to give Crystal hell about not finishing her chores. It was Crystal's day to wash out the diapers, and Vanessa thought she had procrastinated far too long.

"Crystal! Get out here!" But Crystal didn't make a move, so Vanessa stomped off to get the big guns. Pretty soon, we heard the heavy footsteps of Crystal's dad.

"Crystal! Crystal! Where are you?" We buried the magazines deep under the clothes. I curled up in a tight ball, trying to stay out of sight. "Crystal! You better come here right NOW!"

Her father burst through the door to find Crystal sitting on the bed, looking innocent.

* Not her real name.

John Jacobson* was another angry little man, cocky and loud. He had a volatile temper. I shivered in fear, even though I knew I was well hidden. I peeked through a tiny opening in the clothes pile to see what was happening.

Crystal's father was furious. His receding hairline had left him with two widow's peaks, one on each side of his forehead, which made him look even scarier. He grabbed Crystal by the hair and dragged her into the bathroom, which was just off the bedroom. Then he pushed her head deep into a pail of filthy diapers, screaming, "You are going to do what you are told!"

He yanked her head out and she caught her breath. "No!" Her face was covered in muck.

"You are going to make a lousy, rotten wife!" Crystal's father mashed her head back down into the disgusting pail. "I'm ashamed of you!"

He held her head in there, twisting it around this time. Crystal held on to the top of the pail, struggling to raise her head up, but her father was strong. She pounded on the sides of the can with her fists, and her father began beating her on her back, buttocks, and legs with his other hand. I was terrified for Crystal, afraid she would suffocate in there. Finally, he pulled her head out of the pail, reached down inside, grabbed a dirty diaper, and mashed it into her face.

"You have diaper duty for the next month!" he shouted. "If I ever walk into this bathroom and see one single dirty diaper in that can, you will eat what's in those diapers for your food!"

Crystal was sobbing uncontrollably. I wanted to run to her, but I was frozen. If John Jacobson had seen me, he would have beaten me too, just to keep me quiet.

My dad's continual molestation had made me wary of everyone. I did not want *anybody* to touch me. Not so much as a pat on the head. But it seemed that I wasn't safe anywhere.

* Not his real name.

We often took trips to Rulon Jeffs's compound, just south of Salt Lake City, where my father worked as an electrician for some companies owned by the Jeffs family. Rulon was a savvy business-man and accountant. He served on several boards of directors for Utah-based corporations and had founded the very profitable Utah Tool and Die Company. He was also the leader of an esti-mated 1,000 followers of the FLDS church in the Salt Lake area.

His compound was a huge piece of property in an exclusive area at the mouth of Little Cottonwood Canyon. It was like a fortress surrounded by a massive concrete wall, and a far cry from our com-munity of unfinished houses and rooms made out of truck-trailers. Within the compound walls were a half-dozen or so palatial homes occupied by some of Rulon's sons. Rulon's huge house had about twenty-four bedrooms and two large kitchens. When we visited, we always stayed at the house that belonged to his son David.

The Jeffs compound is where I had my first brush with the now notorious FLDS leader Warren Jeffs, one of Rulon's many sons. He was fourteen years older than I was, an insecure, lanky string bean. He looked like the character Ichabod Crane in the Disney movie *The Legend of Sleepy Hollow*, but he had the smarmy personality of Eddie Haskell in *Leave It to Beaver*. He was always sucking up to adults so they'd like him. But the kids knew better. I never liked him, and tried to stay clear of him.

Unfortunately, Warren was not only slimy, he was smart. He was the principal of Alta Academy, the school for all FLDS kids in the Salt Lake area. The school was situated in the center of the compound grounds and advanced the dictates of Rulon Jeffs. Warren was known as a strict disciplinarian. He was soft-spoken and polite to the adults, which made it easier for him to get away with his rigid control over the children.

Warren Jeffs might have fooled the adults, but he was the creepiest guy I had ever encountered. Being around him gave me a panicky feeling—as if I'd walked right into a spider's web and couldn't get the sticky web or the crawling spider off my face.

Worse, Warren was always putting his cold, clammy hands on me and other young children—girls and boys alike. And it wasn't just a friendly hug or a pat on the head.

When I was about ten years old and Warren was twenty-four, I was climbing an apple tree near the school. Warren suddenly materialized behind me, like a ghost.

"Flora," he said, "you know you shouldn't be climbing that tree." I came down slowly, and he rested his hand on my shoulder. "That's better." He stroked my hair. I stood stiff as a board as he moved his hand slowly down my back and onto my buttocks and gave a couple of firm squeezes. Like my dad, he didn't say anything about my not wearing my garment. Then he removed his hand and I took off running, trying to get as far away from him as I could. I had never felt so afraid in my life.

Kids feared Warren. He was like the troublemaking kid in grammar school who would look like a little angel but would be quietly torturing another kid, who would finally start screaming. Of course the other kid was always the one who would get into trouble. That was his technique with children. As principal of Alta Academy, he would torment the students in subtle ways until they broke. Then he'd make them pay.

His favorite methods combined humiliation with corporal punishment. When a boy was disobedient, Warren would make the boy stand up on a chair with his back facing the classroom. With a pointer, Warren would point at the boy's butt and demand, "Flex those muscles." Then he'd make the embarrassed boy flex his buttocks muscles back and forth. He would not hesitate to break a ruler over a kid's head, back, or buttocks.

We all heard rumors that Warren had been kicked out of the compound as a teenager for brutally molesting five- and six-year-old kids. Supposedly, he'd begged forgiveness and promised he would prove himself worthy. Somehow he worked himself back into his father's good graces. As he got older, he became a pro at snowing the adults and adept at manipulating young minds.

Many years later I learned that those rumors were true. Charges and lawsuits had been filed against Warren for molesting little boys. He was accused of sodomizing kids five years old and up. He would tell them, "This is the only way God allows boys to become men." Though he seemed to prefer male children, he also molested girls.

One of my cousins was the mother of one of these little boys. She noticed blood in her son's pants one day, and took him to the clinic. They told her the bleeding was due to constipation. When she pressed for a more thorough diagnosis, she was told she needed to go home, keep sweet, and let the Lord take care of things.

Now that other boys have come forward and testified, my cousin feels responsible and terribly guilty. "You know, there was a part of me that knew," she says. "But because of my religion, I accepted what they told me to believe."

It's hard to comprehend how a skinny, gangly worm of a man like Warren Jeffs could intimidate anyone. But he had his dad's ear, and his dad was very powerful. When Uncle Roy died, Rulon stood a good chance of becoming the next Prophet. Being principal of Alta Academy reinforced Warren's power and gave him a ready-made pool of victims. Warren began setting himself up to become the leader of the FLDS while he was still at Alta Academy. He started planting the idea in his father's head, and it grew deep roots over the years.

But we didn't know any of this back then. At ten I just did my best to avoid Warren and his icy hands. If it wasn't Warren running his hand down my dress, it was my father. If it wasn't my father, it was my brother Theral. He had grown into an emotionally stunted, loner teenager, and he found a unique way to abuse me.

Somehow he'd gotten hold of a funky old computer. After a while he became an expert at the basic kinds of video games they had back then. He kept the monitor and boxes well hidden in his room—we weren't supposed to have that kind of stuff. But we kids all knew it was there. We would sneak into his room and beg him to let us to play games like Space Invaders and Pac-Man. Pretty soon Theral used the computer as a bargaining chip. He would say, "Well, I'll let you play with the computer if you'll let me . . ." Uncomfortable, but dying to play, I would sit at the computer and tolerate my brother fondling my breasts and genitals while I guided Ms. Pac-Man through a course of glowing fruit. Although he has never spoken to me about it, I believe my brother must have been sexually molested too—if not by our father by some of his cronies, other men in the FLDS.

The only place I could avoid the abuse and grinding poverty at home was at my Uncle Fred's house, in Hildale. Most people in Colorado City and Hildale were related. But that didn't mean we were one big happy family. Just as in most of the rest of the world, there were two kinds of people: the haves and the have-nots. We didn't have much. But Uncle Fred was definitely one of the haves—a mover and shaker in the FLDS and rich to boot.

Fred Jessop was my dad's half brother. He was older than my father, and he always seemed like a grandfather to me because of his age. As the bishop of the FLDS, he was very powerful. He controlled the tithing money. Everybody in town gave 10 percent of his or her income to Fred Jessop to manage for the church. No decision was made in that community that did not go through Fred Jessop. He reported directly to Uncle Roy, and later on to Rulon Jeffs and then Warren Jeffs, when Warren became Prophet in 2002.

Uncle Fred was very soft-spoken. He was less than six feet tall and weighed about two hundred pounds, with a potbelly. He always wore a full-brimmed, gray felt hat over his white hair when he was outdoors. His prominent jaw, clean-shaven face, and neat appearance gave him the look of authority. In addition, he dressed like a businessman, with long-sleeved button-down shirts and neatly pressed dress slacks. He was friendly and laughed easily. Uncle Fred looked out for everybody and always had a nice word to say to people. Sometimes, when we went to town, he'd give me a dollar to spend.

But Uncle Fred had one fatal flaw in the eyes of the FLDS: he was sterile, due to a childhood case of mumps. His first wife, Lydia, was childless. Not one to stand still and mourn her fate, Lydia became a midwife who delivered most of the babies born in the twin towns. Fred was also married to Maryett, Permilia, Susan, and Martha. Because Fred was sterile, my dad gave him seven of my sisters at birth to raise as his own—he wanted only girls. Martha Ann, Patricia, Maryett, Mable, Joellen, Mildred, and Annie were all taken from my mother as newborns and handed over to Uncle Fred. It broke my mother's heart, but she did it because my father commanded her to do so. Eventually, Uncle Fred would claim fatherhood for more than a hundred children.

My sisters who lived with Uncle Fred had everything that I didn't have. Their house was finished and well furnished. The carpet was plush and new. Instead of broken-down junk to sit on, they had beautiful furniture and antiques. While the stuffing was coming out of the stained covers on my bed at home, my sisters' beds boasted beautiful pink ruffled bedspreads with matching shams.

Uncle Fred's large, two-story house screamed money. Like the baptismal building, which was located right behind it, the house was built out of local stone. The varied sizes, colors, and textures of the stones gave it the feel of old English architecture. The inside was gorgeous too. Uncle Fred had artisans from the community create beautiful oak cabinets for the kitchen and other built-in cabinetry. If any work needed to be done, the entire community was there to work on the bishop's house.

The only old things Uncle Fred's family owned were antiques. I loved the dark wood rocking chair that had been handcrafted by one of Fred's ancestors. Every now and then, Uncle Fred would wind up his mint-condition antique phonograph and play his old big-band records, blasting out Glenn Miller, Tommy Dorsey, and Benny Goodman.

Everything else was new. Uncle Fred's family always had brand-new vehicles. The wives and daughters always had new dresses and their hair was always perfect. I was wildly jealous of them, and they were aghast at the way we lived.

My sisters who lived in Hildale didn't come down to Mom's house very often. When they did, they didn't stay long. A couple of hours every once in a long while was all they could take. Finally, they refused to come at all. I understood perfectly. Why would they want to sit on the nasty couch with the stuffing coming out of the arms and have nothing to play with and nothing good to eat?

Of Uncle Fred's five wives, I think Martha was his favorite. She was the youngest of the five and a very pretty strawberry blond. She maintained a striking, thin figure. She was also the daughter of Joe Barlow, and she was Uncle Fred's niece. She'd been severely burned as a child and had scars on her stomach. She would never say how she was burned, but the injury supposedly prevented her from bearing children. I thought she was a Goody Two-Shoes, a real prude.

Where Martha was very stylish and standoffish, Susan was frumpy but down-to-earth. She did not have a mean bone in her body. She did all the laundry and house chores. When Susan asked me to help her do something around the house, I didn't mind.

Aunt Maryett was older than Susan and Martha. She ran the local post office. She would bring home boxes of mail, and she and Fred would sit in his office steaming open letters and packages, reading them, and then deciding whether to deliver them. This went on for years. Finally, the postal service opened an investigation and forced Aunt Maryett to retire.

Uncle Fred's wife Permilia was a large, heavyset woman and the Prophet Leroy Johnson's daughter. She operated the cafeteria, where I worked off and on as a child. Permilia was nice in her own way, although she could also be a bitch sometimes. But Permilia didn't hold a candle to Aunt Lydia, Uncle Fred's first wife. Lydia was a viper.

There wasn't a meaner woman in the world than Lydia Jessop. And she was a powerful woman in her own right. Lydia, as I mentioned earlier, was a midwife. She ran the birthing center and the first-aid clinic, which were actually attached to Uncle Fred's house. But she was no angel of mercy. She sincerely believed a woman had to suffer to near death when she gave birth, and Lydia also practiced her own brand of medicine. When the occasional unfortunate outsider—a camper or a hiker—went into premature labor near Hildale and ended up at the clinic, Lydia refused to help them and sent them away. Many of these women wound up losing their babies because of her.

I gave Lydia a wide berth. I'd had a run-in with her on my sixth birthday that set the tone for our relationship from then on. It so happened that I shared a birthday with Uncle Roy. Almost no one in the FLDS celebrated children's birthdays, but there was always a big party for Uncle Roy. Everyone in the community was there. At the party that year, I got a real surprise: my grandmother gave me a Chatty Cathy doll: you just pulled a string in her back, and it magically made her talk. My sisters and brothers and I hardly ever got toys, and I thought that doll was the most amazing present in the whole wide world. I showed her to everyone who came to Uncle Roy's party.

I'd only had the doll for about twenty minutes when Uncle Fred and Aunt Lydia showed up. I ran over to show them my doll, just as happy as I could be.

"Let me see that thing," said Lydia. She snatched the doll from my hands. "That's the most evil thing I have ever seen in my life! Dolls don't talk. They're plastic. It's got Satan in it." Then she put Chatty Cathy on the floor and stomped the life out of her. She didn't quit until the doll was completely destroyed. She scooped up the pieces and tossed them into the garbage, triumphant. I was crying, in shock.

"That's what you do with evil things," said Lydia.

That doll was the only toy I had, and I'd had it for only a very short while. Lydia was not my mother or my guardian, yet as an adult she had the power and authority to destroy my doll. No one came to my defense or tried to stop her. From that point on, I hated her, and tried to stay out of her way.

Nevertheless and despite Lydia's presence in Uncle Fred's home, his place was heaven—a fantasy land. I prayed that I could move there, and I wanted my mom to move there too. I wanted her to have a life like Aunt Martha's, with beautiful clothes and a kind husband and all the food you could eat. At our house, the refrigerator and pantry were sometimes just plain empty. But Uncle Fred's house was a cornucopia of fresh fruits and vegetables that touched the senses with bright colors, scents, and flavors that made my mouth water. The fridge was always overflowing and the candy jar full.

Out of all my sisters that lived with Uncle Fred, I was closest to Patricia. Patricia was a year and a month younger than I was. She and I looked exactly alike and were often mistaken for twins. We both wore glasses, had dark hair, and were about the same size. We would sit and play the board game Hüsker Dü? for hours or play in the playhouse. Sometimes we rode bikes. The kids in Hildale had racks and racks of bicycles to ride. Back home in Colorado City—just a few blocks away, really—bikes were as scarce as food in the pantry.

I envied the life my sisters had. I often wondered, *Why couldn't I have been one of the ones sent up here? Why was I left behind?*

The priesthood tells the outside world that the families of polygamy never feel a single minute of jealousy. What a lie! Everything about growing up in polygamy is about resentment and jealousy. Older sister-wives are jealous of the youth and fertility of the new wives; the new wives are jealous of the power wielded by the favored wives. And sibling rivalry doesn't cease to exist just because the priesthood says it does. Somebody always has more than another person does.

The truth is, competition absorbed our entire life. In a household consisting of dozens or even scores of children, there is constant competition for attention and affection. The rivalry among kids is intense—you have to fight for everything. If you pick the most vegetables out of the garden one day, and Grandpa pats you on the head, that little pat signifies that a fierce battle has taken place and the winner has been acknowledged. That is how emotionally needy children are in polygamy.

Making it worse was the grinding hunger. The less privileged children in town—and they were the majority—were desperately in need of proper nutrition. Most public schools across America provide lunch, but the FLDS schools did not. The priesthood did not want to spend money on feeding kids at school. Lunchtime was supposed to be the family's affair. So the kids were bused home for an hour to have lunch, and then bused back. But that didn't work out according to plan.

In many cases an empty house was all that waited. Often with all parents—including sister-wives—working, there was no one to prepare lunch for the kids. And real nourishment was in short supply anyway, with so many mouths to feed. Besides, most kids had a list of chores to do at noon.

Work was everything when I was growing up. We'd do our chores around the house, but we'd also be put to work as unpaid labor in the church-owned businesses. I worked at Aunt Permilia's cafeteria practically my whole young life—before and after school and twelve hours a day almost every day during the summer—for nothing. It was supposed to be a contribution to the community. Every so often, though, Aunt Permilia would give me twenty dollars, and I'd squirrel it away. Except for the occasional handout, the only other way we kids got money was to literally pick up loose change off the street. In a town where the only law was FLDS law, the church made the most of illegal child labor.

So on the lunch break, kids who were lucky enough even to *go* to school had just enough time to go home, grab a bite to eat, do the dishes and a chore or two, and get back on the bus.

In this regard I was lucky. Because of my family's connections to Uncle Fred, my brothers and sisters and I were bused to his house, where there was food aplenty. Everybody in town envied us for that. When I look back it makes me sick to my stomach. I know there were kids in town who were absolutely starving.

Oddly, Uncle Fred himself was fond of a plig staple from his childhood: homemade bread with milk and honey. He would break the bread into small portions, carefully place the pieces in a bowl, pour on a generous helping of milk, and drizzle honey over the top. The makings of that concoction are often the only food in the cupboard of a polygamous home.

By the time I was eleven, I just couldn't stand being cooped up in my horrible house. I often felt that I'd burst if I didn't escape, and I did so almost every night. Breaking out wasn't easy—my bedroom was on the second floor. But I didn't let that stop me. Before I went to bed, I would drag a trampoline we had then over to the house, just under my window. Then, when everyone was asleep, I'd jump out the window and onto the trampoline, springing up and off into the orchard. Occasionally, I'd land too hard and bounce right into the apple trees.

One night, after a good bounce and successful escape, I headed over to my friend Troy Roundy's house. Troy was my partner in crime. We were inveterate pranksters. He and I had even poured sugar in the gas tank of the car belonging to Sam Barlow, the town marshal, just so he would chase us.

That night, I was sitting on a fence post outside Troy's house waiting for him to come out. I noticed the curtains were open at Leon Prichard's house, next door. Leon was a giant guy with a huge belly. His size alone was enough to scare the daylights out of us kids.

I saw one of Leon's daughters sitting on her bed, dressed in her nightgown. She was a year younger than I was, about ten. As I watched, Leon entered the room and shut the door. He lifted her off the bed and backed her up against a wall. She stood still as a statue, hands balled into fists and arms straight down at her side. Her fear resonated deep inside me. I couldn't stop watching.

Leon began undoing the buttons of her nightgown, and then he pulled it open. He put his thick hands on her tiny breasts, rubbing himself against her, rubbing between her legs. A sick feeling overwhelmed me. I was all too familiar with this sort of father-daughter relationship. He kissed his daughter on the mouth, stepped back, and grinned, pleased with what he had just done.

The girl's expression never changed. She just stared straight ahead. I knew her mind was in another world. I knew exactly where she had to go to save her sanity. Leon, in a parody of parenting, buttoned up her nightgown and patted her on the head like a puppy dog. Looking back at her over his shoulder, he walked over to the door, opened it, and walked away.

I felt like I'd been punched in the stomach. Now I knew for sure I wasn't the only girl in town who was being sexually abused by her dad. It should have been a relief to find out, but it wasn't. I took no comfort in Leon's daughter's suffering. I didn't wait for Troy to come out that night. I just wandered off home.

That girl and I, along with Crystal, Ricky, and many other children I knew, were members of a secret fraternity of abused kids. It was a pretty big fraternity, too. The average age of people living in Colorado City and Hildale is fourteen. The average age for the rest of the country is thirty-five. That means Colorado City and Hildale have a lot of young kids. By my estimate, about 20 percent of the people who live in Colorado City and Hildale are pedophiles and abusers. And these perpetrators are not moving into town from the outside: they are born and bred by the FLDS.

A very few of the kids who are subjected to this horror are able to put up with it and get on with their lives, scarred but not incapacitated. But many more gentle souls are broken in spirit, living lives of quiet despair and submission in the FLDS. For a few the abuse is so devastating that death seems like a better alternative than the hell they have to live in every day.

When I was twelve years old, my dad did something that finally pushed me to that place. Ending my own life seemed like my only escape.

3

The Rape

The FLDS recognizes only two national holidays: Thanksgiving and the Fourth of July. We kids waited for the Fourth all year. It was a chance to cut loose for a day and relax in "the park," a sprawling, open area of cedar and piñon trees nestled in a box canyon a few miles north of town. It was like a county fair—baseball games for the adults, pony rides for the kids. We'd save up our money for months, maybe two or three dollars, and then spend it very carefully on candy and snow cones. After sunset, we'd all go back down to Colorado City to watch fireworks explode in the night sky. It was a welcome escape from life in the crowded, dirty homes most of us lived in. But Dad made sure that July 4, 1981, turned out to be anything but an escape for me.

I'd just turned twelve a few weeks earlier, and I'd been allowed to sew a dress myself—the first and last time that ever happened. The Fourth seemed like a perfect time to wear it. I knew the dress was too short—it hit me just at the knees instead of going the required five inches below—but I'd worn it a few times and no one had said anything. I pulled on a pair of polyester slacks too, just to make sure I was covered.

My family was taking so long! Practically all the people in Colorado City and Hildale had already piled into their cars and trucks and headed for the park. There could not have been more than a dozen folks left in town. Mom said I could ride my horse, Major, to the park if I wanted to. I was thrilled! Major was my best friend, and riding him alone in the foothills and canyons was the one taste of real freedom I had. I didn't wait for her to change her mind: I mounted bareback and hit the trail. But I'd been gone less than five minutes when I realized I'd forgotten my money in my room. I turned Major around and galloped back.

When I got home, it looked as though they'd all left. I could see the backs of their vehicles kicking up dust as they drove off down the road. It felt strange being in an empty house—I'd never been there alone before. I ran upstairs to my room and grabbed what I needed. Just as I left to run back downstairs, I saw my dad standing right outside his office door. I practically jumped out of my skin. What was he doing there?

"Come here, so I can see you." He looked me over slowly, from head to toe. "You're dressed like a heathen. You look like a street whore." His face said he was disgusted with me. "You cannot leave the house dressed like that. Take that off!"

"Dad, look, I'm wearing pants!" I pointed frantically to the polyester slacks.

He ignored me. He couldn't stop talking about the dress. "Where did you get that dress? Who made that dress?"

"I did."

"Well, take it off. Take those clothes off."

I was furious. I loved that dress. But I turned to go to my room to change. Then he said, "Come here!" He pointed into his office. "You can take it off right here."

"But everybody's gone. I need to get up there. Mom will be worried." I don't even know why I bothered. I knew what was coming. As I walked toward him, he reached around in back of me, unzipped the zipper, and untied the sash. "Now take the dress off."

I stepped out of my dress, right there in the office. He didn't even bother closing the door. I was completely naked from the waist up—I almost never wore my garment. I tried to cover my newly budded breasts with my hands.

"Put your hands down, Flora. I want to see you." He sat down heavily in his chair, leaned back, and just stared at me. "Come here."

I took a few steps in his direction and stopped.

He unzipped his pants and pulled his penis out. "Come here and touch me, Flora."

"No. I don't want to." I could see the Fourth of July slipping away fast. Maybe this wouldn't take too long.

"Come here right now!"

So I went to him and I touched his penis with one finger. But that wasn't what he wanted. He wrapped my hand around his penis and then wrapped his hand around mine and started rubbing himself up and down. "This is the way you need to do it." I could feel him stiffen right away. "You know how much it likes you." He moaned quietly.

I waited for it to be over, but he had other ideas.

"Take your pants off, Flora."

"Why?" I felt like throwing up. I just wanted to get to the park.

"I just want to look at you."

So my pants came off. I was totally naked. I felt my mind sort of float out of my body, as it did every time he asked me to do something like this. I remembered the girl I'd seen through her window that night. Did I look like her now?

I wanted to run out of there as fast as I could and never come back, but I couldn't. Instead, I just said in a quiet voice, "I don't want to do this."

But my dad wasn't listening. He patted his knee. "Sit on my lap. Come on, I just want to feel you."

I climbed onto his lap like a little girl, with my back toward him. This was new. I started to get really scared. Suddenly, he was rubbing his fingers inside me. He started breathing harder and harder, and I could feel his hot breath on my neck. Something was really wrong. I started to panic.

He shoved something fat and hard inside me. Oh my God, that was his penis. Then he grabbed my hips, hard, and started sliding me up and down on him. It hurt like hell, like he was rubbing my insides with sandpaper. He started pumping, and I felt a sharp pain, like a knife. He was killing me!

"No! Stop it! What are you doing?" I tried to get away, but he was holding on tight. I don't think he even knew I was there.

"Stop it!" I was screaming and crying. Tears were pouring down my face.

But my dad was in another world. His breath was coming out all ragged now, and he was grunting in my ear.

He was fucking me.

My dad was fucking me.

And he just kept fucking me, faster and faster, and he wouldn't stop and the pain was just so bad. . . .

Then he gasped, a loud high grunt like a sob. He held me tight with his penis poking in as deep and far as it could possibly go and shuddered, shuddered again, and a third time, and then, as suddenly as he'd started, he stopped.

I hurt so bad. I felt like I'd been ripped open inside. I could feel his penis get soft inside me. I didn't know what to do. I didn't know what he was going to do next. I just sat there, scared and in pain, tears streaking my cheeks. I didn't dare move.

For just one moment there was no sound at all except his breathing. I thought about my brothers and sisters, eating snow cones and candy. I thought about Major, waiting for me outside the door. I thought about my mom.

"I'm sorry; I'm sorry." Dad dropped his hands. He was whining now, almost crying. "You must never tell anyone. I'm sorry. I didn't mean it; I didn't mean it."

Why would I tell anyone? Everyone would know what had happened just by looking at me. There was sure to be a sign. I was sure it showed.

I felt so dirty.

Then Dad pushed me off him. "Cover yourself," he said.

I stood up. Nasty stuff ran between my legs, and I looked down and I was bleeding. I thought, *I'm gonna die! He killed me!*

Numb, I picked up my clothes and held them against me, trying to cover myself. I walked to the end of the hall and went into the bathroom and locked the door. I ran a bath. The water was hot and I sank down into it. I scrubbed and scrubbed and scrubbed my body. I tried to scrub away all the signs of what had happened, so no one would know. I didn't want anybody to know. I didn't want to go to hell.

But the nasty, dirty feeling wasn't outside, it was inside.

And you can't scrub inside.

I wanted my mom.

I don't know how long I stayed in the tub. I was so scared to come out of that bathroom, but eventually, I got out of the tub and got dressed. I pressed my ear to the door and listened for the longest time, afraid that Dad was going to be standing on the other side. I didn't hear anything, but I couldn't be sure. So I lay down on the cold floor and looked under the door. I couldn't see his feet. Finally, I turned the doorknob carefully and peeked outside. His office door was shut. I slipped out of the bathroom and tiptoed down the stairs. Then one of the steps creaked, and it scared the hell out of me. I knew if he heard it that I would be caught. I took off running down the stairs, threw open the screen door, and didn't look back.

I jumped on Major's back and rode him as hard and as fast as I could up to the canyon. I wanted to get to where everybody was, because if anybody was around then my dad couldn't hurt me.

The road was hard and dry and rutted, and Major's hooves were kicking up the dust. It was so hot that day. When I finally reached the canyon I'd run Major so hard that he was foaming at the mouth and had sweat running down his sides. I knew I should stop, but I couldn't. I had to reach people.

I finally got up to the park in the canyon under the cedar and piñon trees, and I looked everywhere for Mom, and I looked everywhere for the kids. But I couldn't find them. Then I got so scared that they knew what had happened and they'd never want to see me again, I started to panic inside.

I got off Major and started running around, trying to find my mom. People were starting to look at me weirdly because I was just running in circles, frantic.

I finally found her. She was sitting underneath a tree.

And my dad was sitting right next to her.

He looked up at me and just smiled, like nothing had happened. He patted the spot next to him and told me to come sit down by him.

And I looked at my mother, and she didn't have a smile on her face.

And I knew, I just *knew* she could see what had happened.

And I thought, *I'm gonna have to marry Dad now.*

I knew at the time that that was a crazy thought. But I was so scared, so sick, so ashamed.

The next day was Sunday. I went to church, as on any other Sunday, but nothing was the same. I was so ashamed of what had happened, and I knew it was because of something I had done. If I hadn't done . . . *something* . . . Dad wouldn't have looked at me like that. He wouldn't have made me do those bad things if I hadn't done . . . *something*. But I didn't know what it was.

I managed to avoid my father until he left for work later that day. He was working out of town and would be gone until late Friday night.

Monday, I stayed in my room during the day and went to bed early. I didn't want to play with my siblings. I didn't want to see my friends. All I wanted was my mom, but I still couldn't look at her. I was so ashamed of what had happened.

I had terrifying nightmares every night. Every time I closed my eyes I saw Dad raping me, over and over. And I knew it would happen again when Dad got back.

Tuesday, I knew that I wanted to die.

On Wednesday, four days after the rape, I decided to kill myself. Right away, I felt more focused: I had a mission.

The only way I knew of to commit suicide was to slit my wrists, so I went looking for a likely tool. There were knives in the kitchen, of course, but my mother was there. So I headed for my dad's shed. It was full of junk—he had every gizmo under the sun. I picked out a small crescent-shaped wood shaver with a thin, rusty blade about two inches wide. I tested the sharpness with my thumb, and figured it would do the job. I tucked it into my clothing and headed for the barn.

I knew just the place I wanted to die: up on Canaan Mountain, looking down on everyone in Colorado City. I couldn't think of a better place than this sandstone fortress, where Dad had left Theral to teach him a lesson he never forgot. Some might find the craggy, red-banded rocks forbidding, but to me they were a comfort. And I wasn't afraid of the Gadianton robbers, either. They wouldn't have a chance to steal my soul. If my plan worked, I'd be dead before they could catch me.

Major was glad to see me, and I was glad to see him. I put my cheek next to his soft muzzle and blew gently into nostrils, saying hello. *You're my only real friend in the world*, I thought. We were as close as a human being and an animal can be. During the summer, I would spend all day with him. During the school year, he'd be waiting for me out in the field when I came home, and I would jump on his back and ride him bareback, without a bridle or saddle, just guiding him with my hands on his mane. I hoisted myself onto his back. I knew I could count on him to be with me on my last journey.

It was a hot day, sunny and beautiful. The sky was that bright dark blue you only see in the desert. I kicked Major gently and took off toward the mountains. No one even knew I was gone.

The mountain had always been my place to get away and be by myself. I knew the trails pretty well, and I was pretty sure some of the caves back in there might have been old Indian cliff dwellings, which thrilled me. This part of Arizona and Utah had belonged to Native Americans not so long ago, before the white man drove them out and made them live on reservations. The Native Americans and I were both outcasts in our own land. I felt a real kinship with them that continues to this day.

I took Major up the steep trails slowly. It was hot, and I thought maybe I should have brought some water with me. I didn't want Major to get hurt. I trusted him to find his way home after I died.

We kept going, step by step on the rocky, winding trail, to the point deep in the canyon where it split. One fork went to the park, where the Independence Day celebration had taken place. I guided Major toward the other fork, riding farther than I had ever been before, past where we were allowed to go.

I rode deeper and deeper into the canyon until it narrowed, enclosed by red cliff walls thrusting straight up into the sky. But I wasn't really aware of the scenery. All I could see was my dress on the floor. I could feel my dad's penis pounding away inside me. I could hear his breathing, his hot breath on my neck. I could hear his awful grunt and scream . . . I felt I was going to choke to death before I got the chance to slit my wrists, or maybe my heart would beat so fast I'd have a heart attack . . . The longer I rode, the more anxious I felt, and the more ready I was to get this over with.

In the middle of this narrow pass, I took out my rusty blade and started cutting. I saw myself slice one wrist, and then the other, side to side. I watched the cut swell with blood, trickling red down my arms. Major caught the scent of blood and got skittish, twisting his neck around, dancing on the narrow trail, trying to see what I was doing. I tossed the tool to the ground, brought Major back to a walk, and kept riding.

To my disgust the bleeding slowed down. I'd already thrown away the blade, so I scratched at the wounds to keep the blood flowing. That did it. The trickle of syrupy red blood started up again and increased. Soon I started feeling groggy and tired, really tired. And despite the sun I felt cold, chilled all over. I was very thirsty now, and wondered if there was any water Major could drink. I wanted to die, but I didn't want my horse to die with me.

There was nothing I could do about it now. I slumped across Major's neck, my arms hanging down on either side of his warm neck. I let go of life. A feeling of peace flowed over me like a warm breeze, and I wasn't cold anymore.

The next thing I knew, I had fallen off Major's back onto the trail. I was just so tired. Major nuzzled me, and started licking my wrists, trying to stop the bleeding. I wanted to push him away, but I was too weak to move. I looked up at the reddening sky from where I lay. My thoughts were moving slowly, and going nowhere.

I have to hurry.

I have to hurry.

It's starting to get dark.

It's starting to get dark.

If I am here at dark, then the Gadianton robbers will get me before I die. . . .

I lost consciousness. I don't know how long it was, but I woke with the sweet, smoky scent of fire tickling my nostrils. I heard a male voice, chanting in a strange language, and a thought passed through my mind. *He must be one of the Gadianton robbers.* But his voice was soothing, and I wasn't afraid.

I opened my eyes. The sky was black and filled with stars. My wrists felt heavy and warm, so I looked at them. They were packed with a thick mud paste. How did that get there? All I could think was, *Break it open, it needs to get broke open again.* I started to sit up so I could pick the mud off. Where was Major? I looked around, but he was nowhere in sight.

That's when I saw the old Indian sitting by campfire. He was talking to me. His voice was soothing, calm. And even though he was not speaking English, I understood every word.

"It is not your time, little one," he said. "You must go back. You must go back."

"I don't want to go back," I begged. "Don't make me go back. Don't make me go back." I just wanted to die and get it over with, but what I said didn't seem to have any effect on him.

I stared at him. He had long white hair that hung down his back. His face was wrinkled and leathery, like the simple band he wore to hold his hair out of his eyes. To this day, if I close my eyes I can see his face, crystal clear.

Then I noticed he was cooking something in a little pot over the fire. He poured it into a small leather bowl and brought it over to me, walking slowly, his shoulders stooped a bit. He put his hand on my shoulder and said, "Drink, little one." I just looked at him. Then he sort of stroked my hair, like you'd pet an animal to soothe it. "Drink, little one, drink it all."

"What is it?" I sniffed it and pulled back. It really stank.

He said, "It will make you better." The sound of his voice and the touch of his hand made all my anxiety go away. A peace came over me. I wanted to do whatever he told me to.

So I took a sip and it made me tremble. I have never tasted anything like it, before or since. It tasted of earth, of dirt. It was really bitter. But he just kept talking to me, and petting me, and finally I drank it all.

When the bowl was empty, I lay back down. Then I realized I was lying on some sort of animal skin. The short, dark-brown fur was soft, and I sank into it, just watching the fire while the Indian talked to me, on and on. . . .

The next thing I knew, he had his hand on my shoulder and he was shaking me awake. "It is time to get up, little one. It is time to go home."

"No! I don't want to go home."

But he just shook his head. "You have a lot to do," he said, "but you will never be alone, you will never be alone."

"I don't want to go back."

But he was insistent. "You will never be alone. You need to go home now." He handed me the bowl and said, "Drink." This time, it was a sweet liquid, like berry juice. When I finished, I looked toward the campfire, and Major was standing there.

The Indian helped me up onto Major's back. I looked at my wrists. The mud was gone. The cuts were almost healed. I thought, *That is really strange.*

I turned around to look at the Indian, to ask him what had happened to the cuts. But he just slapped Major on the butt, and Major started walking down the trail. When I turned around to look at him again, there was nothing there. There was no fire.

There was no fire pit.

There was no Indian.

There was nothing there.

Today I have a very faint scar on one arm and nothing on the other.

I'll never know what really happened that night. All I know is that it saved my life. I think we all have spirits that help us, and he was mine. And I never tried to kill myself again—at least, not on purpose.

I wish I could say that life got better after I got back, that Dad never molested me again, that Mom defended me. But that's not the way it worked out. Mom was still sad most of the time, and Dad just kept coming after me. I couldn't do anything about it, so I just got madder and madder. One year later I couldn't take it any more. I decided to get the hell out.

4

The Great Escape

When you're planning to run away from home, it's not all about where you're going: you also have to consider where you are. And when I was growing up, Colorado City was out in the middle of nowhere. There were no houses between Colorado City and Hurricane, Utah, or between Colorado City and Fredonia, Arizona—a thirty- to forty-minute trip by car in either direction. In between was just barren desert. The sagebrush, tumbleweed, and ground cactus weren't much protection from the scorpions and rattlesnakes, or from the humans who'd be on our trail.

But when I was thirteen and my friend Sandy Hobbs* was twelve, we weren't thinking about where we were or even exactly where we were going. We were thinking about what we were running from, and we didn't care what we had to run through to get out.

Sandy and I had been best friends for years. I was a year older than Sandy, but she was bigger—a couple of inches taller and a few pounds heavier—and blonde where I was brunette. We were sort of a Mutt and Jeff team, but we had a lot in common. We both loved horses. We were both little wildcats—she'd already run away and been caught a couple of times. I had wondered if her dad was molesting her, but we had never talked about it. After what happened one afternoon in the spring of 1983, though, my dad put the subject right out in the open.

Sandy and I were hanging around the horses, feeding them and just generally goofing around in my dad's barn. Suddenly, we heard my dad coming in. Sandy dove for cover behind a stall door so fast

* Not her real name.

that Dad didn't even know she was there. He knew I was there, though. He was in a hurry that day, and he didn't mess around. He was all business. He groped my breasts and vagina with one hand and grabbed his penis with the other, jerking hard until he came. I just stood there, waiting for it to be over. It took about two minutes, start to finish. The whole time, I could see Sandy out of the corner of my eye, wide-eyed, frightened, and shocked.

As soon as he'd finished, Dad buttoned up and left. Sandy was shaken. "Flora, are you all right?"

I just shrugged. "Happens all the time," I said, straightening my dress. "Come on, let's feed the horses." I'd learned to keep my rage to myself. Sandy, however, was hysterical.

The Indian had told me to go home, and I had. I'd put up with a lot in the last year, trying hard to keep it together. In addition to touching me, my dad was still raping me from time to time. But after Sandy saw my dad in action, it made what was happening more real. I started looking for any excuse to stay away from home. Soon, I thought I'd found my chance to escape for good.

On Friday nights, the church held community dances at the old school auditorium. Like everything else in the FLDS, the dances had strict rules. You could dance with a person only one time during the entire evening—having two or more dances with the same person was considered a sin on a par with having sex. It wasn't as if we were doing dirty dancing, either. In the early 1980s, when the rest of the country was moving from disco to punk and beyond, we were dancing the waltz, the two-step, and the Virginia reel. But I didn't care. The dances gave me a rare opportunity to socialize with friends without having to sneak out to do it.

I was talking to Sandy and our friend Donia about Friday's upcoming dance when I had what I thought was a brilliant idea.

"You know," I said, "it wouldn't be too hard to sneak out of that dance."

"What are you talking about?"

"I'm talking about getting out of here for good." They were both excited, and we all looked around to make sure no one had overheard us.

Sandy frowned. "We'd have to make some plans, Flora. We can't just run out into the desert with no food."

"You're right," Donia chimed in. "And we'll need different clothes. We can't run very far in these. And they'll give us away." She swatted at her long skirt.

I couldn't believe they'd jumped on board so fast. I was elated. I was prepared to run by myself, but I'd rather have friends with me. Our idle conversation soon became the first of several planning sessions for the great escape.

The next few days were exhilarating. We figured we would be out on the desert for a while, so we'd need plenty of supplies. Our idea of survival gear was pretty unusual. I found some old Indian blankets at my house to fashion into sacks and took them down to the cellar. We carefully wrapped up some bottled pears and peaches and some canned beans. We collected some small pots and pans and filled them with tiny potatoes. We wrapped odd pieces of flatware as if we were shipping expensive designer silverware. But the coup de grace was provided by Sandy. I don't know how she did it, but she managed to come up with three sets of old blue jeans and shirts and squirreled them away at her house.

With everything packaged up tight and ready for the road, Donia and Sandy took their stashes of essentials home and hid them in a safe place. I hid mine upstairs in my bedroom. We were set! We figured that the hardest part would be making it to Hurricane, roughly thirty miles away. Once there, we planned to hitchhike to Las Vegas, where Sandy's dad worked.

Sandy's dad, Don Hobbs,* was gone from home about as much as my dad was, mostly in Las Vegas. Like many others in the community,

* Not his real name.

he didn't see eye to eye with the priesthood, especially about property ownership. Don actually held the title to a few acres the priesthood was pressing him to donate to the UEP trust, and he owned some property in Las Vegas that wasn't connected with the FLDS. Sandy figured that her dad and his friends in Vegas hated the priesthood enough to help us out. I hoped she was right, but I didn't see what other choice we had. And at thirteen, I wasn't really thinking through the consequences.

Finally! The night of the dance. Six o'clock on a warm Friday night in mid-May. I looked around for Sandy and Donia, feeling a rush of adrenaline already starting to build. No one was paying any particular attention to me, and why should they? Mom was home tending to the babies, and Dad was out of town working. The other adults at the dance were watching their own kids or each other.

I spotted Sandy and Donia whispering in a corner. I could tell something was wrong. Donia was crying.

"I'm sorry," she said, shaking her head. "I just can't do it. If my dad catches me, I don't know what he'll do to me, but it'll be bad. I'm too scared. I'm sorry." I was mad, but I understood why she'd chickened out.

Sandy and I looked at each. "Don't worry, Flora," Sandy said, "I'm still going with you."

Sandy and I were as determined as ever to run away. Our plan was to run for it during a break between dance sessions, when we figured no one would miss us. We estimated we had about another hour of sunlight, and a twenty-minute window to make our escape before anyone would miss us.

We tried to act normal, but it wasn't easy. All I could think about was the plan. We danced a bit, and the dances seemed even slower than usual. They went on and on, one after the other. Finally, at around seven, there was a break. We walked outside slowly, as if we were just getting some air. Then we took off running down the bottom of Short Creek—basically, the Arizona-Utah border—which led straight to Sandy's house. Sandy ducked quietly into her house, and I kept going, down a dirt road and through a field that ended at my backyard, and got into my house through the back, sneaking in without anyone noticing. Trying not to make any noise, I grabbed my stuff, tiptoed out of the house, and then made a run for Sandy's again, where Sandy and I changed into the pants and shirts. Then we snuck out and headed for freedom. It was a miracle that no one had seen us.

Yes! We were right on schedule. Another five minutes and we'd make it to the outskirts of town. We giggled like maniacs. Then I heard something that chilled me to the bone.

"Sandy! Flora! Where are you?"

"Flora Mae!"

"Sandy Hobbs! Come here right now!"

More and more voices were calling our names. "Donia must have squealed us out," said Sandy.

"We can't get caught now," I said, looking around for cover.

We heard more and more voices. It seemed as if the whole town was looking for us, and people were coming from all sides. There was nowhere to run. So we did the only thing we could do: we jumped into the creek bed next to Sandy's house and hid underneath a small concrete bridge. Thank goodness there wasn't much water in the creek, but there were a lot of rocks mixed in with the sand. We lay there, flat as we could, so quiet we almost weren't breathing. *Please, God, don't let them find us.*

The streets around Sandy's house were crawling with people, and I assumed it was the same at my house. We'd be here for hours at this rate. Then Becky, one of Sandy's mothers, walked onto the bridge with Sandy's little brother Travis. To our horror, they stopped right smack in the middle of the bridge and started talking. I liked Travis. He was a wildcat, like us. They just stood there and talked for half an hour, as the sun sank down lower and lower. I couldn't believe it. Weren't they ever going to leave? The rocks were pressing through my blue jeans, and we were getting wet.

Still, I was willing to stick it out all night if I had to. All of a sudden, Travis spotted us through a crack in the bridge. *No!* Our eyes locked. He gave me a quick grin and winked when Becky wasn't looking. *All right!* He wouldn't blow our cover.

After what seemed like hours, Becky and Travis walked back to Sandy's house. It was so hard to lie there on those rocks, but we waited until they were out of sight and we were sure that no one else was around. Then we picked ourselves up and ran like crazy down the creek bed, heading for the bridge that crossed it on the highway outside of town. Before we could get there, men in four-wheel-drive trucks started driving up and down the creek bed, looking for us. We had to keep jumping into the head-high brush alongside the creek bottom, hiding from them. I was glad I didn't have to do this in my long skirt and leggings.

Finally, we made it to the highway. We were scared as hell.

"Flora—look." Sandy was near tears. A barbed-wire fence ran across the full width of the creek under the bridge. I wasn't about to let that stop me.

"We can do it." Being as careful as I could, I stretched the strands of wire up while Sandy crawled underneath the sharp barbs, hauling her blanket after her. Then she held them up for me and I crawled though. We finished crossing underneath the bridge and scrambled up the steep bank on the highway's west side.

But we weren't free yet—we could still hear the trucks on our tail, and we knew they wouldn't stop coming after us. "They can track our footprints and find us easy," said Sandy.

Then we had a brainstorm: we'd walk backward, stepping in our own footprints, to confuse the trail. They'd track us to the highway, but we'd be in the desert. They'd never find us.

Walking backward wasn't easy. We kept almost falling over, but we kept at it. We were almost back to the barbed wire when we heard a loud *thwup, thwup, thwup.* We looked up, and froze. Two helicopters appeared over the horizon, out of nowhere, their lights sweeping the desert.

"Are those looking for us? Where did they come from?"

"I don't know. Just stand still. It's dark. Maybe they won't see us." We were scared to death, but we held firm.

Finally, the helicopters passed, and they didn't circle back. I don't know if they were looking for us, but they sure didn't see us. To this day, I don't where they came from.

We kept walking backward, retracing our steps, still lugging our potatoes, canned goods, and pots and pans. If anyone had seen us, they would have died laughing.

But we weren't laughing. We were still chilled from the creek sand and it was getting colder out there in the desert. Still, we weren't giving up. We'd stop for a minute to catch our breath, and then start running again. We were thirsty as all get out from running. For the first time, we realized that we'd forgotten to bring any water.

But even though we were scared, we were laughing our butts off because we were still free. Our fear and adrenaline and our crazy exhilaration because we hadn't been caught made a powerful mix, and it kept us going. We knew they'd follow our tracks to that highway and think that we got picked up. Later, we found out that's exactly what happened. They put dogs on our trail, and the dogs tracked us to that highway and lost the scent. So we even fooled the dogs. Pretty good for a couple of young kids!

We walked for hours and hours. Finally, we got smart and started unloading things. We'd drop a couple of bottles of pears, a couple of cans of beans, a few potatoes. There's probably a row of potato plants out there in the desert right now, and some snakes that are finding shelter under our little pots and pans.

Our feet hurt like hell. "We must be almost to Hurricane by now, right?"

"Have to be." We kept going.

"Man, I wonder how much farther we have to walk. We must be getting to the hill soon, right?"

"Right."

But we were starting to have real doubts. It was pitch-black out in the desert. I was worried I'd step into a damned rabbit hole and break my leg. But we just kept walking and walking, unloading a little bit here and a little bit there until we had hardly any stuff left at all. Those neatly wrapped forks and spoons seemed pretty silly now.

And it kept getting colder and colder. The desert sand doesn't hold the heat from the sun, so after the sun goes down—even on a hundred-degree day—it can get bitterly cold. In the daytime you can die from heat exhaustion, but at night you can die from hypothermia. And we hadn't had any water in hours.

Sandy and I just looked at each other and dropped to the sand, exhausted. We both knew we were done. We didn't have to say anything. We both just wanted to go home and go to bed.

"Colorado City's got to be closer than Hurricane, right?"

"Yeah."

So we turned around, wrapped our now-empty blankets tight around us, and headed for home.

We came walking back in to the far end of town at two or three o'clock in the morning. Everything had settled down and the town was quiet. We were trudging along, thinking how much trouble we were going to be in when we got home. But our adventures weren't over yet.

Out of nowhere, a light-blue, short-wheelbase, jacked-up truck came rolling right up to us and screeched to a halt. Inside were two older teenage boys, Kevin Zitting (his father later became the mayor of Hildale) and his friend, Richard Knudson.

"Hey, what are you girls doing out so late?" They were smiling and laughing. We were dumbstruck. At twelve and thirteen, Sandy and I were impressed that these eighteen-year-olds were even talking to us. We felt wicked and special. And we weren't tired anymore.

"We're going four-wheeling," said Kevin. "Jump in!"

Sandy and I looked at each other and smiled. This was just nuts. "Sure, why not?" We'd never done anything this crazy before, but it had been a day for new experiences.

We climbed into the truck. Sandy sat between the boys, and I sat on Richard's lap. We bounced along the rutted dirt road, and Richard complained the whole time. "Your bony butt is gonna cut my leg smooth off."

We drove a few miles south of Colorado City to Coral Pink Sand Dunes State Park in Utah, which we thought of as a big sand pile out in the middle of nowhere. The rosy dunes are beautiful, perfect for off-roading. We couldn't believe our luck. Sandy and I were laughing, and the boys were drinking beer, spinning the tires, making fancy turns in the dunes. Suddenly, the truck bit hard into the sand, stopped, and rolled completely over. No one got hurt, but it scared us to death.

We managed to push the truck over until it was standing on its wheels again, and we came rolling back into town at about five in the morning, aching, drained, and once again terrified of what might wait for us at home. The boys dropped us off on the dirt road between Sandy's house and my house, and we each headed home. I cut through the field behind the house and tiptoed up to the backdoor. Against all odds, I still had my blanket, and I pulled it tighter around me. I stepped up onto the back porch and looked in the kitchen window. There was my mother, standing stock still. She just stood looking at me. My heart pounded hard. *Oh, my God,* I thought. *I am in so much trouble.*

Finally, I opened the backdoor.

My mother met me on the threshold and didn't say a word. She just wrapped her arms around me, gave me a big hug, and gently pulled me inside. With her arm still around my shoulders, she walked me up the stairs. I was so grateful. I just wanted to fall into bed and sleep for a week.

But then we heard a *bang, bang, bang* on the front door. With her arm still around my shoulders, my mom and I went back downstairs to the living room and opened the door. Becky and Sandy stood on the doorstep, and Becky was mad as hell. I liked Becky. Unlike Sandy's real mom, who could be cruel, Becky had always been very nice. She was the sweet wife in that home, the stay-at-home mom. She was never mean to the children, but she was livid now.

"Flora, you owe everybody an apology for what you did! You frightened us all to death! How dare you run away like that? You owe me an apology, and Sandy owes your mother an apology, and you owe *each other* an apology for talking each other into running away in the first place." She was adamant.

I just listened to her, thinking, *I am not sorry for anything I have done. I am not sorry for trying to run away. And I'll be damned if I am going to apologize to a single soul for this.*

But I didn't say anything, so Becky turned to Sandy.

"I want you to apologize right now to Pat, and I want you to apologize to me."

Sandy looked at my mom meekly. "I'm sorry, Pat." Then she turned to Becky. "I'm sorry for what I've done, and I won't ever do it again." She even apologized to me. "I'm sorry, Flora." She looked miserable.

"Thank you, Sandy. Now it's your turn, Flora. You need to apologize."

I was furious. "I am not going to apologize."

Becky lost it. "Flora, you apologize right now! I'm waiting right here until I hear an apology!"

Sandy stuck her elbow in my side and hissed, "Just apologize so we can go to bed!"

"Fine," I said, when I couldn't take Sandy's insistence anymore. "I apologize to my mother for the scare that I put her through. But I refuse to apologize to anybody else because I do not owe anybody else an apology. And I'm not sorry for trying to get away."

Becky yelled at me for quite a while after that, but I never did apologize. Eventually, she gave up and dragged Sandy home. The sun was just rising, and the sky was growing light.

My mother still hadn't said a word. We walked back up the stairs together. When we got to the top of the stairs, she gave me a big hug and said, "I'm glad you're safe. Go get some sleep."

As I lay in my own bed, safe for at least one night, I broke down, sobbing. The little bit of affection my mom had shown me touched me to the core. Before this, only my grandmother had ever openly expressed her love for me. Only my grandmother had ever made me feel I might be worth something more than living a life as some man's property. Beyond that, my mom had done something truly amazing by not forcing me to apologize, by just letting me get some rest.

According to the FLDS beliefs, I should have been severely punished. Usually, when you don't comply with the rules or adhere to the directives of the priesthood, you're shunned: all love or affection is withheld. I had expected my mother to shun me. By rights, she shouldn't have even spoken to me or acknowledged that I existed. But she didn't punish me at all. Instead, she put her arm around me and just held me.

I knew Mom loved me. I was overcome by that little bit of affection that was normally absent in my life. I cried myself to sleep that night.

But the warm feeling disappeared as soon as my father returned for the weekend. Mom kept the news from him as long as she could, but he soon learned all the details—the story was all over town. True to form, he gave me a royal beating and told me that if I ever tried to run away again, my punishment would be even more severe.

I got punished all right. But it wasn't for something I did. It was because of what my dad was doing to me.

5

Little Runaway

A few months after I ran away, I suddenly became very ill. I was tired and drawn, and I couldn't seem to keep anything down. I was throwing up all the time. After a few weeks, I was really worried and so was Mom. She sent me over to the clinic at Hildale to see Aunt Lydia.

As the clinic's midwife, Aunt Lydia must have delivered thousands of babies over the years. Along the way, she had also become the person all of us in the twin towns went to when we were sick, even though she wasn't a doctor. A lot of people loved Lydia. I wanted to love Aunt Lydia too, especially because she had raised my favorite sister, Patricia. But I'd never forgotten the day she stomped my doll to death. I'd been wary of her ever since.

But now I really wanted to get well, so I trotted over to the clinic. Aunt Lydia asked me a few questions, gave me a shot of penicillin, and sent me home. I knew penicillin worked to cure a lot of illnesses, so I was looking forward to getting better soon.

But the penicillin did nothing. After a few days, I was still throwing up. Now I was really getting scared. Mom sent me back to Aunt Lydia.

I started to sit down in the clinic, where I'd gotten my shot, but Lydia shook her head. "In there," she said, pointing toward the birthing center. She took me by the hand and put me in a delivery room. "Lay down on that table," she said.

"Why?" I asked.

But Aunt Lydia just said, "Open your legs." Then she stuck an icy-cold metal instrument into my vagina and cranked it. I yelped in pain.

"What are you doing?"

"You need a vaginal exam," she said.

"Why?" I was both mortified and mystified. I'd come in sick as a dog, and she had me splayed open on a table for the whole world to see. I'd never had a vaginal exam before. Why now?

Then, without another word, she rammed the business end of a wire coat hanger inside me. The pain was excruciating. I cried out so loud I figured the whole town could hear me. "Stop it!" I struggled, but that made the pain worse.

"You are in pain because of your sins!" Aunt Lydia shouted, poking and probing me. "You have nobody to blame but yourself!"

I had no idea what she was talking about, or what she was doing. The pain was so bad I couldn't think. I thought I was going to pass out. Maybe I really would die this time.

"You are pregnant, you ignorant girl."

What?

I was pregnant. *No!*

That's why I'd been throwing up . . . I was going to have my dad's baby. This couldn't be happening to me. But I knew it was, because I remembered each and every time he'd poked his penis into me in the past couple of months. Dad should have known this would happen! I felt completely betrayed.

As many pregnancies as I'd seen in my thirteen years, as many sex noises as I'd heard coming from behind closed doors, I just hadn't made the connection. I knew nothing about pregnancy, gestation periods, or the act of giving birth. I was just a child. Was I giving birth right now? Were they going to give the baby away? I kept seeing Chatty Cathy, in pieces on the floor. Now Aunt Lydia was taking my baby. Would she stomp my baby to death and throw her in the garbage?

As Aunt Lydia performed the crude and painful abortion and I lay there bleeding, I tried to make sense of it all. But nothing about my life made much sense.

I was in terrible pain. She hadn't given me any anesthesia during the procedure, and I didn't get any painkillers afterward. She just got me up after a few minutes, threw me out, and sent me home. I bled profusely for days. My mom didn't say anything about it, and my dad kept on taking advantage of me whenever he felt like it. My periods went from tolerable to horrible cramping. I hated what dad was doing to me, but there was nothing I could do to make him stop and no way to protect myself.

I knew one thing—I did not ever want to go through the pain of an abortion again. So whenever my period was late, I would beat myself in the stomach until I thought I had done away with the pregnancy. Once, I punched my stomach over and over until I was exhausted. No one knew I used my stomach as a punching bag. I'm not sure anyone would have cared.

The abortion opened the floodgates of the emotional pain I'd been storing up over the years. Over the following months, I began to understand the magnitude of the abuse I was enduring. I couldn't deny it anymore. My resentment, anger, and hostility grew exponentially. I maintained a constant state of rage.

One crisp morning in early December 1983, Sandy and I were walking to school along the dry bed of Short Creek when two teenage boys from prominent families assaulted us. One grabbed Sandy, and the other wrestled with me. They started rubbing themselves against us, saying, "I know you like it. I know you want it."

I struggled and screamed, "Get away from me! Let me go!" Sandy did the same. But they kept right on doing what they were doing.

One of the boys lifted my dress and put his hand on my buttocks, pulling me tighter to him. The other boy did exactly the same thing to Sandy. It was weird. They did everything in unison. It was like they'd choreographed the whole rape beforehand. As they started unbuckling their pants, they loosened their grips on us. We made our break and ran back down the wash to Sandy's house. They didn't follow, and we didn't look back. Sandy was really upset, but for me it was just another day. I was used to much worse behavior at home.

But Sandy couldn't let it go. The next day, in the classroom, she tried to pass a note to one of the two boys. I knew what the note said: "You don't have the right to touch us like that. You tried to rape us. If you ever do that again I am going to tell the police." The teacher snatched it, read it, and sent it right over to Sam Barlow, the town marshal.

Normally, crimes reported to the police in Colorado City were handled in the community, by the priesthood, which accounted for the twin towns' astoundingly low rate of reported crime. But our teacher must have had other ideas, because Sandy soon found herself sitting in the police station in St. George, Utah, trying to explain herself. In short order, the police pulled me in for questioning too. The boys were from high-ranking FLDS families, so the police at first tried to blame us for making up stories. But their questioning took a different turn when Sandy told them that she had seen my father molesting me in the barn.

The police had to bring in the Utah Department of Child and Family Services (DCFS), and they asked Washington County, Utah, district attorney Paul Graff to sit in on my questioning. I couldn't believe it! All this time my dad had been molesting me, and no one had cared. Now it seemed that adults might actually be interested in helping me.

When Paul asked if my father had molested me, I looked him right in the eye and said, "Yes."

Sandy had finally confided in me that her father had molested her too, but now she testified that her father was not molesting her. It was hard for me to believe, but maybe he really wasn't. Maybe when she told me he had, she'd just wanted us to have even more misery to share than we already had. She was so angry now, I thought she would have told the police if her dad had really done something, but I never knew for sure.

They didn't even lock my dad up for questioning. That is how screwed up the Utah judicial system was at that point: a father molesting a child is a felony. But they'd been ignoring what was going on in Colorado City and Hildale for decades, opting to treat polygamy as "religious belief" rather than the violation of state law that it was. And molestation and incest were difficult to prove in any case—let alone with a witness like Sandy, a "rebellious" young girl like me. Moreover, the authorities were afraid of bringing on a confrontation—another Short Creek, only worse. So they let our own so-called police—part of the state system but all members of the FLDS priesthood—take care of the twin towns' problems.

Still, the DCFS did do something. It assigned a caseworker, Chuck Sullivan, to work with me. I met with him once a week— for years as it would turn out. I was suspicious of all adults at this point, but he slowly gained my trust. I opened my soul to that man. I told him about other children who were being abused and molested. I told him about the plural marriages and what went on in polygamous homes. I made it very clear to him that I wanted out of Colorado City and Hildale. He sympathized with me and promised he would do everything he could to get me into foster care. I wanted to believe him.

But nothing happened for a long time. I was still living at home, my dad was still getting after me when he wanted to, and life was getting more miserable by the day. Then Sam Barlow called me into his office. He was a scary guy who could make bad things happen. He said he just wanted to talk about the charges against my father. But his questioning soon took a different and bizarre turn.

"What do you know about penises?" he asked. "What do you know about sex? What does it feel like?"

I could have died! I hated him for asking these awful questions. He bounced up and down in his seat as he grilled me. I know for a fact he was masturbating as he hurled question after filthy question at me. There wasn't one damn thing I could do about it.

In late December 1983, Dad was—to my surprise and temporary relief—finally arraigned in criminal court for molesting me. But then Uncle Fred roared into action. He was a bishop in the FLDS, and as far as he was concerned, the bishop's brother could not be convicted of molesting his daughter. This was nothing new for him—all of Dad's brothers were also child molesters, and Fred protected them too.

Uncle Fred used his influence to have my dad's case removed from criminal court and sent to juvenile court. Adults aren't tried in juvenile court, only kids. The idea of hearing a child abuse case in juvenile court was absurd. The world outside Colorado City had let me down hard: I was still the one who was being treated like a criminal.

In the end, my dad got off easy. He paid the judge a $4,000 "fine," in cash—more of a bribe—and was ordered to stay away from home for a while and to go back to Salt Lake City to work. Dad headed out of town and stayed away for several weeks. When he returned, the abuse began again. In fact, it increased.

One time just before he raped me, he smirked and said, "I told you they wouldn't believe you. I told you to keep our secret. Look what happened." It was always my fault.

I was angrier than ever. Despite the way it all turned out, I wasn't ready to give up. A few weeks later, I tried to get help again.

In early 1984, I was sitting alone in the waiting room of our dentist's office in St. George, waiting to get my teeth checked. All of a sudden, I realized, *No one is watching me.* I ran into the street, sprinted for the courthouse, and ran inside. I pulled open the heavy door to the first room I came to and walked up to a tall wooden counter. "Please," I said to the person behind the counter, "I need help. My dad is molesting me, and I need to talk to somebody." I was scared to death, but apparently I wasn't too convincing.

I was promptly sent to juvenile detention, where I sat for several hours, feeling more and more miserable and neglected. It was obvious that no one was taking me seriously. Finally, someone called my mother to pick me up and take me back to Colorado City. It took her a while to drive the thirty-five miles from Colorado City to St. George, and I could see she wasn't happy about it. We drove home in silence. She did not have a word to say to me, and I had nothing to say to her.

Soon after I returned, I was kicked out of school. The teachers said I was too much of a rebel and caused too much trouble. None of the parents wanted their kids to associate with me. To make things worse, someone told my teachers that I'd been whoring—selling myself for five dollars to young men in town. All of that was more than the school administrators could cope with, so they gave me the boot.

I was completely humiliated. The community as a whole now shunned me. My sisters, my family, and the townsfolk—they all either ignored me or avoided me. They saw me as fighting against God, against God's servants, against the Prophet himself. Everyone saw me as evil except Dad, who continued having sex with me whenever he could catch me.

After I turned fourteen, I had something else to worry about: being assigned a husband. Every FLDS girl understood that as soon as she turned twelve, she could be married off at the whim of the Prophet. At age fourteen, I was prime predators' meat, and every man—no matter how old—was a potential spouse. And what was worse, the majority of the men already had more than one wife. The Prophet's council of old men had been secretly kicking teenage boys out of town for years, fearful of competition for wives and places in the celestial kingdom. The numbers of those poor "lost boys" would only increase as the years went on.

If I had to be married off, I prayed that I would at least be the first wife. Polygamous households tend to follow a strict hierarchy. The first wife usually has more control over her own life than the sister-wives do, and she can boss her sister-wives around. Lydia was the perfect example of a powerful first wife. My own family was really an exception to the rule. Even though my mom was the first wife, she was the one who was abused after Elizabeth married my dad.

Hardly anyone got to marry a boy she was actually in love with. Most girls would settle for somebody who was halfway young. Every time I saw a teenage boy, I'd pray, *Please, God, please, please let me be his wife.* I didn't want to end up married to some man who was old enough to be my grandfather, living in a shack with a million kids, doing all the laundry.

I felt as if I was caught in a vise. The pressure was unbearable—arranged marriage closing in on one side and my dad's unstoppable abuse on the other. I wanted to escape more than ever. I was still seeing my DCFS counselor, Chuck Sullivan, but I couldn't see that he'd done me much good. I still liked him, but he hadn't been able to find me a foster home. In fact, the counselors and lawyers appeared to be as stymied as I was. The states of Utah and Arizona just didn't seem to know how to deal with what was going on in the FLDS.

Because of what had happened at Short Creek so long ago, they had adopted a hands-off attitude toward polygamy and everything that went along with it. Anyway, it was hard to prove allegations of abuse. At one point, District Attorney Paul Graff told me my only real option was to get legally married—by the state, not the Prophet—then I would be automatically emancipated from my family, even if I was a minor. But at age fourteen, and knowing the control of the FLDS, I didn't think this seemed like much of an option at all. Chuck Sullivan had another idea: he said that my only way out was to run away from home. Of course, I'd already tried that. But this time, he said, I'd have some help.

Sullivan put me in touch with an informal, unofficial network of people who tried to help girls escape the cult. He gave me the phone number of a woman called Aunt Jenny, an ex-FLDS member who helped kids escape from their abusive homes. He also gave her my name, so she'd be expecting me to call when I was ready to leave. Then he hooked me up with an FLDS couple, Cornell and Trudy Bateman, who were also willing to help. They lived in Colorado City, just like me, but they'd been on the outs with the priesthood for some time. They wanted to own their own home and had been willing to take a stand against the UEP. Secretly, they were also a stop on this loose-knit "underground railroad."

They took me under their wing and said they might be able to provide me with a safe haven for a short time, until I could find a good place to stay that was further from home. They were good people, and they were risking their lives. I trusted them more than I trusted the state. I started watching and waiting for my moment to run.

One day in early May 1984, a month before my fifteenth birthday, there were only a few people in the house. Mom wasn't in, and Dad was out in the barn. It was just starting to get dark, and I knew that for a few minutes at least, no one would miss me. I saw an opportunity and took it.

I ran out of my room in what I was wearing, just the standard long dress and leggings. I didn't even pack a change of clothes. As I passed my dresser, I scooped up some loose photos of Mom and my brothers and sisters.

In no time, I was standing on the Batemans' porch. "I'm ready," I said, when they opened the door. Fortunately, they were ready too.

"Let's go," they said, heading for their car. There was no time for second thoughts.

I hunkered down in the backseat of their large four-door sedan, trying to stay out of sight as we slowly drove out of town.

When I knew we'd passed the city limits, I carefully raised my head up and peered out the window at the disappearing lights of Colorado City and Hildale. *Oh, my God*, I thought, *it's really happening.* I was torn by conflicting emotions: an overpowering fear that I'd be captured, doubt and guilt about leaving my family behind, and the elation and joy of freedom.

Most of all, though, I felt guilty. All of the FLDS teachings I'd ever had came flooding into my mind: *What if Colorado City really is the kingdom of God's people? What if I'm fighting against God and God's will? What if I'm the one who's wrong?*

We arrived at Aunt Jenny's house in St. George at about nine o'clock. My heart was pounding as we waited on her doorstep. Would she help me, or would she send me home? Jenny Larson opened the door and looked me up and down with an appraising eye. I looked at her too. She was just a regular-looking woman in her late forties. Could she really help me?

"Come on in," she said.

But the Batemans were spooked. They didn't feel her place was safe enough. It was too close to Colorado City for one thing, and too many people knew about Jenny and what she was doing. People in the FLDS called her The Devil, and her family was always telling her she'd end up in hell. The Batemans didn't want to spend any time in her house.

I thought Jenny was a lot like me, and I decided to trust her. She looked me up and down and said, "Let's go."

I looked around to say good-bye to the Batemans, but they were already gone. I didn't blame them. *Cornell and Trudy will be in so much trouble if we are caught*, I thought. *They'll go to jail for trying to help me. I bet they're as scared as I am.*

Jenny kissed her husband, Ronald, on the cheek, and then she and I climbed into the front seat of her car, another big four-door sedan. For the second time that night, someone drove me slowly out of town. This time, we were headed for Las Vegas, Nevada. Jenny told me she was taking me to the home of a woman named Fern Carson* who was willing to take in a runaway.

Aunt Jenny tried hard to put me at ease. She asked me a lot of superficial questions about what I liked, my friends, my horse—small talk. I answered mostly with one-word responses. The rest of

*Not her real names.

the time, I just sat there biting my lip, looking behind us to make sure no one was following us, my head full of shouting thoughts. I really did not feel like talking.

The route from St. George, Utah, to Las Vegas, Nevada, crosses the northwest corner of Arizona, and when we got to the Utah-Arizona state line, Aunt Jenny stopped the car.

"You need to get out here, Flora," she said. "You need to walk across the state line yourself." She pointed down the road. "I'll pick you up on the other side."

"Why?" This made no sense to me at all. Why couldn't we just drive across?

"If I drive you, and someone catches us, I could be charged with transporting a minor across a state line. And I don't want that to happen!"

So I got out and walked into Arizona. She drove across the line and stopped. I got back in the car, and we rolled on. My whole life had been crazy. This was nothing.

As we drove across the desert toward Nevada, I watched at first as the headlights picked out clumps of sagebrush and the occasional lizard making a death-defying run across the road. But pretty soon, I found myself mesmerized by the endless white line in the middle of the road, and I let it lull me. Aunt Jenny was still trying to get me to open up and talk to her, and she did her best to make me feel comfortable by telling me stories of when she was a little girl living in Short Creek. But the stories just made me feel lonely. I missed my family. At that moment, I even missed my father—the man who raped me and abused me.

How could I miss him? Simple. Like every child, I wanted to be loved unconditionally by both my parents. Even though my father had committed the worst possible violation of a human being, I still held out hope that someday he would repent and love me as a father should love a daughter. And sick as it seems, he paid attention to me. To a neglected child, even bad attention can feel good.

As we approached the Arizona-Nevada state line, Jenny pulled over to the side of the road and stopped. This time, she didn't have to tell me what to do. I got out, walked across the state line, and waited for her to drive across and pick me up. It was really an unnecessary precaution—except for the occasional lizard or snake, the dark desert highway was empty under a brilliant canopy of stars.

As we rolled into Nevada, I soon saw an amazing sight: the bright lights of a city were glowing in the midst of a sea of darkness. The artificial brilliance of Las Vegas wiped out the starry sky. A whole city, still awake in the middle of the night. I was so fascinated I almost forgot why we were there.

We drove around Las Vegas for a while, looking for Fern Carson's house. Up close, the lights of the casinos seemed even more incredible. Finally, we found it. Fern, an older, white-haired woman, met us at the door with two tiny, yapping dogs. She seemed nice enough, and her modest home was clean. Fern told Aunt Jenny she would take care of me. We all went into the house. All I could think was that Fern had the most elegant dining room I'd ever seen.

Aunt Jenny gave me fifty dollars. "I hope you'll get a haircut," she said. "And a perm!" she added with a smile—haircuts were bad enough, but perms were taboo in the FLDS community. Jenny really was a rebel after my own heart. We hugged and said goodbye, and I turned to starting my new life.

Fern's husband had recently died, and she lived alone. Fern was a heavy smoker, like my Aunt Mickey, who used to come to play cards with my mother and grandmother. Fern and I played card games too, so I felt at home there.

But when I was alone, I was scared. Fern worked part-time cleaning houses and was gone for long periods of the day. When she was home, she acted very nervous about hiding me. We were both afraid of being caught. She even gave me the code name "Margaret" and called me that whenever she talked with Aunt Jenny on the phone.

I stayed in the house all the time because I was afraid to leave. I slept a lot and ate. Fern always had plenty of food in the fridge. But I grew lonelier by the day. I was always glad to see Fern pull up in her big white Buick, but it was just not the same as being home with my mom and my brothers and sisters.

Fern tried to talk me through some of my fears, but she had no firsthand knowledge of what it was like to be under the spell of the FLDS. She couldn't really understand. I remember feeling stupid trying to explain certain beliefs about apostates, plural marriage, and dress codes. Fern would say, "Come on, now. How could you actually believe something like that?"

"Well, I don't know," I would answer. "I just do."

I had been living with Fern for about a month when I noticed a car driving by the house very slowly. My heart dropped into my stomach: the two men in the front seat were Barlow boys. Maybe it was just a coincidence they were there—lots of FLDS men did business in Las Vegas. But I feared the worst, and I was scared to death for both of us. I knew if they caught me in Fern's house, she'd be in deep, deep trouble. I was really frightened for her safety. I did not want her to get into trouble because of me.

Terrified, and clearly not thinking straight, I ran. Fern had gotten me a few new clothes and other things, but once again I left with only what I was wearing. and headed downtown on foot. Eventually, I wandered into one of the big casinos. Lights were flashing, coins were dropping, and gamblers were yelling and laughing. You couldn't even tell if it was day or night in there. I began to panic even more. I couldn't go back to Fern's. I didn't have Aunt Jenny's number. I had nowhere to turn. Lost and alone, I just wanted to go home.

I saw a dime on the ground, picked it up, and found a pay phone in a nearby store. I called Uncle Fred.

"Uncle Fred? It's Flora."

"Flora! Thank goodness you called. Where are you?"

"I'm in Las Vegas. Can you come get me?" I told him the name of the store, and he told me to stay put.

"Don't move. I'll send someone to get you right away."

I hung up, relieved to be going home, and guilty about letting down everyone who'd helped me along the way. After a month of freedom, I had voluntarily put myself back in the hole I'd just dug myself out of.

But what other choice did I have? As defiant as I was and as much as I yearned to be free of the FLDS and the abuse, I was only fourteen years old. I needed real help, but the only advice I got from those in authority was to run away or get married. Fern was doing her best, but she knew nothing about how to counsel a young girl raised on ignorance and abuse.

The emotional load was just too much for me to carry on my own: the fear of being captured by the Barlow boys, the fear that my actions would harm Fern or Aunt Jenny or Trudy and Cornell, the heart-wrenching loneliness of a month away from family and friends. For fourteen years, I'd been brainwashed into fearing the outside world. What could I do but surrender to what at the time seemed to be unavoidable and inevitable?

All I wanted was to see my mom, to have her put her arms around me and walk me upstairs to bed—as she had when Sandy and I came back from attempting our great escape across the desert. But Uncle Fred's men did not bring me back home. Instead, they brought me back to Uncle Fred's beautiful house. Fred and Lydia were standing at the door, furious.

They didn't wait a second before letting me know exactly what I could expect: "You are a bad influence and have made bad choices. You have disappointed and shamed your parents, the Prophet, and God. You will sever all ties to your friends and obey the will of the Prophet. Is that clear?" said Uncle Fred.

Then Lydia grabbed my hand and dragged me upstairs to the second floor. She shoved me into a room no bigger than a walk-in closet. "Do not leave this room," she said. "I will come for you in the morning."

And right there, my world stopped. For the next two years, I would be their prisoner and slave.

6

The Prisoner

Lydia didn't lock my bedroom door. She didn't have to. The house was full of prison guards. Fred's wives Martha and Susan had rooms on the left side, and my sisters' room was on the right. Uncle Fred's office was on the other side of my sisters' room, with one of the windows facing the same way my small window did. I knew the wives would watch me like hawks. Solitary confinement sent my imagination into high gear. I imagined all the horrible things they would do to me—they'd beat me, set snakes in my room, hang me upside down, strip me naked in front of a crowd . . .

I looked around my new room. The irony of the situation wasn't lost on me. My new prison cell was actually much nicer than my bedroom at home, just as I'd imagined when I dreamed of living here with my sisters. The walls were covered with drywall and painted white. A thick, chocolate-brown shag carpet covered the floor. A nice four-drawer dresser was set tightly in the far corner. A small wooden desk sat under the small window. The armchair, I soon discovered, was a hideaway twin-size bed. But when I folded it out, I couldn't walk around it. I wanted to scream.

I lay sleepless and terrified on the bed all night, waiting for someone to come back and beat me or, worse, humiliate me in front of the family. No one did, at least not on that first day. But as the days dragged on, that would change. Over the following months, I would be beaten severely. Some mornings I would wake to a zombie-like state of distorted and foggy consciousness. Lydia forced me to take pills she called daily "vitamins." But she had unlimited access to medical supplies, and I'm convinced that at least some of these pills contained a barbiturate or benzodiazepine-type drug that depressed my brain and central nervous system. I was always in a stupor, moving in slow motion. I felt as though someone was tromping on my free will. I went through the motions and did as I was told, although it was never good enough for Lydia. The physical, psychological, and emotional terrorism I would endure over the next two years was the worst kind of torture.

Drugged or not, I found every day at Uncle Fred's the same. Like Bill Murray in the movie *Groundhog Day*, I awoke every morning to the same old song. First I took breakfast trays to the women who were in the birthing center, which was part of the clinic attached to Uncle Fred's house. After that the house-cleaning started: wash dishes, vacuum, dust, take out garbage, and do any other chore Lydia could dream up to keep me busy. When I'd finished in the house, I'd go back to the birthing center and clean up anything that needed to be cleaned there. Mostly the people at the clinic seemed well cared for. But way in the back those women who had outlived their usefulness were left to rot. I found one old woman—a mom, an aunt, a grandma—lying in her own feces. I cleaned her up, put ointment on her bedsores, and put her in a hot bath. She cried and cried and ended up dying anyway. This was what the FLDS allowed to happen with the people who couldn't serve them anymore. It made me physically sick.

Laundry—for the family *and* the clinic—had to be done two to three times a week. Sunday school was held at the house every Sunday, and I had to clean the rooms and set up the chairs for that. It was clean, clean, and clean some more. Six days a week, every waking hour was work.

At the end of the day, exhausted, I was restricted to my room. I thought I'd go crazy in there. I often stared out my bedroom window at the playhouse outside, longing for the days when I had scampered around in it with my sister Patricia. I was not allowed to do anything with what little spare time I had: no entertainment, no games, no magazines, nothing. The only thing

I was allowed to do was study correspondence courses for my high school degree, the GED. And the only reason I was allowed to do that was because the state mandated continuing education for juveniles in the DCFS system. Ironically, I would be one of the lucky ones who got a real high school diploma and a thirst for learning rather than a poor education that ground to a screeching halt somewhere around the fifth grade.

I was going stir-crazy. Finally, I ventured outside my room—I just wanted to look out another window and see another view. But Lydia caught me. "Get back in there!" She marched me back to my room and beat the bottoms of my feet with her bamboo cane. It was four feet long and had extra-hard knots every few inches. "Now, just try to leave your room again!" she yelled. I could barely walk the next day. That beating was bad, and worse would come. I'd get to know that cane pretty well.

But for me the worst punishment was psychological: I was shunned. The physical and emotional isolation was unbearable. I was raised in a houseful of people, all of us talking or fighting or just bumping into each other. I especially missed my mom. I even missed my dad. It's not politically correct to say it, I know, but in a household where showing emotion is discouraged and abuse is normal, even a "bad" touch can feel good. All effective jailers and torturers know that depriving prisoners of all touch, of all human interaction, is the best way to break them.

I was made to feel diseased and invisible. My own sisters shrank back when I passed, making sure not to touch me, even by accident. They looked at me through squinted eyes, as if I were the Devil himself.

Often the only words out of their mouths were, "You're an evil, rotten person. I am not going to talk to you. You are possessed by demons!"

I soon learned to keep silent. Aunt Lydia had an old dental chair in her first-aid room in the clinic, where she would perform dental work on the family. After one of my rebellious tantrums in which I continued to voice my "lies" of abuse, I was told Lydia wanted to check my teeth.

Once I was in the chair, Aunt Lydia strapped my arms to it and began drilling into my teeth. I thought I would die. It was not until she was satisfied that I understood the "consequences of my rebellious ways" that she gave me a shot to numb my mouth. I have had an extreme fear of dentists ever since and am very phobic when it comes to the sound of the drill.

After a while I moved through my own life like a ghost. It was truly like living in purgatory or hell. Maybe I really was the Devil.

Late one night when Uncle Fred was away from the house, I managed to slip out of my room unseen and tiptoe into his office. I stood there, gazing out a window at Canaan Mountain, dreaming of the days when I used to ride Major up there and escape from my reality for just a few hours. I wished I could be up there now, living in a cave, the way I thought I would when I was a kid.

Then, as I was sneaking back to my room, I noticed headlights moving up the road toward a cavern. Two medium-duty trucks were parked up there with their lights on. As I watched, all I could see were the headlights on the mountain and the shadows of the men loading some kind of heavy boxes onto the trucks. *Oh my God.* My heart started racing. *The guns for the end of days are being kept in that cavern!* I ran back to bed and hid under the covers.

I thought about the tales of the Short Creek raid that I'd heard all my life. Was there going to be an attack? Were we going to be killed? About twenty years later, I learned that my speculations hadn't been too far off. There were guns in that cavern, and food—preparation for a last stand. If Judgment Day ever came to the twin towns, the FLDS wasn't going to let the FBI and other law enforcement come in without a fight. But at that moment, I wasn't really worrying about the larger meaning of what I'd seen.

I just knew that if anyone found out I'd been out of bed, let alone seen the men moving the guns, I'd be severely punished.

I got away with leaving my room that once. I couldn't get away with much else, but that didn't stop me from trying whenever I had the energy. And I still had at least one friend in town—Sandy. After she'd turned my dad in for molesting me, we'd been forbidden to see each other, and I missed her terribly. One day, to my complete shock, Sandy managed to track me down in the birthing center. I was ecstatic to have someone to talk to—and someone who wanted to talk to me. But she looked dead serious.

"Flora," she whispered, "I have to tell you something."

"What?"

But before she had a chance to say more, Aunt Lydia found us.

She glared at Sandy. "Sandy Hobbs, you know Flora is not allowed to talk to you. Leave here *right now* or you'll face the consequences!" She put her hands on her hips and waited. The clinic was Lydia's domain. Sandy was tough, but she had no choice but to obey. Giving one sad look behind her, she left and didn't come back.

I later found out that she'd come to say good-bye. Uncle Roy had approved her marriage to a forty-eight-year-old man who had molested her—and she'd decided to run away. This time, she managed to get out for good. But I was still a prisoner, at Lydia's mercy. And she was boiling with anger. But, oddly, she said nothing at first. She just led me by the hand into the hospital area and sat me down in a chair. Then she went back to tending to patients while I sat in the hallway, watching. I knew better than to get up from that chair.

At least I wasn't cleaning. The longer I sat there, the more I began to think I'd gotten away with trying to talk to Sandy. I figured that when she finished seeing patients, she would just order me back to work. Instead, she stormed over to where I sat and started screaming at me. "Why don't you listen to me? What were you and Sandy talking about?"

"We weren't talking about anything. She had just got here."

"Why don't you ever listen to me?" she screamed. "What were you and Sandy talking about?"

I didn't understand what she was asking. She kept yelling the same questions over and over, just inches from my face. I tried to tell her Sandy and I hadn't even had a chance to talk, but she didn't listen. She just kept repeating the questions. Every time she screamed she sprayed me with spit. Finally, I couldn't take any more. I screamed back at her as loud as I could, "I didn't do anything!"

That did it. The rage in her eyes scared me more than anything else I'd seen from her yet. She grabbed her cane and started beating me across my back. The cane whizzed by my ear as it came down. It tore through my dress and bit into my back. I gritted my teeth, bracing for each blow.

She was furious and swung wildly, hitting my neck and shoulders. The hard knots dug into my skin, tearing the flesh. That cane was worse than barbed wire. My back tingled and then throbbed in waves of pain. I felt woozy and nearly blacked out, but I was damned if I was going to move. My hatred of her was stronger than my fear of the pain. I dug my fingers into my legs so hard I bruised myself. I didn't think she would ever stop.

I wish I could say that in my heart I knew I was a good person and that I was enduring this brutality for the sake of saving my own life. But that wasn't the way it felt to me at the time. I had been raised to believe that any punishment I received was because of something I had done. I was the guilty party. I hated her for doing it, but I knew deep down that I deserved it. Maybe she really would beat the Devil out of me.

All my life I'd been taught to step on my emotions. Emotions were forbidden—they caused sickness and allowed the Devil to come inside you. So I learned to shut down early on. I'd had a lot of practice keeping still and taking it. Dad had done worse than locking me up and drugging me silly—he'd raped and molested me. This was a piece of cake. As Lydia beat me that day after I tried to talk to Sandy, I didn't cry out, no matter what. I sat in silence as she beat me, thinking, *I was wrong. I brought this on myself. I am a terrible person.*

Finally, it ended. I looked up to see several of the pregnant women staring at me. On top of everything else, I was humiliated.

Lydia dragged me back to my room and left me there bruised and bleeding, with no medication for my wounds. The pain kept me awake most of the night. The next morning the bed-sheets were stuck to my back with dried blood. I had to get in the bathtub and soak the cloth before I could peel it away from my wounds. No one came to comfort me.

I worked that day as usual. I wasn't going to allow Lydia to get the best of me, so I toughed it out and made it through a hard day. Everything hurt. For the next two weeks, I slept on my stomach, careful not to turn over in my sleep. It took about six weeks for those wounds to heal. Emotionally they never did.

One Saturday not long after, I was braiding my hair. I hated this task. My hair was so long, it took an hour to do it right. No matter how hard I tried, I usually managed to leave a few strands hanging down the middle. Instead of starting over, though, I usually just yanked them out in frustration. To this day I have a bald patch from pulling out all those strays.

That Saturday, I found myself wishing I'd taken Aunt Jenny's advice—I should have used her money for a perm. I hadn't even gotten my hair cut—ever. I would have to use it to wash my hus-band's feet someday, a disgusting prospect. In the FLDS, a wom-an's hair is sacred. We are forbidden to cut our hair, doomed to braid it every day for the rest of our lives or wear it pinned up, with that swooping wave in front. We were taught that Mary Magdalene washed Jesus' feet with her hair. To get to heaven, we too had to be able to wash the feet of our master—our hus-band—with our long hair. "You can't get into heaven if you cut your hair," we were told.

Now I parted my long, dark hair down the middle and divided it into two parts, draping one over each shoulder. I carefully separated each part into three strands, pulling them tight to make two long braids. But when I finished the second one, I realized that—as usual—I had missed a big hunk of hair in the back. I wanted to scream! It was too big to pull out. Now I had no choice but to redo an entire braid. I'd be here for another half hour, be late for work, and get yelled at or worse. I pulled the rubber band off one braid and started to shake it out.

A white-hot surge of anger ran right through me. I thought, *This is not fair! I am so sick of braiding my stupid hair!* I stared at myself in the mirror, and then I saw a pair of scissors lying on the dresser. I picked them up and chopped both of my long braids clean off. They fell to the rug like dead birds.

For a split second, I froze, the scissors still in the air. *Oh my God, oh my God, oh my God.* I dropped the scissors on the floor next to the braids and put my hands over my mouth, trying not to scream. I had committed a horrible sin! I desperately tied a scarf around my head, trying to hide the damage.

I walked out, hoping no one would notice. But Martha saw me as soon as I left my room. She frowned, confused. "Why do you have a scarf wrapped around your head?"

"What do you mean?"

Martha, always so perfect herself, pulled the scarf down and began to cry. "Oh, Flora, what have you done? Why did you cut off your pretty hair?" She was nice; I almost felt sorry for her. Later though, she went in my room and picked up my braids from the floor. She saved them for years—maybe she added them to the hair she collected from the hairbrushes of the others in the house—to make a "rat." She'd bundle up the hair in a hairnet, pin it to her head, and wrap her own hair around it, to make her hairdo look big and abundant. Not even hair went to waste in that house.

Lydia's response to my impromptu haircut was true to form: she beat me with her trusty cane. "I am going to purge Satan from you this time!" she said, and beat harder. But my head felt so light without all that hair! I didn't think Satan would be leaving any time soon.

Despite Uncle Fred's easygoing ways, there was plenty of pain in that house. I wasn't the only one suffering. The women delivering babies in the birthing center screamed in agony day and night. Even my mom didn't want to go to the birthing center to have her children. Lydia believed that due to the sin of Eve in the Garden of Eden, women should suffer nearly until death when giving birth. Lydia and her assistants didn't believe in giving any type of medication during birth, no painkillers. It was all "natural."

As I did my chores, I prayed for the screaming to stop. Then I prayed to hear the baby cry. Then I knew it was over. At least until the next birth.

Sometimes after the screaming stopped, the baby never cried. When women miscarried or their babies were stillborn, the families rarely marked the occasion with a funeral. Lydia would deposit the dead baby in a plastic grocery sack, tie it up, and out to the backyard with a spade she would go. She buried these fetuses in the ground behind the clinic. Hundreds of unborn and stillborn babies were buried in those unmarked, crude graves.

I thought it was ironic. Colorado City is built on an Indian burial ground, and Fred Jessop's house was built on their graves. When the workmen dug the foundation, they dug up some of the bones. Lydia had several of these Native American skulls sitting on top of a cabinet in her medicine room. Those skulls weren't just bones to me; they were faces of real people, begging me to put them back to rest. Whenever I could, I would steal them and rebury them. Of course Lydia would beat me for that too when she caught me.

By and large I did the work I was told to do. I didn't make too many waves, and I tried hard to do everything perfectly. But I could never achieve the measure of perfection that pleased Lydia.

The isolation was even harder to bear. My social ostracism, which was already pretty bad, got worse when I cut off my hair. I was like Hester Prynne wearing her scarlet letter—marked for the world to see as the worst kind of sinner.

I wasn't just going to hell, I was already there. Some days I wished I were dead, and some days I wished I'd never been born. The days dragged on and on until I'd been there almost two years.

I longed for my family, especially my mother. But Lydia hated my mom and would not stop talking about how terrible she was. Maybe that was because she was raising Mom's children. I speculated that Uncle Fred was secretly in love with my mother. All Fred's wives, except Susan, treated my mom badly.

One day while I was doing chores in the kitchen, I asked Lydia if I could go see my mother.

"Your mother is worthless," she said automatically. "Your mother has not raised any kids that are worth anything. Her only kids that are going to be worth anything are the ones she gave away at birth."

"I just—"

"Your mother isn't fit to raise kids, and you can't go back there!"

"But—"

"What did I say?"

"I just want to see Mom for a few minutes!"

"Absolutely not. Now get upstairs and clean the—"

"No!"

Lydia started pushing me up the narrow staircase that led from the kitchen to the bedroom area. She was screaming in my ear the whole way, shoving my buttocks with her hand. I'd stumble and she'd grab my arm, jerk me back to my feet, and shove harder. I started trembling inside, as angry as I'd been the day I cut my hair.

Near the top of the stairs, I snapped. I wheeled around and hit her in the eye with my fist, screaming, "You bitch, don't you *ever* talk about my mother like that again!"

Lydia dropped like a felled tree, tumbling head over heels down the stairs. She crashed into a wooden cabinet next to the refrigerator and didn't move.

I was terrified, frozen at the top of the stairs. Lydia lay motionless, her eyes wide open and unblinking. *Oh God, I killed her.* I just stared at her still body for what seemed like hours.

Finally, she blinked. She wasn't dead, just stunned. Relieved, I lit into her again. "If you ever say another bad word about my mother I will kill you! Do you understand? I *will* kill you." I was out of control. I must have looked insane. Lydia just stared at me, stunned. She rolled over slowly and used the refrigerator to pull herself up. I ran into my room, slamming the door behind me, terrified but also thrilled.

Although I was still locked up and treated like a slave, Lydia eased up. She stopped beating me with the cane, and she never said another word about my mother. She told everybody, including Uncle Fred, that she got the black eyes from a fall. I guess even Lydia had begun to realize that she was dealing with someone who had nothing left to lose.

Uncle Fred, who had been gone since the night I saw the trucks on the mountain, finally resurfaced. He began to spend more time around the house and in his office, but he ignored me as everyone else did. Because my room had a window on the front of the house as his did, I could hear him droning out orders in that soft voice of his day and night. I couldn't make out much of what he was saying, but it was clear that he had a lot of influence. I finally understood that he was the real power in the community—more so than Uncle Roy, who was quite old by now. A lot of people thought Uncle Fred or one of the Barlow boys would be the next Prophet. I'd always respected Fred before, and I never really feared him. But after almost two years of captivity, I had grown to hate him almost as much as I hated Lydia. One day I had my bedroom window open. Uncle Fred's window on the front of the house was open too, and what I heard sent a shock right through me: it was my own voice, talking to my Utah Department of Child and Family Services counselor, Chuck Sullivan. I was assigned to see Chuck once a week. He'd gained my trust, and I'd told him everything. He'd told me he was trying to get me out. And all that time he was recording our conversations and giving Fred the tapes.

The depth of Chuck Sullivan's betrayal was shocking. I'd thought he was on my side. I'd thought he was my friend. In that moment he destroyed my faith in state agencies and all other authorities. I lost my trust in everyone. To this day, deep down, I know I can trust only myself.

If Uncle Fred knew everything I'd been telling my counselor, I was in deep trouble. My life was over. I would be in this closet forever. I was a real-life Cinderella, the outcast sister condemned to a life of servitude, deprived of my rightful station in my family, forced to be a maid and servant.

I loathed Fred and his wicked wife Lydia. I hated Chuck too. I felt I didn't care about anything anymore.

A few days later there was a big emergency in the clinic. The wives all ran to help Lydia attend to the situation, and I was forgotten. No one was watching me. Well, I was done being a prisoner, for that day at least. I just walked out the door, sauntered across town on Main Street, and then went down to the creek bed. I was free! But with the faulty logic of kidnap victims, instead of making a run for it, I just sat down on the bank and tossed rocks into the dry wash.

A few minutes later my cousin Phillip Jessop—the son of one of my dad's brothers—drove by. I was surprised to see him here. He'd been living out of town for a while, working construction for one of the FLDS businesses, like so many of the boys. Even more surprising—given the prohibition about talking to members of the opposite sex when no one else was around—Phillip stopped his truck, walked down to the creek, and sat next to me. He was nineteen and really good looking, and he was glad to see me. He didn't know anything about what had been going on.

Phillip told me he was just here visiting his family. Pretty soon, he said, he'd be going back to Page, Arizona, where he drove a truck for Merrill Jessop, a powerful FLDS leader. His brother Ariel lived out there too.

It was a thrill, an incredible treat, to have a normal conversation with a person who didn't think I was the Devil made flesh. But no sooner had we begun our small talk than we saw the God Squad coming—the Colorado City police, all members of the FLDS priesthood. We didn't know if they'd actually seen us or not, but we jumped into Phillip's truck and drove off before they could catch us. That was literally more fun than I'd had in the entire past two years.

Eventually, Phillip said he had to go home and offered to drop me off. But I wasn't about to go back to Uncle Fred's house. They'd find me sooner or later. Why not enjoy myself? I bummed a few cigarettes and some matches off him, said good-bye, and wandered around all night long. I wanted to savor my freedom as long as possible.

When the sun rose, my dad found me sitting on the creek bank, smoking a cigarette. "Get that filthy thing out of your mouth!" He grabbed the cigarette and threw it on the ground, grinding it under his boot heel. He sure hadn't changed in two years. At least he was talking to me.

But I played the rebel all the way, shrugging and lighting up another cigarette. He snatched that one too, threw it down, and crushed it out. So I lit a third one. This time he took hold of my arm, dragged me to his truck, and started driving.

Suddenly, I realized we were headed home. Oh my God, I was going to see my mom! I was flooded with a kind of hope I hadn't felt in two years. But I was confused too; I couldn't help but be wary. "How come you're not taking me back to Uncle Fred's?"

"Because Aunt Lydia doesn't want you back in her house," Dad said, glaring at me. "You're nothing but trouble, you rebellious little bitch! I'm gonna make sure you're locked up in the loony bin for the rest of your life." He looked at me as if I were nothing, sure of his power over me.

Now I was scared. I knew for a fact he could have me committed—that was a typical way for the men to get their women to obey them, and it had been done to plenty of other FLDS girls and women who wouldn't toe the line. The idea of being locked up, maybe for life, was terrifying. I'd already had two years of hell. No way was I sticking around for a lifetime of it. As soon as we pulled up in front of the house, Dad headed inside. Energized by fear, I jumped out of the truck and ran like hell, staying off the street so Dad couldn't easily drive me down.

Even though I hadn't slept the previous night, fear gave me speed. Soon I found myself near an RV park on the outskirts of town. A mom and a dad, two young girls, and a little boy were outside a large motor home—the kind that was outfitted with all the luxuries. I stopped to catch my breath and watched the kids playing, running around after a puppy. The dad picked up one of his little girls and ran across the yard, holding her high above his head. She laughed and laughed. It was so normal it almost killed me.

I sat watching this ordinary family, just in awe of their happiness, for a long time. Then I began to pray in earnest. *God, I want to get in that RV. I want what they have. Please let these guys kidnap me and take me away.* I wanted so desperately to see what it was like to have a real family, a family with one dad and one mom. A family who loved each other, who were nice to each other.

This wasn't a new experience for me. Since I was a little girl, I had scrutinized the outsider families who'd passed through town on their way to somewhere else. They were just tourists, camping at the Grand Canyon or passing through on their way to somewhere else. They looked at us in our pioneer outfits, surprised and puzzled. They had no idea where they were or what went on in Colorado City and Hildale. They'd stop to get a burger at the cafeteria or fill up with gas. Occasionally, an unfortunate woman would go into labor and end up at the clinic. All of them appeared to have a better life than any of us in Pligville. I yearned for their lifestyle so badly it hurt.

But now, no matter how hard I prayed, I wasn't magically transported into that RV. Maybe I really was invisible. It never even occurred to me to walk over and talk to them. Dejected and miserable, beyond exhausted, I turned around and started walking back to town, ready, at last, to give up.

I didn't have long to wait. Dad had finally caught up with me. "Get in!" he said, and I climbed back into the truck. But instead of driving toward the state mental institution, we were headed back home. He was dead quiet. "You're getting married."

"What?"

"Your Uncle Fred says that you're going to marry Phillip."

"What? No!"

He just grinned at me. "Your choice, Flora. Either you get married or I have you committed, right now. The mothers at Hildale do not want you back up there because of your continued rebellion, and they are worried about the bad influence you are beginning to have on your sisters."

"Why does Uncle Fred want me to marry Phillip?" My tired brain was having trouble catching up.

"You *know* why."

I *did* know why. The God Squad had seen me talking to Phillip and they must have reported it to Uncle Fred, so now I had to marry my first cousin. It was Uncle Fred's decision, and I'm sure it was a no-brainer for him. FLDS logic in action.

In the FLDS, as I've mentioned, any type of association—a friendly conversation, more than one dance—with a member of the opposite sex who is not immediate family is cause for matrimony. Most nonpolygamous societies consider a first cousin to be immediate family. In the United States and most of the world, marriage to first cousins is considered incest. It's against the law. But in FLDS communities, first cousins—along with stepbrothers, half brothers, and stepfathers—are commonly considered potential spouses for girls as young as fourteen. So the fact that Phillip and I were first cousins was never even a consideration for Dad or Uncle Fred.

"I've made the arrangements," Dad said. "We're going to Las Vegas. Now." Everybody knew you could get a quickie wedding in Vegas. People did it all the time.

So this was going to be a real, legal wedding, like most first weddings in the FLDS. The husband had one legal wife, and all the children of that mother were legal too—which made it easier to apply for welfare or food stamps. After that the wives were under the state radar, and their children were ghosts. I could see my life stretching out before me now. I stared at it in horror as I tried to get my brain to think clearly.

The last twenty-four hours had been surreal. I had stayed out all night and hadn't slept, Uncle Fred had refused to let me come back to his house, and now I was getting married. I didn't even have time to think about it—not that I had the option to say no.

We got out of the truck at our house. "Come on," said Dad. "We're going in the car." As we got into the car another truck pulled up—Phillip had arrived with his mother and stepfather. We just stared at each other, two scared kids with no way out. Elizabeth was walking out the door of our house, ready to go. My mom, hugely pregnant, was right behind her.

"Mom!" I wanted to run to her, but Dad wouldn't let me out of the car. Then she clutched herself and let out a cry. Her water broke. Right there, she went into labor.

"Come on," said Dad, as Elizabeth got in the car beside him. "You're getting married. She can take care of herself."

Phillip squeezed in next to me in the backseat. His folks were already turning their truck around to follow us to Vegas. No one ran to help Mom. Why should they? She was always pregnant, always having babies. That was her duty. Besides, there were lots of kids in the house. As we drove away, I watched my mom get smaller and smaller. The older kids were waving at me; the younger ones didn't even know me.

As we bumped out of town and onto the highway, Phillip gave my hand a squeeze. I leaned into him, dead tired and grateful for a shoulder to lean on. Now that we were getting married, Dad and Elizabeth didn't care how close we were. Maybe God hadn't completely forsaken me. It was a foregone conclusion that I had to marry someone—and soon—and the odds were stacked in favor of my husband's being some kind of relative. Phillip was my cousin, but at nineteen he was kind and young, and best of all, I would be a first wife. He wasn't some abusive old man with other wives and dozens of kids. And he was the sweetest guy in the world—in my world anyway.

Phillip gave me a shy smile. "I love you, Flora," he whispered. "Everything will be fine."

A ray of real hope broke through the darkness in my mind. For two years, I'd been Cinderella. Now Prince Charming had come to rescue me. I suddenly remembered what District Attorney Paul Graff had told me: marriage was a genuine opportunity to escape my abusive family. I was still a minor, but if I married Phillip with my parents' consent, I would be legally emancipated—an adult! And Phillip and I would be living out of town, where the people of Colorado City couldn't' tell me what to do.

Now I grinned at Phillip and he grinned back with real love in his eyes. For the first time in years, someone was looking right at me and not seeing the Devil. I was beyond grateful to him for that tiny scrap of humanity. Maybe I loved him too.

Part Two

Apostate

Write it down in your notes: **An apostate is a person that turns against the prophet. They turn away from him at first then they turn to fight him in the end.** . . . *I'm trying to show you what happened because of the apostasy.* **When people fall away, they become dark and filthy and low** . . .

—FLDS Priesthood History for 3rd–8th Grade Students, taught by Warren Jeffs, Alta Academy[1]

7

Married

In Las Vegas, Phillip and I dutifully filled out the marriage license application and handed it to the woman behind the counter. She got only as far as the first line before she put it down and smiled at me.

"No, dear," she said patiently. "We need your *maiden* name."

What was she talking about? "Jessop *is* my maiden name."

She looked at the form again. "You're *both* Jessops?"

Phillip and I looked at each other. "Yep."

"Are you're related?"

"We're cousins," I said, trying to help her understand. "His dad and my dad are brothers."

"Well, that makes you first cousins," she said. She handed us back our application. "I'm sorry, but you can't get married."

Phillip and I just stared at each other. Was she kidding? "Well," I said, "try and tell my dad that."

"I don't care *what* your dad says," the woman said. "You can't marry each other in the State of Nevada!"

Dad and Phillip's folks were waiting outside. When we told Dad the bad news, he stormed inside. After about an hour, he finally came back. "Come on," he said, "you're getting married now."

Somehow, he'd worn her down. The only thing I can think of is that he somehow convinced her we weren't *really* first cousins because even though Phillip's dad and my dad were brothers, they had different mothers—so they were only *half* brothers. Maybe in Nevada, cousins of "half blood" can legally marry. At any rate, he'd talked her into giving us a license and we were getting married.

In fact, we were going to get married right there at the marriage bureau—no looking for a wedding chapel. The clerk, with a weary look, pointed us down a long, dark hall. At the end, a justice of the peace stood waiting in a small room cluttered with dusty storage boxes full of files. It was a cubbyhole, no larger than my tiny prison cell at Uncle Fred's. A lovely place for a wedding.

Phillip and I faced each other, me in the same long calico dress I'd been wearing for days, still dusty from sitting on the river bank. Dad and Phillip's folks stood by impatiently. The justice of the peace took us through the "quick and easy" wedding vows: "I do," "I do," "I pronounce you man and wife."

And just like that, on May 3, 1986, a few weeks before my seventeenth birthday, I was married. We all "celebrated" with dinner at a cheap family restaurant and headed back to Colorado City.

As we drove back through miles of barren desert, I sank back in my seat and felt the weight of the world drop off my shoulders. I was married! To Phillip! I knew he would never hurt me. It was an awesome feeling to be free from slavery and abuse. I got goose bumps just thinking I might have a future. That happy thought seemed to trigger an abrupt nosebleed—the first one I'd had in years. It was so bad that Dad had to pull the car over to the shoulder while I fought to stop the bleeding.

Finally, the bleeding slowed and we rode on, my head tilted back and a tissue stuffed up my nose. I leaned into Phillip hard, and he had his arm around my shoulders. I couldn't believe what he had done for me—not that either of us had really had a choice in the matter. Still, I was pretty sure he was my ticket to freedom, and I wanted him to know I loved him for it. Even better, we were not returning to Colorado City to stay—just to pick up my hope chest and Phillip's truck. Phillip had been living and working in St. George, and that wasn't going to change. Soon we'd be moving in with Phillip's brother Ariel and his wife, Ann. It all sounded so grown up.

We returned to a houseful of excitement. My siblings—who'd been forbidden even to speak to me the day before—greeted me with big smiles, saying, "Congratulations, Flora! We're so happy for you!" A new baby was wailing in the background. While we were gone, Mom had given birth to a little girl, my youngest sister, Ruby. Fifteen years later, my efforts to help Ruby would mark a turning point in my life: the beginning of my life's work and the loss of my mom, maybe forever. But on this, my wedding day, I barely paid them any attention. I was focused on getting that hope chest and getting the hell out.

We girls in the FLDS all knew that marriage was our destiny and—along with making babies—our sole reason for being. So from a young age we began making and collecting items we'd use to set up our homes. My hope chest was a large, military-style metal trunk filled with linens—pillowcases I had sewn as a child, towels, a tablecloth, and the like. I even had a set of dishes from a restaurant that had gone out of business. As I watched Phillip carry the heavy old trunk down the stairs, I was grateful to Mom for saving it for me while I was a prisoner at Uncle Fred's. I also thought about the girls who weren't lucky enough to be their husband's first wife. Their new houses had plenty of linens and dishes already, and their hopes died in their hope chests. At least I'd be able to use my own dishes.

As Phillip shoved my hope chest into his truck, I jumped into the passenger seat, anxious to leave. I wanted to get out as fast as I could. I half expected it was all a dream. I wasn't really getting out; they were going to throw me back in a cell. Yet I was raring to go, ready for a taste of freedom. I didn't realize then how much of a loss this move would be for me later. My mom's love for me had been large even though she was emotionally and psychologically too battered to give me much support. I didn't know then how hard I'd have to fight to see her and Ruby in the years to come. But it's just as well that we can't see the future. If I had, I might have been too numb to leave.

The numb feeling set in soon after my departure. Looking back, I know now that I was suffering from the first moments of post-traumatic stress, and there would be years more of it to go.

But that night, I just knew I was married and free, and I didn't really feel much else.

We spent our "honeymoon" in a hotel. Phillip was an absolute doll, and for the first time in my life, someone really cared about *me*—about more than what I could bring to the kingdom. But at the same time, we were both Jessops! He was family! I'd been taught from birth that it was evil to touch someone's body, even your own. I'd been taught that sex was disgusting and horrifying and only good for making babies. And my only sexual experience had been repeated molestation and rape by my father. So how the hell was my wedding night? Embarrassing. My shame was so huge it's wiped out the details. Basically, I just wanted to get the sex over with and go to sleep. It had been a very long day.

Overnight my life had changed dramatically. We headed back to Ivins, Utah, a suburb of St. George, and moved in with Ariel and Ann. I thought I was a married woman, a grown-up. I thought I was free, that I could do whatever I wanted. But as I've worked for years now with the children who run for their lives from the FLDS, I've seen how every single one of them regresses in age, mannerisms, speech, and thought processes. The age most are going back to, even the twenty-year-olds, is about eight—because that's when the baptism takes place and the heavy indoctrination starts. When I look back, I can see that I did exactly the same thing.

I was like an eight-year-old kid with a husband. How much could I have really comprehended about what was going on? I had no way to understand the way the world worked, what was happening to me, or even *how* to make those choices I was so eager to make. I'd been used to two things: being told what to do and then either doing it or rebelling against it.

Yes, I had the freedom I'd never had before. Yes, I got rid of my dresses and bought myself tight blue jeans and the shortest shorts I could find. But I was terribly embarrassed about all of it. I was in full-on rebellion but self-conscious about everything. It was clear

even to me that I had no clue how to behave, and I felt lost—
completely lost. I struggled every minute with the idea that I was
going to hell. And I was on my own. Nobody understood what
I was going through. Hell, most people *still* don't understand how
being raised in a cult like the FLDS can destroy your sense of self.

For two weeks, Phillip and I played house. I stayed home with
Ann while Phillip and Ariel went off to work construction. When
Phillip came back from work, we'd laugh a lot—more than I had
in years. Our biggest treat was to go out for frozen yogurt. We
couldn't get enough of it. That's how innocent we were.

But I knew it couldn't last. Phillip was falling more and more
in love with me in every way—I could see it in his eyes and in
the way he treated me. For him, at least, marriage was working
out great. My mom and dad, and Uncle Fred, were happy too.
They were positive I'd be pregnant soon, and then we'd have no
choice but to move back to Colorado City and live the Principle
and keep sweet, like everyone else. I'd be broken, like one of dad's
horses. It was only a matter of time.

But if I was a horse, I was more like a wild mustang who
couldn't be tamed. As two weeks turned into three, I started getting cabin fever, and it worsened by the day. I got some sleep and
some food and some fun and some real affection, and it made me
stronger. I'd been a captive at Uncle Fred's house for two years.
Before that, my father had held me in another kind of captivity.
I appreciated everything Phillip had done for me and his sweet-
ness to me. I loved him for the genuinely good person he was, and
I do to this day. Still, after three weeks of marriage, I was bursting at
the seams, ready to experience whatever life had in store for me. Like
any eight-year-old, I wanted what I wanted and I wanted it *now*.

And I had a plan. Ivins was a small town, and it was full of
people like me and Phillip—FLDS refugees. Everybody knew
everybody. Before long, I found out that Sandy Hobbs was living
in Las Vegas, in a house her dad owned there. I wanted to see her
so bad! I knew if I could just get to Vegas, I'd be OK.

Sandy and I had been amazingly close as children, and we'd lived through some of our best—and worst—moments together. Everything in me focused on reconnecting with her. When you are eight years old, you just want to go play with your friends!

I knew Phillip would be upset that I wanted to leave. He genuinely thought we could make our marriage work. I also knew he loved me enough to help me. "Nobody can tell you what to do, can they, Flora?" He looked so sad. I hugged him, and he held onto me like his last hope. But I couldn't help it; I was leaving, and he couldn't stop me.

We were kids—cousins!—who had no business being married. I'd never been encouraged to have friends; a girl's only friends were supposed to be her sister-wives. Any friendships you have as a child are supposed to be severed when you get married. But I had been lucky enough to find a real friend, and we'd been through a lot together. Now, being with Sandy was the most important thing in the world to me. I wasn't so much saying good-bye to Phillip as I was saying. "I'm going over to my friend's house to play, and no one can tell me I can't!"

It broke my heart to leave him, but Phillip understood. He probably thought I'd come back to him when I'd had enough. "OK," he said, "I'll let you go. But you have to let me drive you to Vegas—I want to make sure you really get to Sandy's house. No way you're wandering around there on your own!"

I packed my new clothes—some shorts and underwear and skimpy tops—some makeup and soap and a book to read, into a backpack and was ready to go. For years after, I'd never carry more than I could fit into that pack—I wanted to be ready to pick up and go on the spur of the moment, and I wanted to travel light. I left my heavy hope chest with Phillip, still loaded with linens. I wouldn't need it where I was going.

I didn't know Sandy's address, but I'd heard that her dad hung out at Binion's Horseshoe Casino, so that's where we headed. As we drove down the strip, Phillip and I couldn't miss it—it had a giant neon horseshoe on the sign. I found Don Hobbs right away.

He was surprised to see me, but he shrugged and gave me Sandy's address. He'd been on the outs with the FLDS for a long time, and he wasn't about to do them any favors by telling my dad I was here.

Phillip drove me to Sandy's house, and I ran from the truck and threw my arms around my best friend. No matter how much time we spent apart, we could always pick up as if we'd seen each other yesterday. It was that kind of friendship. When I hugged Phillip good-bye for the last time, I know he could see that I wasn't planning on coming back to him.

Over the years, we stayed in touch. He'd send me money from time to time when I needed it. He stayed single for years, hoping that some day I'd come back to him. At one point, discouraged, he went back to Colorado City for a while. But after so many years away, he couldn't take that restricted and fearful way of life. We're good friends to this day, and I never stopped loving him— for his goodness and for what he did for me. But I was done with being married to my cousin. I was done with playing house. I was damned if I was going to get pregnant and end up like my mother. I was done with the FLDS and everything connected with it.

My marriage had lasted three weeks. As I danced into Sandy's house to start my new life, I didn't even look back to watch Phillip drive off.

Sandy was staying in her dad's house, but Don wasn't living there on a regular basis. He wasn't there for the first week or more after I joined Sandy, which was kind of a relief for me. I'd always been confused about Don. Sandy had once told me that he'd molested her, but as I described earlier, I wasn't sure that was true. When she'd ratted out my dad for his abuse of me, she told the police her own father wasn't abusing her. We'd been kids; when she had confided in me maybe she was just trying to keep me company in my misery or maybe she just didn't want me to have something she didn't have.

Now we reveled in each other. With no one to answer to, we had the kind of long, uninterrupted talks that had never been possible back home. It was like one long slumber party.

Phillip sent me some money, but I needed to be on my own. I got a job at a nearby movie theater working the concession stand. If there was one thing I'd learned how to do at home, it was work. But soon I also learned how to party. A house full of teenage boys lived down the street from Sandy, and one night after work a bunch of us went to a party there. I'd had a few sips of beer in the past and had been on a first-name basis with cigarettes for a long time. But this was my first experience with unlimited amounts of alcohol, and I was a willing victim. Before long, I was commode-huggin' drunk. I could hardly walk.

Somehow, I made it safely back to Sandy's house and passed out on a bed. The next thing I knew, I woke up to find myself in Don's room and Don on top of me, pounding away, raping me. Sandy walked in, let out a gasp, and ran out of the room.

Don, of course, wanted to marry me right away. Indoctrinated all his life with the belief that if you can achieve intercourse with a girl she is your wife, what else could he do? When I said that no way in hell was I marrying him, he left and didn't come back.

Sandy laid the blame squarely on me. "This is *your* fault!" she yelled. "I didn't let you stay in my house just so you could sleep with my dad!"

Sandy's sister told me years later that Sandy had actually created the situation that night. I'd been so drunk that I'd crashed in Don's room, not mine. Sandy had given Don a drink that knocked him out, and "helped" him to bed, dropping him down next to me. When he woke up, in a bleary stupor, he'd figured I was there waiting for him and took advantage of the situation. In my life so far, this barely registered as abuse.

But it did disturb me, and it spurred me to action. If I was going to leave home and start a new life, I needed to get as far away from these FLDS refugees as I could—maybe to another part of the country entirely. But I had no idea how you did that. So I patched things up with Sandy as best I could and returned to work at the theater while I tried to figure out exactly how I was going to make it all happen. Then somewhere between filling the popcorn popper and pouring someone a large Coke, I got a phone call that would change my life.

"Is this Flora Jessop?" a woman asked.

"Yes . . ." Who would be calling me at work? I didn't recognize the voice at all. But the next thing she said blew my mind.

"This is Patti Hassler. I'm a producer for 60 Minutes, the CBS news show, and we'd like to interview you for a piece we're doing on polygamy."

"No! How the heck did you find me? What do you want with me?" I hung up, terrified, before she could respond. I'd never been allowed to watch anything on television other than Disney videos, and I had no clue what 60 Minutes was. Anyway, we'd always been taught that it was evil to talk to the media.

Mostly, though, I couldn't figure out how this total stranger had found me. As far as I knew, Mom and Dad still thought I was living with Phillip in Ivins. He'd promised he wouldn't tell them I'd left, and I'd trusted him. As it turned out, he hadn't betrayed me—I'd done it myself. But I wouldn't find that out for months.

I was in a white panic and completely irrational. I thought, If 60 Minutes can find me, Dad can find me. He'll lock me up in the loony bin for sure this time. I was ready to leave town. Right now.

I turned to my friend Jerry* who worked with me at the theater. He was from Kansas City, Missouri, and he'd been telling me that he and a friend were planning to drive back there for a visit.

"Take me with you," I said.

"Right now? We have to finish our shift." He laughed, but I was dead serious.

"I want to go with you to Missouri."

"OK," he shrugged.

And the next day, just like that, we were headed out of town.

---

* Not his real name.

8

Gone for Good

As we drove out of the Southwest toward the Plains states, the world began to look a whole lot different from anything I'd seen before. The craggy mountains flattened out, and the desert I'd always known was replaced by rolling hills and grasses.

Jerry and his friend Mark were good company. Their car didn't have a stereo, but I had a little cassette player with a speaker and one tape: *Best of the Beach Boys*. We listened to it all the way from Las Vegas to Kansas City, and we were sick to death of "Surfin' USA" by the time we got out there.

Kansas City was a shock—it was humid as hell all day, and it didn't cool off much at night. Coming from the desert, I'd had no idea what high humidity could be like. And it was a big city, nothing like what I was used to. It made Las Vegas, which was the biggest place I'd ever been, look small.

Jerry—who hadn't even tried to kiss me up to that point—suddenly asked me to be his girlfriend. I declined—I didn't need any more boyfriends. He was good about it though. He arranged for me to stay with him in his grandmother's basement. Right away, I got a job as a cashier at a grocery store so I could help with the rent. When I had a chance to catch my breath, I felt like crying. I was far away from home and very, very lonely. I was a fish out of water here, and I missed Sandy, crazy as my last days in Vegas had been. And even though I was sure nobody knew where I was, I couldn't help looking over my shoulder.

On a break one day, I went outside to smoke and saw a fellow cashier talking on a pay phone. After she hung up, she walked over to me. "I'm Terri Routh," she said, smiling.

"Flora Jessop." I smiled back.

We started talking. From then on, we were friends. She was my first real friend outside polygamy.

Terri was young—just twenty-one—but she had a motherly way about her. I trusted her right away and opened up quickly. I told her that I was from a polygamous family and that I had more than twenty brothers and sisters.

"Bullshit!" she said, laughing. She thought I was the biggest liar this side of the Mississippi. But rather than calling me a fraud, she just said I was a "good storyteller."

"You have the wildest imagination I have ever heard in my life," she said. "How can you talk about this wacky weird Third World crap and claim it's going on in the middle of America? Come on, get real!"

At work, Terri would tell our coworkers, "Don't believe a word she says. She's just good entertainment. She has some wacked-out ideas about where she's from, but it's all bullshit. Just humor her."

Terri was far from alone in her disbelief. Hardly anyone outside the Utah area knew about polygamy at that time. In Missouri, everybody looked at me as if I were nuts when I tried to explain about it. They just said, "This is America. Nobody lives like that here."

I was glad to live in a place where polygamy wasn't an everyday reality, but it was also frustrating. Polygamy was real! Why couldn't I get anyone to believe that there were kids out there who needed help? That really dangerous people were after me? Nevertheless, whether she believed my tales of Colorado City and Hildale or not, Terri and I were growing closer and closer.

One day Jerry met me in the grocery store parking lot. He wanted rent money. I gave it to him, but he wanted more—I don't know what he was going to use it for. When I wouldn't give it to him, he started punching me and knocked me down. I couldn't believe it. He'd never been violent before; he never even got mad at me. But when I thought about it later, I realized I'd just missed the clues. From the beginning, I hadn't liked the mean way he treated his grandmother, but I'd shoved it to the back of my mind. I was far too used to men being abusive, and anyway, I needed a place to stay.

Now though, he was really hurting me. I was on the pavement, screaming and sobbing. Then Terri ran out of the store, yelling at the top of her lungs.

"Get off her! Get out of here right now, or I'll call the cops!" Her shouting ran him off. Then she turned to me. "Are you OK?"

I nodded, still sobbing.

"That's it," she said. "You're moving in with us, Flora. Today." She called her husband and told him the story. After work, she went with me and watched while I picked up my few belongings. And then she took me home. Her husband, David, and their two kids, Christine and Bethany, made me feel that I belonged. I'd finally gotten a monogamous nuclear family to take me home with them! They felt like family from the first day.

The Rouths were a loving young family, struggling to make it. Terri was only four years older than I was, but we were worlds apart in maturity and sophistication. I didn't know the first thing about life in the real world. I looked at her more as a mother than a friend, and I respected everything about her.

The one place we didn't see eye to eye was about religion. After seventeen years in the FLDS, I hated God. I didn't know much about Jesus—He didn't really figure in the Book of Mormon, especially our fundamentalist beliefs, the way He seemed to figure in Christianity. I didn't care what Terri said about Jesus—I wasn't about to turn my life over to another man, Son of God or not. All the evil that had been done to me was in the name of God, and I despised Him for it. God's love? I sure hadn't seen it. Anyway, I'd been assured I was going straight to hell when I died. That didn't make me love God any more.

It was many years before I understood that there might be a difference between the kind of religion I'd learned living in a cult and the kind of everyday religion most people practice. When Terri would try to tell me about Jesus' love, or about how good God was, I'd just walk out of the room. What did she want from me? I had just escaped from one cult that preached God; I wasn't going to get into another one. Thankfully, Terri never took my ranting about religion personally. I guess she thought I'd see the light someday.

Nice as she was, she didn't give me a free ride, and I didn't expect it. As part of my rent, I agreed to help take care of her two children and do some of the cooking and cleaning. This was a breeze for me. I'd been taking care of kids all my life, and I loved her two little girls. Plus I could cook for a family of thirty. The hardest part was having to cut the recipes down for a normal-sized family. After two years of slave labor under Lydia's cane, I found Terri's dusting and dishwashing assignments painless. Day by day I was beginning to adjust to a life where the people I lived with liked me, and I actually got to make my own decisions—good or bad.

One night soon after I moved in with Terri's family, I looked at myself in the bathroom mirror. I hadn't cut my hair since I chopped my braids off at Uncle Fred's, and I could feel its weight dragging me down again. Although it was still scandalously short for an FLDS girl's hair, it was too long as far as I was concerned. I hated hair and everything it stood for. The hair had to go! I rummaged around in the drawers for an electric shaver and went to work. *Zip! Zip!* Giant clumps of hair fell into the sink. My smile got bigger by the second. When I finished the buzz cut, I had only a quarter of an inch of hair on my head. I'm tiny, and people had always told me I was waif-like. Now I probably looked more like a concentration camp survivor. But I didn't care. I felt so light I thought my head would float right to the ceiling.

A few days later, the phone rang at Terri's house. No one else was in the room, so I picked it up.

"Hello, Flora?"

"Yes?"

"This is Patti Hassler, from 60 Minutes."

"Oh, hi." *How do they keep finding me?* But I guess I must have felt safer now, because I listened to what she had to say. She still wanted me for a 60 Minutes show on polygamy, and this time she added an incentive. "Hang on a second," I said, and put the phone down.

Terri was taking a shower. I ran to the bathroom door and started pounding on it. "Terri!" I screamed. "That lady from 60 Minutes is on the phone, and she said they'll fly me and one other person to New York City! Will you go with me?"

She laughed her head off and yelled back, "Flora, you tell them that if they want to do a damn interview with you, they can come here!" Later, she told me she thought I was making it up; that it was just another one of what she called my "stories." But I took her at her word.

I told Patti what Terri had said. "Flora," Patti responded, "we'd be happy to come to you, wherever you are."

"I don't know," I said. I was already so paranoid I got scared when the little girls wanted to play outside. I was afraid that if I were seen on television, Uncle Fred's FLDS thugs would find me for sure. But I just didn't know how to say that to this nice lady from TV.

Patti wouldn't take no for an answer. "Would you think it over, Flora? I'll call back, and we can talk about it again."

"OK," I said. "I'll think about it."

I hung up with no intention of doing the interview. I knew very little about television programs and didn't see what good it would do to appear on 60 Minutes. It sure couldn't do me any good. Then the phone rang again. This time, it was someone I knew: Don Cox and his wife, Katie. Their daughter Trudy and her husband, Conell Bateman, had driven me to Aunt Jenny's when I ran away at fourteen, and I'd kept in touch with Trudy and

Conell, letting them know where I was each time I moved. Now Don wanted to know if I'd agreed to do 60 *Minutes*. How the hell did the Coxes know about that? It turned out that it was Trudy and Conell who had given my phone numbers to Patti and had also let Don and Katie know where I was.

At this point, both the Coxes and the Batemans were moving away from the FLDS and the priesthood. Trudy and Conell, along with several others, were still fighting with the UEP for ownership of their homes—a case that would drag on for many years—and their lives were being threatened. All four of them had agreed to do the show, and they really wanted me to join them.

That put a different light on things. "I'll think about it," I said. If they were going to do it, it might be OK. But it took one more call to convince me. This time, the call was from a woman named Janet Johansen. I didn't know her, but I understood her story. Janet told me that she and her sister had left polygamy and had taken their kids with them. But then her sister found out she was dying of cancer, got scared, and thought God was killing her because she'd left the sect. Terrified, she took her six children back into the FLDS, married a man, gave him custody, and died soon after. Now Janet was fighting for custody of her nieces and nephews, and she thought I could help by appearing on 60 *Minutes*. The idea that I could help free six children from that world finally changed my mind.

When Patti called me back, I said, "OK. You can interview me."

"Great!" she said. "We'll be at your place on Tuesday morning." We?

The 60 *Minutes* crew showed up at six o'clock Tuesday morning. Five people—along with their cameras and assorted sound and lighting equipment—appeared at Terri's door ready to start setting up. That's when Terri finally realized I wasn't making it up.

"Oh my God," she said. "Who are these people?" Terri then asked Patti not to use her name or give the location of her house during the interview because, finally, she feared for her family's safety.

Terri may have been in shock, but I was having a blast. The crew spent about a week with us, and I ran around the whole time asking questions about everything. Everything about it fascinated me. I had never experienced anything remotely like this, and I wanted to learn how everything worked.

I also wanted to know these people. I'm a people watcher by nature, and at that time I watched everyone closely, to see how "normal" people behaved so I could try to act like them. One thing was clear: they all got along with each other really well—even though they were not all men or all white. This was a huge revelation to me.

I especially liked Dick Wiggins, the lighting guy. He was a big black man with a bushy beard and the first African American I'd ever met, a kind and funny guy who was far from the "evil satanic Negro" I'd been taught to fear. This in itself was an instant education about just how many lies I'd grown up with. I was learning fast that it was the teachings themselves that were inferior and evil, not the outsiders.

Finally, the fun was over and the day of the actual interview arrived. I was really excited because I was allowed to do my own wardrobe and makeup—by this time, the crew probably realized they couldn't have stopped me if they had tried. My basic theory was simple: the more makeup and the fewer clothes the better. Partly, I wanted to make damn sure any relatives who were watching would go into shock when they saw me. But a lot of it was just sheer ignorance about what looked good.

My hair was a no-brainer—I'd already buzzed most of it off. But I went wild with makeup, which we'd been forbidden to wear at home. I slapped on orange-tinted makeup pancake-thick and painted my eyes with tons of dark-blue eye shadow. I thought I looked great! Forced all my life to wear my sleeves below the wrist bone, I chose to wear a tank top—and I made sure that my bra strap was showing. Finished off with pierced ears and nail polish, I was the perfect apostate. I loved my look, and the crew didn't say a thing.

Finally, the equipment was set up and everything was ready. At the last minute, a big black limo pulled up outside and out stepped Harry Reasoner, an imposing man with bright white hair. Of course, I had no idea who he was, but everyone else sure did. When Terri opened the door to let him in, she almost fell over.

I'd been nervous up to now, thinking that I didn't want to say anything stupid. Then they sat me down in a special chair across from Harry Reasoner, in front of the bright lights and camera, with the big silver screens to soften the light. The crew and Patti were smiling at me in encouragement, and the Rouths were standing around watching, pretty impressed that all this excitement was because of me and my crazy stories . . . and I suddenly realized I was still having fun, just as I had all week. This was my moment to let the world know what kinds of abominations were going on out there in the Arizona-Utah desert. Then Harry Reasoner nodded at me encouragingly, and the director said, "Roll tape." It was happening.

As the tape rolled, I relaxed. The crew hadn't really prepared me for what he might say, but Harry Reasoner asked me questions I knew the answers to—What was it like to get married to your cousin? How many brothers and sisters do you have? What were relationships like in your polygamous family? I desperately wanted to talk about the rapes and abuses, but I was too afraid, and he didn't ask.

When he asked if I'd ever go back, I shook my hairless head no: "There's not a chance I'll go back there," I said.

When it was over, they told me what a great job I'd done. Terri gave me a hug. And then the crew went home. I didn't know it then, but that was just the first of many media interviews I'd do and the beginning of my lifelong passion to tell the world the truth about polygamy and its abuses.

The interview aired on October 5, 1986, a few weeks after the taping. Until the moment we all watched it in Terri's living room,

I really hadn't understood what a big show *60 Minutes* was and how many people would see it. Once again I became obsessed with the idea that Uncle Fred would find me and kidnap me. I had been driving Terri crazy with my fears, but she became fearful too when she finally realized that I hadn't been making up stories, and she started watching over her shoulder for any of Uncle Fred's men who might have tracked me down.

My fear affected everything. When I babysat her girls, I wouldn't allow them to play in the front yard. I constantly peered out the windows, wary of every passing vehicle. And when Terri and David would leave the house, I would say, "Make sure nobody follows you." After a while, Terri was almost as spooked as I was.

Terri had her hands full with me. I may have been seventeen, but I was closer to an embryo in terms of social development. I was so naïve. People could talk me into anything. Terri tried to set appropriate boundaries. She insisted on knowing where I was going, whom I was going with, and how long I was staying out. If she caught me violating her rules, she gave me consequences— grounding or extra chores. But I didn't feel I was in prison, as I had at Uncle Fred's. Her boundaries were nothing compared to what I'd grown up with.

Terri didn't treat me like a child, but she didn't treat me like an adult either. She cared for me as the young teenager I was and gave me rules to follow. But when I bucked those rules, I felt I could still go back and be forgiven. That was something I had never felt growing up. Terri extended unconditional acceptance to me. I love her for that to this day.

9

No Boundaries

The 60 Minutes interview had been a big deal for me and Terri, but no one from work mentioned it. And even though the neighbors must have wondered what was going on with all the trucks parked outside—and Harry Reasoner's appearance on our doorstep—no one said a word. The FLDS, too, was ignoring me.

After a while, I stopped worrying about every car that drove up the block. Life returned more or less to normal.

Eventually, boys started asking me out. My first real date was with a nerdy kid from work, a real sweetheart. We had hamburgers at a Sonic drive-in, and then went to an Air Supply concert. I thought there must have been a million people at that outdoor arena. I loved every minute of it. The band played all their hits—"Lost in Love," "All Out of Love," "Sweet Dreams," and "Making Love Out of Nothing at All."

My first concert, holy cow! I was blown away. I had never imagined there was a world like that outside the FLDS. And the best part was that none of the lyrics contained the lines, "My daddy is the best man in the world. My daddy is so good because he does the things he should. . . ."

Beyond the music, it was refreshing just to be able to hang out with a guy without having to marry him. My date expected nothing more than my company and a good night of music. I was in heaven.

If I could have stayed at that stage of my experience, just mellowed out for a while and accepted life as it was served up, I would have saved myself a lot of grief. But I'd been abused for so long I didn't know how to handle such prosperity. I wanted to get out and do everything I'd been denied. I wanted to experience everything in life in one day—and what I couldn't fit into a day, I would try the next day. No one was going to tell me what to do anymore.

I'd built a hard shell around myself, chain-smoking Camels and talking tough, but inside I was intensely shy, emotionally vulnerable, and socially clueless. Today, young girls I've rescued sometimes tell me, "If you really cared about me, you'd beat me." I was the same way—I was so used to abuse it seemed like love. So it wasn't surprising that even with Terri behind me, trying to show me what real love was, I managed to get into one scrape after another. I would sneak out after curfew, wander the streets, and inevitably meet the wrong people. It was a pursuit that took me down a dark path to sex, drugs, and rock and roll, not necessarily in that order.

Darren was in his late thirties—much older and more experienced than I was—and owned a garbage business. I'd moved on from the grocery store to a better-paying job behind the counter at a gas station. Darren used to come in every morning to fill up, grab a cup of watered-down coffee, and flirt with a girl half his age.

He looked right in my eyes and didn't look away. It was thrilling. "What's your name?" he asked.

"Jessie," I replied, without missing a beat. Around that time, I'd picked up a nickname. People would say, "Hey, Jessop! Jessie—get over here!" Before long, I was Jessie to all my friends. I loved having a new name. Being Jessie allowed me to let go of Flora and all Flora had been raised to be and failed at so miserably. Flora was damned to hell. Jessie was bursting at the seams to experience life full on.

Terri didn't like Darren at all and tried her best to keep me away from him. But I was unstoppable. He made a good living, he was rough and good looking, and he owned his own house.

But what really won my innocent teenage heart was the fact that he was in a rock band.

Pretty soon I was spending most of my time at his house smoking weed and watching the band practice. I was mesmerized by the drummer—twirling drumsticks, a cigarette hanging from his mouth, black t-shirt, long hair slinging sweat. I have no idea if they were any good, but I thought they were the greatest band in the world.

And we were bad, really bad—so bad that I was in heaven. His house was set way back from the street, with a crop of marijuana growing in the yard and a church next door. Every Sunday morning, we'd open all the doors and blast Black Sabbath albums at the churchgoers during services. I have no idea why they put up with it, but they did. I could do anything I wanted to do there, like a real grown-up.

No question, the new Jessie was a wild chick. In no time, I became a user, boozer, and loser. I drew the line at using needles, but there was no drug I wasn't willing to try. Cocaine, LSD, hallucinogenic mushrooms—and lots and lots of marijuana. Then I discovered freebasing. I loved the whole process. We'd heat a mixture of cocaine, ether, baking soda, and water in a glass pipe until the ether evaporated, resulting in freebase. I'd stick a cotton swab into the glass bowl of the pipe, light it, take a hit . . . and within seconds, I had an intense high. But after ten or fifteen minutes, I'd already be jonesing for the next hit. And I'd do anything to get it. Anything. I'd crawl around on the floor picking up whatever I saw that was white, stick it in the bowl, and light it, hoping it was an overlooked rock of cocaine. We would have marathon smoking binges and smoke until we ran out of cocaine. We were just damn lucky we didn't blow ourselves up.

When I wasn't too stoned to function, I'd call Mom. In November 1986, she told me, in tears, that Uncle Roy had died. She was distraught, and for good reason. We'd been taught that Leroy Johnson, our Prophet, was going to live forever and take all the people in Colorado City and Hildale to heaven. When he died, the entire town believed that God had forsaken them. Then my dad grabbed the phone.

"This is your fault, Flora! You have forsaken this family and caused us all to be damned!"

The sad part is, I believed it. I felt fully responsible that Uncle Roy had died a few months after I had left. When Grandma Bertha died, my family told me the same thing: I'd killed her because of my shameful behavior. If it wasn't for me, she'd still be alive.

I buried my shame, guilt, and fear under a mountain of drugs. For a while, drugs were not just a way of life; for me, they *were* life. Like any addict, I lied, hid, and snuck around to conceal what I was doing. But Terri could tell when I was high. And she had her babies to protect. She didn't even have to kick me out. She just looked at me sadly and said, "You know what, Flora? You can't come back here like this."

I felt I had really let her down, which of course just made me want to get high again to dull the pain. When I got really high, I just wouldn't go home. Sometimes I'd be gone for a couple of days. But Terri would always track me down and take me home. There were times I would think, *Damn, can't she just go home and tend to her kids? Quit coming over here. I can't smoke this joint if you keep coming over here.* She did her best to keep me safe. It's taken me years to appreciate it.

Drugs introduced me to some people I never would have met in Colorado City. The flat out most unlikely friend I made was a man named Tony Fanelli.* His daughter had died not long before I met him, and he said I reminded him of her. We had a real friendship, no strings attached. I told him all about myself, and he believed all my stories. It was a year before I found out what he did—he was connected with the Midwest Italian Mafia. He didn't like it, he said, but that was his life:

*Not his real name.

"Once you become part of my family," he told me sadly, "you can't get out."

It was an interesting relationship. He called me his "little Mia," and I thought of him as a dad. He was just trying to stay alive. But the way he chose to do it was a little strange: for years he supplied me with free drugs—anything I needed he got for me. I would go to his house, and he would fill my order. I never had to buy a thing. When I finally kicked drugs, I was angry with him.

"Tony, why would you give me this stuff that's killing me?"

"Oh, my little Mia, you make me so proud today. I prayed for you to get off this devil's stuff. I always knew you could do it. But I knew that if you didn't get it from me, you would end up in the projects getting it."

Of course he was right. I was already freebasing in the projects. Plenty of the girls I was smoking with were prostitutes, and I have no doubt I would have ended up the same way to get more drugs.

But despite Tony's efforts to protect me, I was still hanging out with the wrong crowd and getting involved in bad activities. I saw stabbings, shootings, prostitutes, jail—and I had some narrow escapes. Once the chemicals in a friend's Jheri-curled hair caught on fire while we were smoking—blue flames were shooting off her head three feet high. She didn't even notice. She called me a bitch as I beat the flames out. It's a miracle we didn't all die.

Terri and I had changed jobs together. Now we were both waiting tables at Shoney's, a big restaurant chain in the Midwest and South.

One day, in the middle of my shift, I started having sharp pains in my abdomen. I told the manager I was in agony, but he told me to suck it up and get back to work. It was Terri's day off, so I had no one to make him—and me—see that I was really sick. Anyway, I thought, maybe he was right. I had experienced similar attacks for years as a child. The FLDS believes in very limited medical care, so my mother would lay me on the couch and pack my belly with ice until the pain subsided. Now I automatically reverted to my FLDS training—I absorbed the pain and finished my shift.

But by the time I got home, I was doubled over. I finally realized this was much worse than any stomach pain I had experienced before. I collapsed at the foot of Terri's bed, holding my stomach and moaning, rocking from side to side in excruciating pain.

When Terri came home she was horrified and took me right to the hospital. It turned out that I had acute appendicitis and needed emergency surgery. But there were some catches: I had no insurance, I was underage, my parents were out of the picture, my husband lived in another state and I didn't have proof of our marriage, and Terri was not my legal guardian. I begged Terri not to call my parents. I was more concerned about their finding me than I was about dying.

Finally, the doctors decided they couldn't wait for the paperwork—I had a severely inflamed appendix, and it had to come out before it burst. Afterward, the doctors told Terri that if they had waited another half hour the appendix probably would have ruptured and killed me.

During my recovery, I got terribly homesick. All the feelings I'd been stuffing down with drugs came welling out of me. I missed my mother and my younger brothers and sisters. And I was worried about my mom's emotional well-being. I knew that after Uncle Roy died, she was dreadfully scared. I may have felt responsible, but I also knew my mom was blaming herself, thinking she'd somehow failed in her one task: to become the faithful saint. If Uncle Roy didn't lead the FLDS community to heaven, maybe it was her fault. Even if it was my fault for all the terrible things I'd done, maybe it was also her fault because I was her daughter. She should have kept me in line.

Worse, although everyone in Colorado City and Hildale had assumed that the new Prophet would be Uncle Fred, it wasn't. The new Prophet was Rulon Jeffs—father of the creepy school principal, Warren Jeffs. Uncle Rulon had a neat solution to the problem of why Uncle Roy had died and left everyone else behind: "God took Uncle Roy so he could prepare a place for us," he explained. "He's going to come back for us soon." Rulon's words sounded ominous to me. But they calmed the flock. Still, I wanted to make sure Mom stopped blaming herself.

I called home to talk with my mother, but Dad answered the phone. "Let me talk to Mom," I said.

"No," he said. He was angry. "And don't call back here!"

Well, I was angry too. "You can't keep me away from my mom!" He hung up on me of course.

I called back several hours later, and Mom answered. I started crying as soon as I heard her voice.

"Mom, I miss you so much. I love you so much. How are the kids doing? How are you doing?"

"We're all fine." Her voice sounded tired and flat.

"You know I want to come home to see you."

"Well, you are going to have to talk to your father about that."

"There's no way I'm talking to Dad about that!"

"Well, Flora, you've made your own choices. If you want to come back, you are going to have to talk to your dad and Uncle Fred about it and see what they say." Nothing had changed. My mom was still just a woman who had to answer to the men.

"Are any of the girls married yet?" I asked. I was afraid that after I left, my sisters would have been married off quickly.

"Oh, they're fine," she said vaguely. "They're not here right now, but they're fine." She didn't answer my question, and that worried me. But I knew I wouldn't get anywhere by pressing the issue.

"OK, Mom."

"Call Uncle Fred, Flora. You need to talk to Uncle Fred and Uncle Rulon." Her words hit me like a body slam.

In her roundabout way, she was making it clear to me that this wasn't a family matter; it was a church matter. But it wasn't the church I wanted to have back. I understood the rules: in order to go back to my family, I would have to go back to the church. But I didn't want to go back to the town, the church, and the enslavement. I just wanted my mom to hold me. I wanted what every kid wants and deserves—his or her parents' unconditional love.

So I was angry. "I am not going to call Uncle Fred! And the only thing I'll ever call the Prophet is a liar!"

"Flora!" My mother was horrified.

"God, Mom, why can't you just *love* me? You know, just love me for me, and don't tell me all that crap when I call. Damn. Just talk to me."

Every time I talked to her, I would get off the phone trembling and weeping. My mother was brainwashed, and I could not break through the nonsense. Finally, frustrated, I would just give up and not call home for a month or more.

One day, I again felt an urgent need to call my mother.

"Hi, Mom," I said, fully expecting her to hang up on me. But she didn't.

"Flora?" she whispered.

Oh God. Something's wrong.

"Uncle Fred is coming for you, to bring you back. Please, whatever you do, don't meet him."

Crap. Uncle Fred had bullied my mom into giving him my phone number. It felt good to know that Mom loved me enough to warn me, but she was never strong enough to stand her ground with men.

I was back to looking over my shoulder again, and I told everyone I knew, just in case.

A few nights later, Uncle Fred called.

"Hello, Flora, how are you?" He was very friendly. I wanted to spit through the phone at him.

"I've got your sisters Mabel and Mildred with me, Flora, and they miss you. They want to see you. Don't you want to see them?"

Well, of course I did. But I knew what he was up to. He said that they wanted to meet me in a deserted parking lot at the LDS temple in Independence, Missouri. Despite Mom's warning and against my better judgment, I agreed to meet them—I really did want to see my little sisters.

"OK," I said. "But I'm not meeting you there." I told him to meet me at a nearby gas station in a shopping center and gave him the directions.

As soon as I hung up, I began to feel panicky. I had no doubt he would try to kidnap me, and I was terrified. I called my friends Pridgette and Chris and begged them to go with me. They agreed immediately. Of course they had no idea what they were in for.

Pridgette and Chris were a married couple in their forties. I'd met them soon after I got to Kansas City—they lived around the corner from Mike, one of the boys I'd driven to Missouri with. I knew just seeing them would freak out Uncle Fred. Pridgette was white, the daughter of a Southern Baptist minister. But her husband was tall, well muscled—and black. They both drove city buses. Pridgette's son from her first marriage, Charlie, was my age. When Charlie heard where we were going, he wanted to come along—and so did his friend Terrance,* who was also black. They were ready to protect me with their lives and brought a couple of tire irons along for good measure.

Despite the tire irons, these were all basically just nice people who wanted to help. I knew my smiling Uncle Fred would be there with his goons who would not hesitate to do whatever they thought needed to be done to snatch me. So I also called Tony and told him about the meeting.

"OK," he said. "Don't worry. I'll have somebody out there keeping an eye on things. If it gets out of hand, they will step in."

We packed into Pridgette and Chris's little four-door economy car and drove into the parking lot at about eleven o'clock.

*Not his real name.

We parked about fifty yards away from Uncle Fred's RV. Even though it was sitting at the furthest edge of the lot, you couldn't miss it. It looked like a mini–school bus, with rows of bench seats that would accommodate about twenty-five or thirty passengers. I looked around for the man Tony was sending, but I didn't see anybody likely, just people filling their cars with gas.

We stayed inside the car and waited for Fred to make the first move.

Finally, Uncle Fred stepped out of the bus and walked over to the car. He smiled, just like the old Uncle Fred I used to think I knew. "Flora, it's good to see you." Somehow, he managed not to flinch when he saw my lack of hair. Maybe he'd already seen me on TV.

"Come on out and say hi to your sisters," he said, slowly taking in the fact that I was in a car with two black people.

I stayed put. "Tell my sisters to come over here and say hi to me." No way was I going over there so they could grab me.

At first he refused, but then he said he would allow them to come over.

I started to get out of the car, and Charlie and Terrance started to get out of the backseat to follow me—my bodyguards. But Uncle Fred just put his hand on the door and glared at the two boys. He was a man who was used to being obeyed.

"I didn't invite you," he said. They stayed put.

I looked over at the bus. James, who drove my uncle around all the time, was standing in the bus doorway. I saw more men seated inside the bus, but I couldn't tell how many or identify any of them. It was too dark and I was too far away. My sisters were standing on the steps of the bus, but James wouldn't let them come any closer. Uncle Fred just kept saying, "You need to come over here and say hi to them, Flora." He was smiling.

"No. This is far enough, bring them over here." I stopped halfway between the two vehicles. This was a scene right out of the movies.

Uncle Fred gently nudged me closer.

Suddenly, a stranger appeared out of the darkness. He was a huge man wearing an expensive suit, and he was sloppy drunk, stumbling all over himself. He walked over to the bus, stepping between Uncle Fred and me. "Hey, lemme on this bus!" he said, slurring his words. James pushed him aside, but with a drunk's persistence, he just kept trying to get on board.

"Is this the ride out of here to the casino?"

That did it. Uncle Fred grabbed my arm and jerked me closer to him. One of his hoods ran out of the bus and guarded Chris's car to make sure the boys didn't try to get out again.

"Hey," yelled the drunk, stumbling toward us. "You sumbitches can't just take a girl off the damn street. Not in KC! What the hell are you thinking?" The people who were filling up their tanks at the gas station all stopped what they were doing and stared at us.

Uncle Fred dropped my arm and turned to the drunk. "You need to get out of here, sir," he said. "This is of no concern to you." As soon as he let go, I ran to the car and dove in. Chris floored it and we fled.

We passed two sets of flashing blue and red lights as we sped away. The gas station attendant had called the police. The drunk stood around to talk to them, and they sent Uncle Fred and his entourage packing. Later, Tony told me that the drunk was one of his men, pretending to be drunk so he could break up the attempted kidnap. It hadn't even occurred to me.

Now I was really worried. Uncle Fred and his team of goons had been there to abduct me. Very likely, they knew where I lived and worked. It would only be a matter of time before they tried again.

About a month later, James suddenly appeared outside the restaurant where I was working. He sat in his pickup truck outside for a couple of hours, then simply vanished. I wasn't sure whether he'd been there to terrorize me or kidnap me.

He had definitely accomplished the terror part. The urge to travel hit me hard.

So one morning, instead of going to work, I grabbed my backpack, headed for the highway, and stuck out my thumb. I didn't know where I was headed, I just wanted out of Missouri. I hitched a series of short rides, mostly with truckers, and managed to get hundreds of miles west on I-70. After several hours, I made the bold—or crazy—decision to sneak into Colorado City to see my mom. With the help of the truckers and their CB radios, I hopped one truck after another at truck stops along the way.

My route took me through Denver, Grand Junction, and then St. George, where a young man stopped for me, gave me a lift into Colorado City, and dropped me off at my mom's house. She was floored when she opened the door, and shocked at my skimpy clothes and lack of hair. But I could tell she was happy to see me. I hugged her long and hard. I didn't want to let go. The littlest kids looked at me curiously, unsure who I was. Then my dad came down the stairs and stopped dead.

"You're not welcome here," he said.

"Then get the hell out of town," I snapped back. "Because I don't care. I'm not here to see you." He walked out the backdoor. I was thrilled with the way I had stood up to him. Secretly, I think Mom was too.

Mom and I talked for an hour or so. She said I looked thin and sickly. I knew it was the drugs, but I didn't want to tell her that. She kept insisting I talk with Dad and Uncle Fred about returning.

"That's not going to happen, Mom."

I had to get out of town before the God Squad came for me. Against her better judgment, Mom drove me a few miles outside of town and left me on the shoulder of Highway 59, where I figured I'd catch a ride. She was worried about me, as she had every right to be.

"Don't worry, Mom," I told her. "I'll be safe. I'll call you real soon." We were both crying as she drove off, back to Colorado City. I lit a joint and felt sorry for myself while I waited for some traffic to come down that lonely road.

10

The End of the Road

I finally caught a ride with an eighteen-wheeler heading north. After two transfers and five hours, I ended up back in Las Vegas.

I walked aimlessly down a street just off the Strip, still consumed with sorrow for my mom and fury at my dad, ranting at him in my mind. Suddenly, a huge guy stepped from a dark alley, grabbed me, and dragged me back into the alley. He started rubbing his big, filthy hands over my body. *No way.*

"Hey!" I yelled. "I didn't say you could touch me!" He grabbed my shoulders with both hands and picked me up off the ground. I kicked him wherever I could and hit him with my fist, twisting and spinning as I tried to break away. I fought him with every ounce of my strength, screaming nonstop. It didn't faze him—he just backhanded me across my face, knocking me to the pavement.

Lying there, dazed, I felt something in my back pocket pushing into my hip. It was a box knife I was carrying for protection. The only truckers I'd met had been nice guys, but I hadn't been taking any chances. Well, I needed protection now—he was coming at me again. I got up off the sidewalk and pulled the knife out behind my back, sliding the blade forward and locking it. Then I just rushed at him and started swinging, slashing away. He must've thought I was crazy, and I probably was. I was making deep cuts in his arms and hands, slicing off pieces of flesh, blood spraying everywhere.

"Get away from me!"

I was in a black rage and couldn't stop. I wanted to kill him. I hoped I'd kill him. I had gone somewhere in my mind I'd never been before.

The next thing I knew, I was sitting on the curb watching the flashing lights on the police cars, dead calm. There were cops everywhere. My assailant was in handcuffs. One of the cops told me that the guy was a serial rapist, and there was a warrant out for his arrest. They had been looking for him for a long time.

It took them a couple of minutes to sort it all out and to realize I was the one who had done the cutting. I thought for sure I'd be going to jail, but they saw it as self-defense—they actually thanked me for finding the guy. He was moaning in agony as they loaded his bloody body into the ambulance.

God, I thought. But a few seconds later, I realized that I could have killed the guy and it wouldn't have bothered me at all. The most disturbing part was the absolute calm that I felt. I'd gone from an adrenaline-fueled rage to a place of complete detachment. That scared me more than anything.

The cops asked me if I needed a doctor, but I shook my head. I told them I had someplace to go, and they told me to stay in town. But I walked away, heading for the highway. I soon found myself in another big rig heading down another highway.

"Where are you headed?" the driver asked. If he noticed the blood on me, he didn't say anything.

"Same direction you are," I said, getting in. I just wanted to lie back and go to sleep.

"Well then, you're going to Arizona," he said.

Fortunately, I knew someone in Phoenix. Phillip had introduced me to Michelle, a young woman in her early twenties, and I still had her phone number in my address book. As soon as I got there, I gave her a call. She let me stay with her for a few days, and we had a great time together. But suddenly, I didn't want to be on my own anymore. I missed Terri and her family. I said goodbye to Michelle and hitchhiked for twenty-four hours straight to get back to Kansas City.

I dragged myself into the Rouths' house expecting to be yelled at for taking off without telling anyone. But Terri just threw her arms around me. "Thank God you're safe!" she said. Later, she told me she thought she'd never see me again. She was pretty close to being right.

I settled back into my job at Shoney's and all of my bad habits. My drug abuse increased, and Terri was more and more frustrated with my erratic behavior. One day I came home with multiple piercings in my ears—way ahead of my time, as always. She was horrified.

"Jessie"—by now, I'd trained all my good friends to call me Jessie—"you're doing all of these crazy things to your body. You don't have to put holes in yourself! And the drugs you're putting into your body—this is not what God has in mind for you."

The God talk pushed my buttons. "How do you know what God has in mind for me? As far as I can see, I'm going to hell anyway. So what's the difference what I do?" If it had been anyone but Terri, I'd have spit in her face.

At this point, I was buying insurance to make *certain* I went to hell. Terri hated to hear me talk like that, but she backed off. She knew I'd had enough religion for a lifetime already. If she pushed it down my throat or even tried to get me to church, I would go missing again—for good.

That the Rouths put up with me the way they did is the real miracle. I lived with Terri off and on for about two years, hitching a ride out to other parts of America now and then, and moving in and out of the Rouths' house. But Missouri was my base, and Terri's family was my family. No matter what I did, she always took me back. For a while, though, I moved in with Pridgette and Chris. When my father found out I was living with a black guy, he finally came calling.

One cold day in early winter, Chris was at work, driving a city bus. Pridgette and I were just hanging out around the house when someone knocked at the door. To my shock, it was Dad and Elizabeth. Pridgette just stood there open-mouthed, staring at Elizabeth in her pioneer clothes. She'd never seen anything like it.

None of it fazed Dad. "I'm bringing you home," he said to me, walking right in. "It's my duty to save you from the demon black heathen you're living with." He looked at Pridgette, who was as white as he was.

I just started laughing. I was scared of Uncle Fred, but Dad and Elizabeth were something else entirely. Elizabeth sat down on the couch, stony-faced and out of place in her long dress and pinned-up hair, trying to ignore me and Pridgette in our tight jeans and sweaters. What a contrast.

Pridgette couldn't believe her eyes. She just stared at them as though they were from outer space. I couldn't wait to see what Chris would do when he got home.

Dad was spoiling for his showdown with Chris. "When he gets here, I'm going to have a few things to say to him! And then you are going to leave with us."

"Not this week," I said.

"I find it disgraceful that you're living with a black man. Aren't you worried about being damned to hell? Don't you know those people are Satan's people?"

"Dad, you can deal with Chris when he gets here."

He started pacing around the room. "I'll handle that nigger," he said, growing angrier by the second. "Then I'm going to haul your ass out of here." Pridgette was jumping out of her skin by this point, but she kept quiet.

It was a long afternoon. Finally, letting in a blast of cold air, the front door opened and Chris walked in, innocent as a baby. Dad turned to confront the evil black man—I have no idea what he thought he was going to do. But even in his bus driver's uniform, Chris looked like a linebacker for the Kansas City Chiefs. Next to him, my dad looked like a jockey.

Chris just stood there staring, trying to figure out what these farmers were doing in his living room. Pridgette and I could barely contain ourselves. "Chris," I said, "this is my dad and my other mother, Elizabeth."

Chris put out his hand. "Nice to meet you," he said.

Dad, meanwhile, was just staring up at Chris. The look on my dad's face was priceless. His head didn't even come up to Chris's chin. Finally, he took Chris's hand and shook it, dropping it quick. It probably almost killed him to do it.

"Nice to meet you," he said, grabbing his coat. "Sorry, we have to run. Come on, Elizabeth." And they were out the door.

We were in stitches after they left, but once I stopped laughing, I was scared. If Dad had found me, Uncle Fred—or worse—wouldn't be far behind. I said good-bye to Chris and Pridgette and hitched a couple of rides back to Phoenix, ending up at Michelle's again. After two days there, I wasn't ready to go back to Kansas City and Michelle was ready to roll. So in a moment of dumb inspiration, we decided to hitchhike out to California and find some fun in the sun.

We hit the freeway, two cute young girls on the road. Right away—no surprise—we were picked up by a truck driver from Texas. He said his name was Steve. He was middle-aged and overweight and seemed harmless. He was super nice in the beginning, but he couldn't stop talking about his ex-wife. He was still in love with her.

"You look just like her, honey," he said. He couldn't take his eyes off me. "You have the same hair, the same eyes. She was tiny, like you." I looked at Michelle—we both knew this was trouble. But we were in the middle of nowhere, driving and driving and driving. It took six hours to get to LA, and he talked about me and how much I was like his ex the whole way. Finally, he pulled in to an LA warehouse and dropped his load.

"Thanks for the ride," we said, ready to jump and run.

"Where are you going?" He wouldn't let us out of the truck. "I'm not done yet. I have to go up to Frisco, and you girls are coming with me." We were freaked out, but there was nothing we could do.

We started driving north on Route 5; I was sitting next to him and Michelle was by the door. He just kept telling me how much he loved me. He started rubbing my leg with an oily hand.

"Dude, get away from me," I said. "Don't touch me. Keep your hands to yourself."

But he just laughed. He was convinced that he was going to make me fall in love with him. I was scared, but I wasn't about to let him know that.

We were on the road for hours. When we got to San Francisco, he picked up another load, and we turned around and headed back to LA. The whole time, he never let us out of his sight, even guarding us when we used the truck stop restrooms, one at a time. Finally, we got back to LA and he pulled into a truck yard surrounded with razor-wire fences. Huge Doberman pinschers, mean yard dogs with clipped ears and docked tails, barked and growled. No way were we getting out of the truck there. He left us trembling in the cab.

A buddy of his walked over to the truck, wanting to flirt. "He won't let us go!" Michelle blurted out.

"What?" He looked over his shoulder. We told him about the unending trip from Arizona to San Francisco and back to LA. "Look," I said, pleading with the guy, "you need to help us get out of here."

"I can't let you go," he said, shaking his head. "He'll kill me."

Steve returned with a fifth of vodka and commenced to get drunk. He offered us some, but we declined. He finished it himself and passed out in the sleeper. Michelle and I jumped out and grabbed his friend. We finally talked him into driving us to San Diego in Steve's truck. Steve was dead to the world, we told him. What could happen? It was a really stupid plan. Of course the guy agreed to do it.

At the San Diego city limits, as we pulled up at an intersection, Steve came to, roaring. Then our driver began freaking out, probably wondering why he'd thought this was such a great idea in the first place. Michelle and I leaped out of the truck and ran down the street, with Steve staggering behind us. But two young, lean teenagers could out run a drunk, fat trucker any day.

Our narrow escape, instead of teaching us a lesson, empowered us. We laughed our heads off at our good fortune.

Looking back, we were two girls without one whit of common sense between us. But at the time, it seemed like a pretty good adventure. San Diego was sunny and warm and beautiful—it sure wasn't snowing here. We ended up in Pacific Beach, a seaside town with a boardwalk and a beach and surfers. I loved it there. But Michelle and I were broke. We had no money and nothing to eat. And we weren't staying in a fancy hotel. We hung out with the homeless guys on the beach. We slept on the beach at night and combed through seaweed in the morning, occasionally finding a few big crabs that we sold to restaurants for pizza money. Sometimes we'd dumpster dive or dig through garbage cans to find something to eat. Every once in a while, we would talk someone we'd met on the beach into letting us take a shower at their place.

When beachgoers forgot their towels, we'd make a bed with them and sleep on the sand. But warm as it was in the daytime, it got cold at night, as it did in the desert. Many times, we would take a couple of shots of whiskey before falling asleep, trying to keep ourselves warm—we could always find alcohol or other drugs to get us through. Toward the end of the week, we spent a couple of nights at an abandoned house not far off Pacific Beach with other homeless people.

That did it for us. A week of Pacific Beach was enough "fun." We thumbed an uneventful lift back to Phoenix. I said good-bye to Michelle and headed home to Missouri.

My last ride while going home was with a suicidal driver in a Peterbilt truck who barely stayed on the road while driving through a blizzard. When I got back to Terri's, I was done in. I knew I couldn't get away with living like this much longer. I stared at myself in the mirror. It was not a pretty sight. Despite a week at the beach, I looked gaunt and pale. My hair, what there was of it, had lost its shine. My eyes were sunk so far back in my head you couldn't even tell what color they were. I had let drugs rule my life for too long. It was time to give them up—and I did.

11

Shauna

I went back to my waitress job at Shoney's and promptly met a customer who stole my heart. Terrel—everyone called him Terry—was tall, with long hair and tattoos. And he had something else that appealed to me—a young son, Kris. It was really Kris who stole my heart.

I fell head over heels in love with Kris. Just eight years old, he was a sweet little blonde-haired, blue-eyed kid. But one look at him and you knew he was lost. Both his parents—they were never married—were wild partiers, staying out all night and sleeping all day, and he bounced back and forth between their two houses. Sometimes his mom would lock him in his bedroom while she and her friends had wild, drunken orgies. She usually forgot to give him dinner first, so at age seven he learned to pick his bedroom lock so he could get into the kitchen and find some food. His grandmother, Terry's mom, did a lot of the heavy lifting— she tried as hard as she could to be there for her grandchild. But with those two as parents, it was hard. All in all, he got more neglect than love.

Terry and I moved in together right away. Our first apartment was a small two-bedroom in a funky little complex—six single-story buildings facing each other across a courtyard. Now that I was off drugs, I wanted a family. Moreover, the Rouths had shown me a great example of stable family life. I was no saint; but I tried my best to be a stabilizing element in Kris's life, and he soaked up what love I could give him like a thirsty sponge.

I'd kicked hard drugs, but I was tolerant of others' drug use. Still, I had one rule: no needles. One day, a friend of Terry's roared into town on a motorcycle, looking for a place to stay. I knew he was trouble when he insisted on parking his bike in the middle of the living room. I soon figured out that not only did he do drugs, he used needles.

"Nobody does needles in my house," I told Terry. "If he uses needles, he needs to leave my home. Don't bring him in here."

"Get over it, Jessie," Terry said.

"No. There's no way."

"He'll be all right. I'll talk to him."

That night, I was woken from a deep sleep by a bloodcurdling scream from the bathroom. I jumped up and ran to see what was happening. It was a pretty horrific sight. Kris had gotten up around midnight to go to the bathroom. When he opened the door, he had slipped on a pool of blood and fallen on Terry's biker buddy who had hit a vein while shooting up and was spurting blood all over the bathroom walls and floor. Kris couldn't stop screaming; blood was spraying out of the guy's arm—I lost it.

I grabbed Kris, walked him back into his bedroom, and sat with him until he settled down. He'd stopped screaming, but I didn't think he'd forget that bloody scene for a long time. Then I stormed back to the bloody bathroom, where Terry was wiping down all the walls. His buddy was collapsed against the shower, looking glazed. I was disgusted. "Get this son of a bitch the hell out of my house!"

"You just need to chill out."

"Chill out?" I wanted to kill him. "Your kid is freaking out because of what that son of a bitch did! I'll be damned if he's going to die in my bathroom. I don't care if you have to haul that piece of shit out to the middle of a field and dump him! No way is he staying in this house!"

"You can't kick my friends out of my house!"

"Oh, hell yes I can. You go look at your son and tell me I can't kick this fool out." Meanwhile, the biker was starting to stir. I began

Joseph Smith Jr., the founder of the Latter-day Saint movement. In 1830 he published *The Book of Mormon*, after announcing that he had discovered and was translating a set of golden plates, which he claimed described a visit by Jesus to the "indigenous peoples of the Americas." Scandals and conflicts chased Smith and his new followers from Ohio to Illinois; Smith himself was assassinated by a mob of non-Mormons in 1844 while attempting a run for the United States presidency.
CREDIT: Library of Congress

Nicknamed "The American Moses" for leading his people through the desert into their version of the Promised Land (the Utah Territory), Brigham Young gained control of the Church of Jesus Christ of Latter-day Saints in 1847, holding the position until his death in 1877. Many of his teachings follow suit with current FLDS beliefs: the building of a "Zion," plural marriage, and communication with God.
CREDIT: Underwood & Underwood/CORBIS

One of the only photos I have of myself as a baby. Even though I was so young, my eyes already look sad and lonely.

CREDIT: Courtesy of Flora Jessop

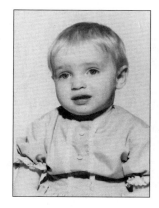

My sisters and I, around 1974. From left to right (seated on couch): Daphne, my oldest sister; Martha Ann; me; (seated on floor, right to left): Patricia, Fawn, and Maryette, who was the youngest at the time.

CREDIT: Courtesy of Flora Jessop

This photo was taken in 1985, shortly before I escaped the FLDS for good. I put on the bandana and the glasses to show everyone what I thought it meant to be cool and rebellious. I knew so little about it at the time, but even then my version of "cool" was different from everyone else's.

CREDIT: Courtesy of Flora Jessop

The only photo I have of my whole family, circa 1996. I'd left the FLDS by then but returned to pay my disrespects to Aunt Lydia, at her funeral—to spit on her grave, really. These are all my brothers and sisters, and my dad's second wife (and mom's younger sister), Elizabeth, and her children. My dad is seated in the second row; Elizabeth is on his left. I'm standing in the second-to-last row, behind Elizabeth. Mom is on Dad's right; Ruby is kneeling in front of Elizabeth. Of all the people in this photograph, I am the only female who has left. These women remain; some married to the same man. But all the males, my brothers, have broken ties with the sect.
CREDIT: Courtesy of Flora Jessop

My first big interview with Harry Reasoner, in August 1986, shortly after I'd escaped for the last time.
CREDIT: Courtesy of Flora Jessop

Tim and I on our wedding day, February 24, 2001.

Shauna and I in 1991, just
after we moved to Phoenix.
She was such a happy baby.
I loved carrying her; for me,
being pregnant was a joy.

Mom and I in 1992. She managed to leave Pligville for a week, to come visit me in Phoenix. She brought Ruby with her, and Lyman, my youngest brother. We did all the things she never got to do: go swimming and go to a bar.

CREDIT: Courtesy of Flora Jessop

Mom and Ruby in 1988. Ruby is about two years old here.

CREDIT: Courtesy of Flora Jessop

FBI TEN MOST WANTED FUGITIVE

UNLAWFUL FLIGHT TO AVOID PROSECUTION - SEXUAL CONDUCT WITH A MINOR, CONSPIRACY TO COMMIT SEXUAL CONDUCT WITH A MINOR; RAPE AS AN ACCOMPLICE

WARREN STEED JEFFS

Warren Steed Jeffs, the "Absolute Ruler" of the Fundamentalist Church of Jesus Christ of Latter Day Saints (FLDS), was placed on the FBI's Most Wanted list in 2006 after unlawfully fleeing Utah when charges of arranging illegal marriages between church members and underage girls were raised against him. He was eventually captured and is still behind bars.
CREDIT: Tom Fox/*Dallas Morning News*/CORBIS

Live *Court TV* interview outside the Washington County Courthouse, during Warren Jeffs's trial in 2007. I'm on the far right; Gary Ingles, special investigator for the Mojave County Attorney, is in the middle.
CREDIT: Courtesy of Flora Jessop

Polygamist sect leader Warren Jeffs is flanked by Las Vegas Metropolitan Police SWAT officers as he listens to Judge James Bixler during an extradition hearing at the Clark County Regional Justice Center in Las Vegas, Nevada.
CREDIT: Steve Marcus/Reuters/CORBIS

The two Fawns: Fawn Holm (left) and Fawn Broadbent (right), in Salt Lake City, around 2005. They had been free of the FLDS for some time but were still in hiding, so I made regular trips to visit them.

At Zion National Park in Utah, 2007.

Tim and I on Thanksgiving in 2007.

CREDIT: Courtesy of Flora Jessop

pushing and dragging the idiot out. "This dude is shooting up speed, coke, and heroin in my bathroom!"

Terry finally sent the biker and his motorcycle on their way. He never apologized for any of it, but after a while things settled down. Sort of.

By now, Kris was like my own kid. I never wanted to see kids hurt like he was, ever. I cared about him, and I spent a lot of energy trying to build him a home. But I was swimming against the tide. And Terry wasn't any better at staying in one place than I was. After three or four months, we moved to Springfield, Missouri. Kris's mom was happy to send him with us, and I was happy to get him away from her. I got a job working at Tiny's Barbeque. Tiny was a great big old grumpy guy. Everybody was afraid of him, but he and I got along very well, and the food was incredibly good.

Nine months later, we moved again—this time to Marionville, Missouri, not far from Branson. Terry worked as a housepainter, and I got a job at a rest home. I got along with all the old folks, and I really liked my job. I'd helped a lot of patients at Aunt Lydia's clinic, but this time people said thank you and meant it, and they paid me for my work.

In my mind, anyway, I'd settled into a family life of my own, and I loved it. I thought we were a happy family. Kris was maturing. Even though he had such deep sadness in his life, he was still a well-behaved kid.

Almost a year into our stay in Marionville, I got pregnant. I was so skinny and my cycles were so erratic that it took me almost four months to figure it out. Kris was thrilled about the idea that he was going to have a little sister or brother. Terry was happy too—at least, he acted the part. We told everybody the good news, except my family in Colorado City.

Anyone could have told me that Terry was trouble, but I was in no place to pay attention to good advice. It had to be shoved right in my face before I saw it. One night, two weeks after I found out I was pregnant, Terry didn't come home. I put Kris to bed and told him his dad had to work late. But when I woke up in the morning, Terry still wasn't there. It wasn't like him to stay out all night, and I was worried sick that he'd been in an accident.

I didn't know what to do about Terry, so I went to work as usual. To my great relief, he was there when I got home that afternoon. When I asked him where he'd been, he shrugged and said that he'd just decided to go visit his mother in Kansas City on the spur of the moment. He apologized for not letting me know.

"That was a damn stupid thing to do. We were worried to death about you."

"I know I made a mistake," he said. "It's the first and last time." It was—at least for a few weeks.

At five months pregnant, just starting to show, I was cooking breakfast in the rest home. Suddenly, the smell of bacon frying made me so sick that my boss sent me home. When I got to the house, Terry's truck was parked out front. What was he doing home from work?

"Terry?" I called his name a couple of times, but he didn't answer. Then I rounded the corner to our bedroom and stopped dead in my tracks. He was in the middle of screwing a young girl. In our bed. The girl saw me first. Her eyes got wide, and she screamed. Terry stopped and looked up at me, stunned. Several seconds went by before any of us could move or speak. I was shaking, and I felt like throwing up. Finally, I said, "When the two of you are finished, I need to speak to you, Terry." Then I turned around, shut the door, walked into the living room, and sat down on the couch. I felt I was in a bad dream.

Terry came flying out of the bedroom, pulling up his pants, "It isn't what you think, Jessie," he said.

"Oh yeah? Why don't you explain to me what I think it is?" By this time, the shock had worn off. I was just pissed.

He backed off and put his hands up, pleading. "Don't cause a big problem for us, Jessie. You know I love you. It was just this one time."

"You know what? It doesn't matter how many times it happens. You might as well move her in here, because I'm done. It's over."

Then he lost it. He started stomping around, screaming at me, smashing things. The young girl just stayed in the bedroom, probably scared out of her wits. I stayed calm, given the circumstances. I'd been through worse. The hardest part wouldn't be leaving Terry; it was Kris I'd miss the most. But he'd always be my baby's big brother. I swore we'd never lose touch, no matter what. And we never did.

I packed my car and headed back to Kansas City. When I got there, I called Terry's mom to let her know I was back in town and that I wasn't going to stop her from seeing her grandchild. She wanted me to move in with her until the baby was born. I agreed to stay for a while but didn't want to hang around too long. I liked her, but staying with her put me just too close to Terry.

She was furious with Terry for the way he had treated me. I also found out from her that that day he'd gone missing, he'd showed up at her house with a young woman. He had also lied to her, saying that I was not pregnant and that I had moved back to Utah to be with my family. I was stunned. I should have known Terry was a scumbag, but I didn't.

A month later, Terry was back in Kansas City asking to move back in with his mom. "You get the hell out of here!" she said. "You are not welcome in this house." Unfortunately, his response was to get drunk and wreck his truck, nearly killing Kris. Poor Kris ended up the way he'd started, bouncing back and forth between his mom and dad like a Ping-Pong ball.

Terry completely lost it after that. He went from at least trying to be a stable family man to a womanizing drunk in no time and hit bottom fast. One night he called me from jail after being arrested for soliciting prostitution during an undercover sting. "I want you back, baby," he moaned. It was pitiful.

"Oh yeah, that's going to make me come back to you. Trying to pick up a prostitute, of all things."

Finally, in a last-ditch effort to show me how much he loved me, he had my name tattooed on his chest.

"You're such an idiot," I said when he came by to show me. "You think I'm going to come back to you because you got my name tattooed across your chest?"

Everything he did after I left made me even more determined to remove him from my life completely. But Terry saw it differently. I was having his baby, and he wanted to be my Lamaze coach. That was never going to happen. Before we'd left Kansas City for Springfield, we'd made friends with a couple named Mark and Rachel. Rachel and I had gotten close, so I asked her to go with me to Lamaze classes. I refused to let Terry attend.

Finally, I had to leave Terry's mom's house. The longer I stayed, the more I'd have to deal with him. Terri Routh and I were still in touch of course, but taking in a pregnant girl while managing her own family was more than she could handle. Still, she wasn't about to let me down. During the last four months of my pregnancy, Terri arranged for me to live with her sister, Sherry.*

Sherry was managing a Subway sandwich shop in Eudora, a small town just east of the University of Kansas campus. In exchange for being able to stay with her, I took care of her baby daughter while she worked. She also got me a job working part-time at the Subway, alongside college students. It was good for me to be around college kids at that point, to see kids my age who were getting an education. I lived the college life vicariously through them. We were all about twenty-one and had much in common—except, of course, that they were in college and I was barely educated and pregnant.

Even when I was six months pregnant, I didn't show much. I still wore my regular jeans. I just had to leave the top button undone and slide the zipper down a couple of inches. But at about seven months, I finally popped out of my jeans. If I even burped, those college kids worried about me. They just knew they were going to have to deliver a baby on the floor of Subway.

*Not her real name.

In the final few days of my pregnancy, I stopped working and moved in with Mark and Rachel. Rachel wanted to be right there when I went into labor so she could go to the hospital with me. She didn't have long to wait. I got up to go to the bathroom one night and my water broke. I woke Rachel.

"Let's go!"

We drove for an hour and a half to the Humana Hospital in Overland Park and got there about 1 A.M. By the time they examined me, I had dilated to five centimeters. Then I stopped.

The contractions were more painful than I'd imagined, despite the literally hundreds of pregnancies I'd seen in my life. The nurses asked if I wanted an epidural.

"Hell no!" I said. "Get that away from me. Just let me up out of the bed."

I was tough. My mom had babies on her own—how hard could it be? If the women at Aunt Lydia's birthing center could do it without painkillers in that horrible place, I could handle it in a nice hospital with doctors and nurses looking after me.

So I got up and started walking around the hospital. I walked for six hours. Every time I had a contraction, I'd lean against a wall and tough it out until it passed. Finally, about 7 A.M., the nurse came looking for me. She just shook her head and said, "I've never had to hunt down one of my patients before." She was about to go off shift and wanted to make sure I was okay.

But when she checked me, I'd dilated only one more centimeter. "Oh, you'll be here for another few hours," she said, disappointed. "I guess the day-shift nurse will get to catch your baby."

But the second she stepped outside the door, I felt the baby drop. "Rachel," I said, "get her back in here. This kid is coming right now!"

"But she just checked you," Rachel said.

"Rachel, trust me, go get her. Now." I'd never felt such pain in my life.

Rachel dragged the nurse back into the room. "I just checked you," she smiled. "Relax. You're not going to have that kid until later tonight."

I said, "You better get me the hell into somewhere because this kid is coming right now."

She took another look. "Oh my God!" She ran for a gurney and got me on it. We barely made it into the delivery room before the baby came. The doctor didn't show up until thirty minutes later. My beautiful daughter was born at 7:09 A.M. on November 12, 1990. I had a lot of names picked out for her, but when I looked at her, I knew none of them was right. Her name was Shauna. She was the best thing that ever happened to me, and from that first moment she became my whole world.

Shauna and I moved in with Pridgette and Chris. From time to time, Terry would come over to see his daughter. Sometimes he'd bring Kris, and Shauna and Kris bonded right from the beginning. He loved his new sister, and she loved him.

Terry never gave up. He was always asking me to get back with him, swearing to me that he'd changed. But I knew better. As I began to adjust to being a single mom, I had to think about what kind of role Terry would play in my baby's life. I swore that I would never tell her anything bad about her dad, and I kept that promise—even when, over the years, she begged me to get back together with him. Like any child, she wanted her mom and dad living in the same house. But I knew that for her sake and mine, it would be best to put some space between us and Terry. And that meant leaving Missouri.

I'd never lost touch with Sandy. She was living in Phoenix now, with her boyfriend and her two young kids, a four-year-old girl and a three-year-old boy. I thought she and I could help each other with our kids, and she was all for it. So in January 1991, when Shauna was two months old, we headed back to the Southwest.

Shauna had changed my life more than I'd ever thought possible. But I had no idea what was coming up.

12

No One's Property

Sandy's boyfriend owned a big construction company, and she was working with him there during the day. When she offered me the chance to live at their house in exchange for watching her kids, I jumped at it. This would give me exactly what I wanted: a chance to be a stay-at-home mom.

Sandy and I picked up our friendship as we always did—as if we'd just seen each other yesterday. Her kids welcomed us in too. They loved Shauna, especially Sandy's little boy. When I nursed Shauna, he would grab a doll and sit down and nurse his doll. If Shauna started crying, he'd ask his doll why *she* was crying. I tried to give Shauna the love and affection I had always craved, and I was content to just be her mom and watch her grow.

But even though Sandy and I were both moms, we were still struggling to grow up. After sixteen years in the FLDS, five years on the run, and almost a year of being responsible for a precious human life, I was still a socially retarded adolescent. Sandy and I had been held down for so long, we were thirsty for experience. We loved going out dancing at Mr. Lucky's, a popular bar in Phoenix that featured live country music upstairs and rock-and-roll DJs downstairs. It was a far cry from the dance we'd run away from a lifetime ago. I was so shy that it always took me a couple of drinks to loosen up. Even so, we danced and partied way too much. I guess we were both trying to experience a life we'd never had.

Then Sandy and her boyfriend broke up, she left his company, I needed to find my own place, and we both needed to find work. I came across an ad in the paper for a new club that was just opening up—Tiffany's Cabaret. They were looking for waitresses, bartenders, and dancers.

When we applied for the waitress jobs, the manager told us that Tiffany's was upscale, a "gentlemen's club." They were going to cater to business lunches and expense accounts—a business-man could bring in a client and buy him lunch and a table dance on the company credit card. Then he told us how much money we could make as topless dancers and offered us the job.

Dancing topless would definitely seal my deal with hell, and it was about as far away from FLDS beliefs as I could imagine. I looked at Sandy. "Let's do it!"

She snorted. "You? You can't even get on the dance floor at Mr. Lucky's without a couple of shots of tequila!"

"I dare you."

"You're on."

We both tried out for the job. Sandy hated it and didn't want any-thing to do with dancing topless. But despite the fact that I was pain-fully shy, I loved it. To my complete surprise, I got hired on the spot.

I started working at Tiffany's the day the club opened its doors. My first day was Tiffany's first day, which made it a lot easier for me. There weren't a lot of customers, and no one was expect-ing anything spectacular from me. And that was a good thing, because the first time I walked on stage and took my clothes off, I was completely, totally embarrassed.

I thought I was going to fall right through the floor. I wasn't cold—the adrenaline was pumping through me like crazy—but I was frozen to the spot. I just stood there and swayed on the stage for the whole song, trying not to make eye contact with the cus-tomers. I was a flat-out horrible dancer.

But as time went on it got easier. I lost myself in the pounding beat of the music. When I danced, all the bad things that ever happened to me just disappeared. I wasn't Flora, the stupid run-away from Pligville. I was Jessie, the tough little girl who would dance only to rock and roll. When the music was Bob Seger's "Turn the Page," the customers knew Jessie was coming on. They didn't know anything else about me except what I showed them. It was a kind of freedom I'd never experienced before.

I started out working the day shift—from eleven in the morning until five in the afternoon. The day shift was less pressure—the lunch crowd still had to go back to work. The night crowd was wilder, and the money flowed more freely. Eventually, I followed the money. I spent the day being Mommy. At night, Shauna went to child care and I was Jessie.

I had regular clients, men who came in specifically to see me. Some of the guys had a lot of money, and they didn't mind spending it on their favorites. I was certainly not the typical stripper! I was tiny, and flat as a board. All I had on was a G-string and my glasses—I can't see if I take them off, so they stayed on. And I think that's one reason I did so well—I fit a certain fantasy that is shared by more men than you might imagine. Customers often told me, "Oh my God, you look just like my third-grade teacher! I was so in love with her." And the dollar bills would flow.

Whatever the reason, I made a mint in tips wearing those glasses. Most of the time, I'd clear at least $200 a night. On a good night I could pull in $600. Sometimes I traveled to Las Vegas on my day off to guest dance at various clubs, and I would bring home $1,200 to $2,500. I guess I was a natural.

The one thing I did not like to do was table dances. Without fail, a customer would reach around and grab something he wasn't supposed to touch. I'd just stop dead and stare at him. "Do I look like public property?" I'd say. "Do that again and I'll break your fingers." After a while, they knew better than to touch me unless they were stuffing dollar bills in my garter.

After six months, I left Tiffany's to work at a tiny bar called Excalibur. The owner and his girlfriend were cool, and I liked working there. It was just a hole in the wall, but it was always busy and I made a lot of money.

I'd been dating a guy named Dave for a while. He was a real psycho son of a bitch, although—as usual—it took me a while to realize it. He rode a Harley and hung out with another biker named Gary. Gary was a member of the Vagos, a San Diego biker club. Ever since I'd met him, Dave had claimed that he was in the Vagos too. I didn't really care one way or the other.

One day, I'd just finished my shift at Excalibur when Gary came into the club with three gigantic bikers. They were all wearing Vagos jackets. I hadn't even had a chance to put my clothes on yet. What the hell was going on here?

"Hey, Gary, what's up?"

"You need to step outside with these guys and talk to them."

"Dude, I'm working. I need to get some clothes on. You want me to walk out the door like this?"

Gary really didn't care. "Just do what I'm telling you, right now."

I grabbed a shirt and stepped out the door with the giant bikers. One of the guys leaned in close. "You know Dave, right?"

"Yeah, I know Dave."

"Well, he's going around threatening people and telling them the Vagos are gonna make good on the threat." He slammed his fist into his hand as he talked. These guys were really pissed off. What the hell was Dave doing?

"Hey," I said, "I don't know anything about that."

"Did he ever tell you he was a member of the Vagos?"

I nodded. "Yeah . . . You mean he's not?" That's all they needed from me. When they found Dave, they beat the crap out of him and told him he had twenty-four hours to fix the problems he'd caused them.

But I didn't know anything about that. I just knew that when I got off work that night, Dave was waiting. He grabbed me, threw me in his car, and then forced me into his house. He took my clothes and shoes and started beating me, yelling, "You're going to tell these guys you lied to them!"

"Dude," I said, "I didn't tell them anything they didn't already know!" I tried to shield myself from his blows, but he was twice as big as I was.

"The hell you didn't!" He just kept punching me. If he kept going, he'd kill me; it was just a matter of time. So I ran for it, lunging headfirst, shattering the glass, and plunging straight through his front window. I stood outside, stunned and bleeding, shards of glass all around me. Dave just stared at me in shock and let me go. I stumbled away and walked halfway across town naked and barefoot, landing in the hospital, where they found I had a concussion. Nobody stopped to help.

That was it. No man was ever going to treat me like that again. Maybe abuse and love weren't the same thing after all.

The guy who owned Excalibur died suddenly, and the place was sold. The new owner and I didn't get along, so I left to work at a club called Centerfolds. After Dave, I'd had it with guys who like to use their fists on women. And I had a new zero tolerance policy for customers who thought they could do whatever they wanted with me just because I was taking off my clothes for them.

If anyone touched me while I was dancing, I'd give him one warning: "Don't touch me. I'm not public property. Don't put your hands on me." If he grabbed at me again, that was it. I'd just haul off and deck him. If he was foolish enough to keep trying, I made sure he went over backward in his chair. I had quite a reputation for taking care of myself. The bouncer, a former football player for the New York Giants, used to say, "Jessie, if a fight breaks out in this place, I'm gonna make sure to be on whichever side you're on!"

By 1994, I'd spent a year fighting off the customers at Centerfolds. I was tired of this life. One day, I just couldn't do it anymore. I'd had enough. I'd been a topless dancer for two and a half years, and I was burned out. It was time to quit, and I did.

It was also time to quit running—from town to town and job to job. I'd run and run and run from the FLDS. This was no way to live. I could not continue to run and protect my baby. Anyway, they seemed to have stopped coming after me lately—maybe because I hadn't caved in. I'd begun to realize that the men in this cult are like schoolyard bullies. They only like to pick on people who are weaker than they are—people who've learned fear from birth. I was twenty-five years old. If I'd stayed in the cult, I'd probably have given birth to three or four babies already, or maybe I'd have finally found a way to kill myself. After eight brutally hard years in the real world, I'd begun to have a glimmer of hope— maybe I really was worth something. I might be destined to burn for eternity, but I sure as hell was here now.

I'd never give up what those first years on my own taught me. For one thing, I finally began to grow up. I learned that thinking for myself wasn't such a bad thing after all. If I hadn't put myself out there, no holds barred, fighting for what I wanted and surviving, I never would have known just how strong I really am—and I might not have had the guts to fall in love with a truly good man and accept the life that would soon find me.

The end of dancing and the beginning of love came at the same time. It was so random it could only have been fate. I had to pick up Shauna at child care, but my car had broken down. I asked a friend of mine to drive me down to collect Shauna after my shift was over. On the way home, he said, "I just need to stop by this guy's house before I drop you off."

He went in the garage to talk to his friend, and Shauna and I went inside the house to wait; both of us were exhausted. We settled down on the couch to watch TV, and the next thing I knew, it was morning. Shauna and I had fallen asleep in front of the TV. The guy who'd brought me here was long gone, but another guy was sitting there, smiling at me. "Good morning!" he said.

And that was how I met Tim.

13

Family

We hit it off from the minute we met.

Tim had his own business. He worked as a boat mechanic, fixing engines in his garage and also driving around to service people's boat engines on site. Kids growing up in the FLDS were taught to fear the water—we never went near it. Satan lived down there, and if we weren't careful, he'd pull us in. Hardly anyone in the FLDS can swim. Never in a million years would I have imagined I'd fall in love with a man who had anything to do with boats.

But I did fall in love, and so did he. He loved Shauna, and we both had little girls. His daughter, Megan, was two years older than Shauna, and she lived with his ex-girlfriend, who had custody. He didn't get to see Megan nearly as much as he wanted, and he worried about her. His face lit up when he told me about his daughter; he was missing her terribly. My heart went out to him.

Tim was what I'd always wanted—a normal guy. He told me he was born and raised in Arizona. His mom, Carol—in fact his whole family—lived in Phoenix. He was the black sheep, he said, grinning. "What about you, Jessie? Is your family from around here?"

"Oh," I said, "I don't have any relatives." It seemed a safe enough lie. My family would be enough to make any halfway decent guy run as fast as he could in the other direction. But Tim didn't run—even after he found out about all my crazy relatives, which happened pretty quickly. When I told him what it was like growing up in the FLDS, he couldn't believe it. Most outsiders couldn't. But instead of calling me a liar or making excuses for my relatives, he just held me closer. He was angry at all of them on my behalf. And he didn't really care about my past or about what I'd done. He'd done some things he wasn't proud of either. We were starting over, together. I'd never met a man like him before.

So for once, I didn't run either. Before long, I'd moved in with Tim. Legally, I was still married to Phillip—I'd had no reason to divorce him and really hadn't thought about it. I knew Phillip only wanted the best for me, and he'd never asked anything of me. But I loved Tim so much. I wanted our relationship to be real. And I needed to move on from everything that connected me to the FLDS. So I filed for divorce.

Phillip was a rock. He was sad that I'd never gone back to him, and in some ways I felt that he'd waited around for me to change my mind a little too long. But he understood, and he wished me well. When we signed the papers, Tim and I spent a weekend with him at Lake Powell, where friends of ours lent us their houseboat.

Phillip did one more incredible thing that week—he snuck into Colorado City and got my mom and my brother Joe. They stayed with me, Tim, Phillip, and Shauna for a couple of days. So they got to meet Tim, which was so important to me. I loved my mom so much for coming—she could have gotten in a lot of trouble if anyone had found out where she was. As it happened, we had a lot of fun that weekend. And Satan didn't reach his hand up out of the lake once.

Right away, Tim and I had started a custody battle for his daughter, Megan—a three-year battle that we won, even though we weren't legally married yet. She came to live with us when she was about six. From the beginning, we were a real family. Megan was my daughter, and she and Shauna were sisters.

And Tim's mom, Carol, was like a real mom to me. Her calm demeanor, pleasant smile, and grandmotherly quality drew me to her and made me feel peaceful. We'd sit at the kitchen table, and she'd talk to me about her faith and love of God. I respected her, and I didn't want to offend her with my opinions, but the way I felt about religion was no secret.

Carol was never appalled, never self-righteous. After hearing about my childhood, she said, "I can see why you feel like you do about religion. I'd feel the same way if I was brought up like you were."

She kept asking us to go to church with her—we were her family, after all. But the thought of stepping inside a church made me shudder. I was really afraid I'd lose it and embarrass all of us. Before I'd met Tim, when I was crazy on drugs, I actually went and sat in churches, and I'd stand up in the middle of the service and say, "You guys are all out of your minds! God was such a bastard! Go to heaven! Leave me in hell!" and storm out. When Mormon missionaries came to my door, I'd taunt them. "I believe in Satan," I'd say. "I'll read your Bible if you read mine!" I'd tell them *exactly* where they could put their God.

So when Carol asked me to go to church, I was polite but firm. "No thank you, Carol. I don't do church. I don't do God. I don't do religion. You know I think it's all hogwash. It's not something that's part of my life anymore, and I refuse to have it as part of my life. If Tim wants to go, that's fine with me. But I won't go."

It was just a fact: I hated God and found Him worthless. I couldn't understand why she believed in Him. She was such a great person. Why would she believe in something that was so disgusting to me?

We never argued about it, but we had some frank discussions. I'd try to convince her how evil God was, and she'd try to persuade me to see how good He was. I did my best to explain the FLDS and polygamy and all the abuse I—and so many others—had suffered in the name of religion. Until she met me, Carol had never even heard of the FLDS. She was fascinated and asked a million questions. I guess everything she heard, rather than making her agree with me, just made her more determined to share her faith with me. Finally, she found an opportunity.

"It's not a service," she said, "just a little function, nothing unusual. My church is small—it's not intimidating at all. I would really like for both of you to go with me." By the time she left that day, I was tired of saying no.

"OK, Carol, I'll go. But if the roof caves in, it's not my fault." I didn't want to go. I thought, *I'm going to go to the church because Tim's mom wants me to go. I don't want his mom to hate me, so I'll go.*

I was uneasy as we walked through the doors of Church of the Valley, a small Southern Baptist church in Phoenix. My radar was full on as I scanned the people who were already in their seats, but I couldn't understand what I was seeing. This was not like church as I knew it. No one was dressed in his or her Sunday best—some women were wearing pants, a lot of people were in blue jeans. The pastor greeted everybody in the same warm way. Kids were wiggling around in their chairs, talking and laughing, and nobody was smacking them on the back of the head. Nobody looked at the parents as if they were worthless because the kid was wiggling and talking.

A little boy a couple of rows away was talking to his mom. I was tense, waiting for some man to slap the mother for not controlling her kid. I thought, *Oh, please, please stop, please stop, so your mom doesn't get in trouble.* But all that happened was that the mom leaned over and said to her son, "Talk quietly, please."

Everybody listened to the pastor's sermon calmly, without fear. I listened carefully. Pastor Larry was talking about . . . I don't know, something normal. Incredibly, not a single time did he tell us we were going to hell because we didn't walk, talk, and dress the way we were told.

I started to realize this was something different, something good. As Carol and I walked out of the church, she said, "So it wasn't so bad after all, was it?" I couldn't even answer her.

It wasn't like a lightning bolt struck me or a burning bush suddenly appeared. I didn't drop to my knees and accept Jesus Christ as my lord and savior. I just knew that when I left that church

I wasn't tense anymore. I wasn't afraid for my eternal soul. I felt . . . peaceful. As time went on, we accepted Carol's invitations to go to church with her more often than not. I wasn't born again, but for the first time since I'd left Colorado City, I no longer felt the urge to spit in the face of anyone who mentioned God.

My divorce became final in 1995. Tim had already asked me to marry him—in 1994, soon after we met. But I was happy just to be in this relationship: I was committed to it, and I didn't need to have the piece of paper from the government to know I'd stay. For the next six years Tim and I and our girls enjoyed a typical family life in our low-profile Phoenix neighborhood. For the first time in my life, I had the luxury of not working. Tim supported us with his business, we took family vacations, and I got to stay home and raise the girls.

I grew up with my kids, experiencing school and learning about a normal life through their eyes. When they'd ask what it was like for me growing up, I'd tell them. Not all the details; not even Tim knew all the details. They were just too painful. But my kids learned enough about large families, long dresses, and sister-wives to understand just how different my childhood had been from theirs.

Because I'd had to follow so many crazy rules growing up, I made sure Megan and Shauna had a lot of personal freedom. I wanted them to learn to trust their instincts and think for themselves. I taught them two important life rules: if they didn't understand something, they were allowed to ask questions. And if the answer didn't satisfy them or made them feel uncomfortable, they didn't have to do what was being asked of them. Bottom line, they didn't have to do something they didn't want to do just because some adult told them to do it.

Naturally, I ended up in the principal's office a lot!

"Why am I here?" I'd ask the principal.

"Shauna won't obey what the teacher's telling her to do," she'd say.

"But she wants to know *why* she needs to do it."

"In this school, we teach the kids that that they need to do what the teacher tells them to." She was being pretty patient with me, so I patiently explained my position right back.

"Well, my kids have been taught that they don't have to obey any adult without an explanation. I don't think a child asking 'Why?' is back-talking, do you?"

It took a few visits to the principal's office, but I finally made my point: my kids—and the other kids—had a right to know the reasons behind what they were asked to do. The kids were thrilled that I'd supported them and that the school had listened and understood. And I was thrilled to find out that I could make a small change in the system. We all learned a lesson from that.

As my girls grew up, I encouraged them to bring their friends home. Our house was considered the safe house—all the kids came to my house and hung out, and they felt free to talk about all kinds of issues. I loved my life.

By 2001, that life had settled into a comfortable groove. I consider my neighborhood to be part of my life, and I want to be sure it's a safe place for me and my kids. So I walked around and met my neighbors; I introduced myself to new people who had moved in or who just hung out here. Recently, I'd gotten involved with some neighborhood cleanup.

A number of our neighbors are elderly; some are also disabled. Around that time the city of Phoenix was cracking down on homeowners, fining people thousands of dollars for zoning violations, including weeds that were too tall and houses that needed painting and fixing. For the elderly and disabled, complying with the city's rules was often completely beyond their resources. I hated seeing these people suffer, so I got involved with Fight Back, an organization helping to bring services to those who needed them, pitching in to do the work that was needed. We painted houses and cleaned yards for the elderly. We also worked with the adult probation department, getting the help of people who were working off their community service hours. I was grateful for these people, but I had one demand of the department: "Don't send me a sex offender."

One weekend, I came home tired and dirty from working in a neighbor's yard. The girls were both at a sleepover, and Tim surprised me by having a full dinner prepared: a huge batch of crab legs, which he knows I love.

Dinner was wonderful. Afterward, Tim said, "Hey, go look in the closet." He followed me into the bedroom. When I opened the closet door, I almost fell over: a gorgeous wedding dress was hanging in there. Before I could even catch my breath, Tim put his arm around me and whispered, "Let's go to Vegas and get married."

"We can't go to Vegas," I said.

"Oh," he said, "so you don't want to marry me?"

I squeezed him tight.

He smiled. "So what's wrong with Las Vegas?"

I pointed to the closet. "You get me this dang dress and then you want to take me up to Vegas where nobody's going to see it?"

"OK," he said, "what do *you* want to do?"

"I want to get married at Church of the Valley." I couldn't believe those words were coming out of my mouth.

Neither could Tim. "What? You?"

"I know—it sounds pretty weird coming from me, the God hater." Tim laughed. But it just felt right. This time, I was marrying the love of my life, the man who had felt like family from day one, the person I knew would support me and never hurt me. And I guess I wanted to make Carol happy too.

"I'm fine with that," Tim said. But he still couldn't believe it. And he wasn't alone. Everybody who was close to me, except maybe Carol, was shocked that I was willing to get married in a church. Most of our friends were just shocked that we were getting married at all. They joked, "Aren't you doing this backward? Everybody gets married, stays together for seven years, and then gets divorced. But you stayed together for seven years and now you're getting married."

Before we could get married at the church, Tim and I had to meet with Pastor Larry. I laid it all out to him, telling him how I felt about God—I didn't hate God anymore, but I wasn't too happy about religion, either. By way of explanation, I told him the short version of my life story and what I'd suffered in the name of God.

By this time he was crying. "I can't believe, after the story you just told me, that you're even willing to walk through these doors."

"This is what I'm struggling with," I said. "But I've seen nothing but good in your church and in you. And because I love my mother-in-law so much, I want to get married in the church—for her."

I invited my whole family too. My five brothers had all left the FLDS by then, and three of them came. My sisters still thought I was poison and stayed away. My mom couldn't get out, although I suspected she might want to. And my dad didn't want anything to do with an evil church or with my marrying outside the faith.

Over the years I have been lucky enough to have made many good friends, and since I had no idea how to plan a wedding, everybody stepped in. Our friend Donnell helped with every detail of our wedding and her sister Elaine made all of the flower arrangements and decorations. Tim's best man, Ron Parker, provided the entertainment with his band, and his parents, Don and Jackie, allowed us to use their home for the reception.

Another good friend, TJ, who owns a landscaping business, completely redid our yard so it looked wonderful, and another friend, Big Mike, let us use his '57 T-Bird as our "getaway" ride. Rather than getting individual wedding gifts, everyone chipped in so Tim and I could go to Jamaica for a week on our honeymoon.

On the day of our wedding, the church was packed with friends and Tim's family. It was the most gorgeous wedding, an amazing service. And I looked great in my dress. After I took it in just a little, it fit perfectly. Because I was not sure beforehand if any of my family would come, I had asked Tim's brother Ralph to walk me down the aisle. Tim and I wrote our own vows, and it was a day like no other. Pastor Larry pronounced us man and wife, and that was it. We were married.

I was finally, and officially, part of my own nuclear family: one husband, one wife, two kids, a home of my own. I was finally ready to live my own life. I was starting to believe that somebody—maybe not the vengeful, hateful God I'd grown up with but a more personal spirit—had been looking out for me over the years—just as the Indian had promised me. How else could I have survived to see this day? I'd never felt happier in my life.

That was in February 2001. Two months later, my baby sister was forced into a marriage she didn't want, and I declared war on child abuse in Colorado City.

Part Three

Outlaw

Living as a small child
in fear each night of sleeping
and every time I went to sleep,
I'd pray I'd not be waking.
I do not want to cry no more
so tired of the pain,
wondering how to get through life,
a child raised in shame.
Tho' physically the scars are few
they healed in little time.
It's the ones that eat my heart and soul
that I keep hiding from.
If I asked for your help
would you put out your hand?
Or is helping these children
beyond your power of command?
If you would just listen
those cries that you hear
are cries of desperation,
cries of pain and cries of fear.
Just remember your risk
is backed by a life force
and LIFE should always be
worth risking for.

—Flora Jessop, 1994

14

Ruby

Ruby was born the day I married Phillip and escaped Colorado City forever. I always thought of her as my "freedom baby." But for Ruby, freedom had never been an option. While I'd been going wild on the streets and slowly learning to take care of myself, she'd been growing up in Colorado City. I felt bad about leaving my little brothers and sisters to that life, but I didn't have much choice. I tried to call Mom as much as I could, but mostly I just stayed away.

Soon after Shauna was born, I was ready to at least try to make some repairs in the fabric of my family. Not long after I moved to Phoenix, I begged my mom to come down to spend a week with me and get to know her new granddaughter. Somehow, she managed to get away, and she brought her two youngest children, Ruby and Lyman. That was my first opportunity to get to know Ruby. She was a sweet little girl who wore glasses, just like me. We loved each other right away and struggled to stay in touch as she was growing up.

I also stayed in touch with some of my sisters but for a much sadder reason. Like so many children born in the twin towns, many of my sisters' babies had birth defects. Of my own siblings, two have cleft palates, and one of my sisters was born with dislocated hips. But it could have been much worse. Because of inbreeding, Colorado City and Hildale have the world's highest rate of fumarase deficiency—more than half the cases of this enzyme deficiency in the world are right in my home town. These babies have terrible seizures. None has an IQ over 25. Some have brains that are literally half water.

The care children with birth defects needed was way beyond the scope of Aunt Lydia's clinic, and everyone knew it. My sisters brought their babies to be treated by real doctors in Phoenix, and we'd visit. I'd take them to secondhand shops and buy their kids clothes. For a while, I had a pretty good relationship with most members of my family—better than could be expected for an unrepentant apostate like me.

I started getting to know Ruby better when she became a teenager and hit puberty. She'd call me on the phone and share the kinds of problems she was forced to keep to herself—girl talk, mostly. She told me that her period brought violent cramping—the result of benign ovarian cysts, which run in my family. Each period brought so much pain she couldn't walk. Finally, she was hurting so much she went to the clinic for help with getting the cysts removed. But Aunt Martha, who was a nurse, told Ruby nothing could be done until she was married. Martha also told her the reason nothing could be done was that she was a virgin. The doctors would have to go in through the vagina to remove the cysts, which would ruin her virginity. So, of course, it was impossible. Ruby was devastated.

She was also suffering, and now without hope. Each month she'd call me, sobbing, and I'd do my best to try to comfort her. We'd talk on the phone for hours. I pleaded with my mother to send her down to Phoenix to stay with me so I could get her real medical help. But of course it never happened.

One month, Ruby called crying so hard I could barely understand what she was saying.

"Slow down, Ruby. What's going on?"

"Oh, Flora"—by this time, only my FLDS relatives called me Flora—"Uncle Rulon kicked Dad out of the community . . . and Mom's been reassigned to Uncle Fred!"

I wanted to throw the phone across the room. I didn't care what happened to Dad, but I was not having my mother be one of Uncle Fred's wives. I knew what would happen to her there.

I told Ruby to put Mom on the phone. "Mom, that is such bullshit! You know better. You can't go to Uncle Fred."

"Flora," she said, ever the obedient wife, "that's what I've been told to do and that's what I'm *gonna* do." She was matter of fact about it. She knew how life worked in the FLDS, and she didn't have the strength to fight. Besides, if Uncle Rulon told her to do it, he was speaking for God.

Uncle Fred just kept collecting wives, and those wives all brought children with them. Fred eventually ended up with many children living in his home, most of them the kids of men who had been kicked out of the FLDS. It was ironic that this man who couldn't create children of his own wound up claiming so many. It was even more ironic that my mother—the mother of seven of his children, hated by all of his wives—was going to end up as one of those wives.

I lost contact with Ruby right after that phone call. I called often for three solid months, at all times of the day and night, trying to talk to her. But every time, Mom would say she wasn't home or was busy. I was really worried.

One Saturday in May 2001, I came home tired from helping one of my neighbors weed her yard and plant some flowers. I had just opened a bottle of water when the phone rang.

"Flora?" It was Ruby.

"Ruby! Where have you been for the last three months? Is everything all right?"

"Not really." Ruby began to cry.

"What's wrong? Where have you been?" I could feel my chest getting tight.

"I had to marry Haven Barlow last month. I didn't want to, Flora. They made me."

Ruby was fourteen years old. "What? Who's Haven Barlow?"

"He's our stepbrother. His mother's a Jessop, she's our cousin. His father was a grandson of John Y. Barlow." John Y. Barlow, a cofounder of the FLDS, was the Prophet from 1935 to 1949. It seemed as if everyone in Colorado City and Hildale was somehow related to John Y. Barlow or to Joseph Smith Jessop, who founded the sect. But Ruby was still talking.

"Uncle Rulon kicked out Haven's father, the same time he kicked out Dad, and his mom got reassigned to Uncle Fred too. I hate Haven! He's horrible."

They'd been living as siblings, and now they were husband and wife. I wanted her out of there, fast.

"Ruby, whoa, back up. What happened? Why'd you end up with Haven?"

"Because they caught me kissing Joe Rohbock," she sniffled. She told me that Joe was a boy she really liked. It was the same old story. Because their relationship wasn't sanctioned, Ruby and Joe were both branded as evil. In the twisted arithmetic of the FLDS, kissing equals sexual relations. Now she was tainted.

She had been terrified that Uncle Rulon would assign her to share a husband with one or more of her sisters. (To my intense sorrow and anger, nearly every brother-in-law I have is married to two of my sisters.) Ruby hadn't wanted that, so she went for the next best option—she asked Rulon Jeffs for permission to marry her love, Joe Rohbock. But true to form, he immediately assigned her to twenty-one-year-old Haven Barlow. It was a typical power play by Rulon. It didn't matter whether or not Joe was a suitable husband otherwise. Because it was something Ruby wanted, Rulon would not allow it. She told me that Warren Jeffs had officiated at the ceremony. I felt sick about it.

"Are you still in school?" Very rarely, a woman's husband might allow her to finish high school and perhaps even to go to college. But most girls in the twin towns are made to leave school after the eighth grade—if they get even that far.

"No, I'm not in school. They made me leave."

"Have you had sex? Are you pregnant?"

"On my wedding night; I had just started my period and it hurt really bad." She was whispering so softly that I had to ask her to repeat herself several times.

"I begged and begged him not to touch me," she said. "But he ripped my dress off and shredded my clothes. He told me he owned me, and I had to obey him. I screamed for hours. Everybody heard me."

"That son of a bitch raped you?"

"Yeah . . . he did." She was really quiet now. I could tell she was extremely embarrassed and didn't want to talk about it.

"I tried to get help," she sobbed, "I really did. But I couldn't remember your phone number. No one else would answer their phone. I couldn't get hold of anybody!

"After, I got really sick. When I felt better, I just ran to our brother Joe's house. He took me in. He was really good to me. Then Patricia, Martha Ann, Mabel, and Susie found me and tried to force me to go back to Haven. But our brother kept stepping in the way. He finally made them leave." I was proud of my little brother.

"Where are you right now?" I asked.

"I'm at our brother Joe's house. I'm going to try and stay here for now. I have to get out of this mess, Flora. I can't go back. I just can't go back to him."

I was ready to head out the door. "Hang on," I said, "I'm coming to get you."

"You don't have to come this minute," she said, sniffling. "I can stay here. I'll be OK. We're going camping this weekend. At the lake." I knew what a forbidden thrill that was. "You can come get me after that."

"No, Ruby. We need to get you out of there now." I was so furious with everybody—my mother, Haven, and Uncle Fred. Even Ruby, for wanting to go camping instead of getting to a safer location. "Look, put Joe on the phone."

Once I got on the phone with my brother, I told him, "I'm coming to pick her up right now."

"I promised her we'd go camping at the lake," he said. "She really wants to go. Just come on Monday. She'll be here. Anyway, I'm her big brother. What can you do that I can't do?"

"You don't get it. They're not going to let her stay with you! I need to come get her now."

But Joe wouldn't budge. He was convinced that he could protect her. He promised he'd call later. As much as I wanted to jump in the truck right then and go get her, I knew I couldn't force her to leave. She was going to have to make that decision herself.

I got Ruby back on the phone and said, "What is it you want to do right now?"

"Well, I want to go camping." She wasn't crying anymore at least. "I think I'll be OK here. Joe is keeping everybody away from me. So can we talk when I come back from the lake?"

"Yeah, OK. That's fine. But what do you want to do about leaving Haven?"

"I don't want to go back," she said. "I want to get away from here for good. I want to be free, like you."

"OK, then. I'll do everything I can to keep you safe—I promise."

We hung up. I was distraught. I wanted to do something right then, but my hands were tied. So I called my mother and yelled at her.

"Mom," I said. "What are you doing? Why did you allow this to happen to Ruby?"

But I got the same tired answer. "Well, you just don't understand, Flora."

"You're right, Mom. I don't understand. Explain it to me. What are you thinking, letting her marry her stepbrother? And you listened to her scream for what, three hours? And you didn't do a damn thing?"

"She belongs to him, Flora . . ."

I felt sick to my stomach. "When is it going to be time for you to protect your kids, Mom?"

But she just kept repeating the same old excuse. "You don't understand. You just don't understand."

"Mom, for my whole life, I've made excuses for you about why you didn't protect me, why you said nothing when you knew Dad was raping me. But Ruby is your baby girl. This is your last chance to do the right thing. What's stopping you from standing up for her?"

Silence.

"I love you with all my heart, Mom, but I can't do this anymore. If you won't stand up for your babies, then I'm going to have to do it for you. I love you, but I'm done defending you."

The phone went dead.

I called right back, but my sister Martha Ann answered. "What the hell did you do to Mom?" she asked.

"Just let me talk to her," I insisted.

"Well, Mom's left. You have no right to interfere in this. Just leave it alone and stop meddling!"

"Listen, Martha Ann, I'm going to tell you the same thing I told Mom. If you won't protect Ruby, then I will!"

She hung up on me.

That was the last time I ever spoke to Mom or Ruby. If I'd known that then, I might never have been able to keep going.

But I still thought I was going to save my sister. I was jumping out of my skin all weekend. On Monday, I called my brother Joe's house. "Hey, let me talk to Ruby. Is she ready to come home with me?"

Silence.

Oh, shit. "What's wrong?"

"She's gone, Flora."

He told me they'd gone camping at Quail Creek Reservoir with another of our brothers, as planned. They parked the cars in the lot, away from the lake, and carried their gear down there. While my brothers were setting up camp, Ruby walked back to the car to get something. She never returned to the campsite.

Freedom

Heart racing, sight dimming,
as footsteps near the door,
Trembling beneath the covers,
no escaping from the horror

Brutal words, stunning blows,
nothing I can do
My husband has the priesthood's blessing
to beat me black and blue

Blood oozing, torn flesh,
so cold, so hot, so sore,
Fourteen years old and forever changed,
a virgin never more

Heart racing, they're coming,
the men are hunting me
Safety is finally within my sight,
run faster, Oh God, help me get free.

White hot fear, blinding pain,
blood flowing down my face
No memory, just shadows, running for life,
knowing now I've lost the race.

Five years passed, still I'm chained;
I've babies now to free
Must listen closely, keep them safe,
protect them, protect me

My sister fights the evil here,
no backing down, she shows no fear
My dimming dream, barely alive,
cries only my sister can hear

The nightmare will soon be over,
freedom, light, and peace abound
My sister's voice I long to hear,
freedom comes only from that one sound.

Give me strength, my mind grows weak,
just hold on little ones
The pain is nearly over,
darkness turns to light, she comes

Freedom, a foreign word I chant inside my head
Freedom, I dream, I wait,
Freedom, please come before I'm dead.

April 20, 2005, by Flora Jessop. Dedicated to my sister Ruby.

My brothers looked for her everywhere. Finally, they drove out to Uncle Fred's house and saw Ruby through the kitchen window. They banged on the door. One of the Timpson boys, one of Uncle Fred's strong-arm goons, told them to leave the property immediately. He said that if they tried to contact Ruby, they would be arrested and charged with trespassing and attempted kidnapping.

This was so completely twisted I couldn't even wrap my mind around it. Apparently, Ruby had run into her boyfriend, Joe Rohbock, in the parking lot and had started talking to him. Then the little son of a bitch had kidnapped her and turned her in to Uncle Fred. I was livid.

As soon as I was through talking to Joe, I called the Utah Department of Child and Family Services. I was desperate enough to call the government agency that I felt had screwed me over when I ran away at fourteen.

"My sister Ruby was forced to get married at fourteen, and her so-called husband raped her. She tried to get away from the FLDS, and now she's being held against her will," I explained. "She's only fourteen years old! You've got to go to Hildale and get Ruby and put her in state custody immediately until we can sort it all out."

The person at the DCFS told me that the agency couldn't do a welfare check without a report from the sheriff's office and that I should call that office. I did, but then Steve Stovall with the sheriff's office told me to call Julie Wilden—a caseworker with the DCFS in St. George. Julie told me she needed a sheriff's report first. I felt like a dog chasing its tail. "Julie, can I talk to your supervisor?"

She put me on the line with Gene Ashdown, the director of the DCFS in southern Utah. I gave him the lowdown on Ruby's situation, and we set up an in-person meeting—me, Gene, and Julie Wilden—to hash it out.

Then I got an e-mail from Les Zitting. His sister Carolyn* had become my Dad's third wife, shortly before he'd been kicked

*Not her real name.

out of the FLDS. Dad had finally met his match in Carolyn. She was a molester too; she had molested Les. I'd never known Les in Colorado City. He'd been kicked out of town as a teenager, one of the hundreds of so-called "lost boys"—young teens expelled from the FLDS and forced to leave. They were not really lost, though; they were abandoned because the priesthood saw them as competition. Now Les had become an advocate for children. He hadn't lost his sense of humor, either. The first time I met Les, he walked up to me and said, "Nice to meet you! I hear my molester is married to your molester."

Through the grapevine, he'd found out I was fighting for Ruby. He e-mailed me that he and his friend Jay Beswick were offering to help. Jay was a tri-state representative with For Kids Sake, a child abuse prevention organization working out of Southern California. He'd grown up just outside the twin towns, and knew all about what was going on there. Because they were familiar with the officials I needed to work with and had been involved with a couple of high-profile media cases, I wanted Les and Jay to be a part of the meeting, and they agreed.

Now I had to tell Tim exactly what was going on. I don't know what I expected, but my husband was right there with me, as mad as I was. He told me he'd drive me to the meeting at St. George. I was agitated—worried about Ruby and very nervous about dealing with the Utah DCFS again. I'd been screwed over by these people more than once, and they didn't have a great record for protecting the kids in Hildale. The whole state of Utah, in fact, had just ignored the place since the Short Creek fiasco. There hadn't been a case made against those polygamists in fifty years. I decided to tape our meeting, so I could throw their words back in their faces when they let me down.

A couple of days later, we made the trip to the DCFS office in St. George. I felt freaked out from the beginning—the place even smelled the same. Everyone else was already there.

"Hello, Flora," said Gene Ashdown, rising to shake my hand. "This is Julie Wilden." I was too nervous to be very polite. Jay and Les just smiled tightly and nodded.

I set my jumbo cup of Mountain Dew on the table, slipped my microcassette recorder behind it and pressed the button to start taping. I don't think anyone saw it; at least, no one said anything.

I was feeling angry and nervous, and I was more than a little obnoxious. Right away, I started on the offense: I asked Gene Ashdown if Chuck Sullivan still worked there.

"Chuck Sullivan was one of our very best caseworkers," he said with pride. And then added, sadly, "Chuck died several years ago."

I'd liked Chuck, at first, until the day I'd heard the recordings of my conversations with Chuck coming out of Uncle Fred's office. "Well, good," I snapped back. "Then I won't have to kill him, because I owe him for several beatings I took."

It was hard for anyone to be nice after that. I felt I needed to keep my guard up or the cell door was going to close on me again. I didn't realize how traumatized I'd been by my first experience with the DCFS until I stepped back into that room.

Gene clearly didn't know what to make of me, but he kept his cool. He promised that as soon as DCFS or law enforcement people located Ruby, agency staff would take her into state custody and protect her until they could get the details on her case. I walked out of the meeting trying to convince myself they would keep their word. I had my tape, just in case.

When Tim and I got back in the truck for the long drive home, I lit a cigarette and sank back into my seat, exhausted and crying. I was emotionally drained. I identified with Ruby completely— I knew exactly what she was going through. I felt as if I had walked backward in time, and this crap was happening to me all over again. I feared for my sister. I kept thinking, *Ruby, just hold on, hold on, hold on. I'm coming, I'm coming.*

I was quiet on the ride home, obsessed with Ruby and what she was going through and feeling powerless to stop it. She was at Uncle Fred's—and I knew exactly where they were keeping her. They may not have put her in the same brown-shag cell; but spiritually, mentally, psychologically, and emotionally, they were locking her in a prison. I was so terrified for Ruby. I'd been fighting the FLDS for a long time, and they almost broke me. I wasn't sure my sweet baby sister would have the strength to take the psychological mind screwing, the emotional terrorism she was about to receive.

Over the years, I've heard several journalists say they're amazed that the women who have come out of the FLDS can tell their own horror stories without any emotion, but the minute they start talking about their sisters or other family members, they break down and cry. That doesn't surprise me. Ruby's abduction provoked the most genuine emotion—besides anger—I'd felt my entire life. For the past ten years I'd been tough little Jessie—I hadn't allowed fear to be a part of my life. Yet when Ruby was taken away, the fear came out of nowhere and just knocked me to my knees.

It's as if my own emotional wiring is disconnected but I can feel the pain of others loud and clear. Maybe that's because in the FLDS we're raised to keep sweet—no emotions allowed. Keeping sweet was hard for me—my independence translated into anger, rage, and rebellion, which always managed to get me into trouble. At the same time, my more vulnerable feelings were so suppressed I hardly knew they existed. By the time I married Phillip, I was numb. I didn't care whether I lived or died. It was eight years before I could even let myself cry.

When we got home from St. George, the phone was ringing.

"Hello?" I was hoping against hope that Ruby had escaped. But it was Jay Beswick, the For Kids Sake representative.

He cut right to the chase. "Flora," he said, "I'm sorry to call so soon after the meeting, but I need your help. I've got a sixteen-year-old runner, Chery Beth Taylor. She's from the Salt Lake City FLDS group."

I was puzzled. "Why are you calling me?"

"Because the folks in your state contacted me. I don't have a place for her, and she needs to get as far away from Salt Lake as she can. Can you help us out?" he asked.

I was floored. He was asking me to be like Aunt Jenny, like Fern—two women who had risked everything to help me save my own life. I couldn't do much about Ruby right now, but I could put my fear and anger and my love for her to some good use.

I didn't even hesitate. "Sure. Send her to me. I'll protect her."

"We'll drive her up tonight."

"OK."

Chery arrived on my doorstep looking worried, sad, and lost. Like so many girls, boys, and women I and others would rescue from the FLDS in the years to come, she had no concept of the outside world or of the skills she would need to survive.

"Hi, Chery," I said, welcoming her in. She looked at the woman who had driven her here from Salt Lake City. I thought she was going to cry.

"It's OK, Chery," said the woman. "This is Flora. She's going to take care of you now."

"Come on in," I said, smiling.

But Chery just stared at me. I stared back, puzzled. Tim and our two girls stood behind me, waiting. What was wrong with this girl?

We finally got her into our house and set her up in the living room with a blanket and pillow. The girl was full of questions she didn't ask. By the time we got to sleep that night, we were all exhausted. It had been a very long day.

And just like that, I was thrust into activism big-time. Before we turned out our light, I turned to Tim. "When I first met you, I told you I didn't have any family at all . . ."

"Yeah, I remember."

"Now you know more than you ever wanted to about just how nuts they are."

"Yep." We were both quiet, just breathing.

"I've got to do this."

"Yes, you do."

"What about the girls?"

"We'll all back you up."

We lay there, both of us thinking about how this was going to change our lives.

15

Lost and Found

Taking care of Chery Taylor gave me someone besides Ruby to worry about. And I did worry about Chery. Sometimes, I wondered if she was mentally challenged. As we got ready to go out one day, I asked her to pick up before we left—her clothes and shoes and bedding were all over the living room, where she'd been sleeping. In our tiny house we didn't need any more messes.

In response she gave me the same blank look I was getting used to from her. I was frustrated, and concerned.

"Chery? Please pick up in here so we can leave."

Her response this time was to begin turning in slow circles. I must have watched her do this for five minutes. It went on and on and on. I couldn't imagine what was going on in her mind. "Chery? What's wrong?"

She stopped, almost in tears. "You told me to pick up the living room . . . but what . . . pick up what?"

A light went on. She'd been told how to do every little thing from the minute she was born—if she made a mistake, there'd be hell to pay. Thinking for herself was not a safe option, so she'd just turned off that switch. Someone had to tell her specifically every move she was supposed to make. "I need you to pick up your dirty clothes and put them in the hamper," I said gently. "Then pick up your blanket and fold it. Put it on the couch with your pillow. Get your shoes out of the middle of the floor and put them together, out of the way. Then we'll be ready to go."

"Oh, OK!" She brightened up and got to work.

That's how severe the cognitive thinking disabilities can be with these kids. It wasn't until I worked with several runaway girls that I realized it wasn't just Chery.

Chery ran away from home because her family, like other FLDS families living in Salt Lake City, had been told by Warren Jeffs that they had to move down to the twin towns. Warren was starting to consolidate his power, but Chery didn't understand that. She just knew that she didn't want to leave her friends and Salt Lake to move down to the sticks.

Warren couldn't have cared less what Chery or anyone else wanted—he was intent on becoming the next Prophet. Even though Uncle Rulon was still alive, Warren had made significant inroads toward power. A few years back, a news article had described Warren as the "primary gatekeeper for access to the prophet."[1] I wondered how Uncle Fred felt about that.

Personally, I had found the news chilling. But there was nothing I could do about it. I'd dropped everything else I'd been doing, and redoubled my efforts to find Ruby. I had realized that the Internet might be a good way to get my message to more people. If I could get her picture out there, somebody might recognize her.

I found out that ex-Mormons had online discussions on Internet message boards, so I posted a message asking for help getting started. Right away, a man named Jim Ashurst e-mailed me and said he could help. With his assistance, we posted her photograph, with a story about what had happened and a plea for help finding her. Right away, people started asking what they could do to help. Maybe it was Ruby herself that made people reach out: she looked so young and innocent. With her sweet smile, her wire-framed glasses, and her blue dress with the big white collar, she looked like a girl from another century.

Practically before I knew what was happening, we had started a nonprofit grassroots organization of volunteers that we called Help the Child Brides. Soon, I began to hear about other women and girls who needed help, and we put their stories up on the Internet too. I began opening my house to more and more refugees from the FLDS—runaways, like Chery; young girls fleeing from arranged marriages; and young mothers and their children running from abusive polygamous homes. My small house was sometimes overflowing. Growing up with so many brothers and sisters, it seemed normal to me even though my friends couldn't understand how we fit them all in. I just shrugged and said, "We know how to stack 'em up in polygamy!"

Help the Child Brides was riding a small but swelling wave of interest in American polygamy. Slowly, people on the outside were beginning to question the idea that polygamists who married little girls were really exercising their freedom of religion. They were beginning to think that the girls might have rights too.

What started out as a Web page about Ruby quickly evolved into a Web site addressing the bigger picture: helping all of these girls get out of bondage. Ex-FLDS members and folks interested in the antipolygamy movement began to contact me, and before long I was making new friends and talking to people I hadn't talked to in years. After all those years of feeling alone, it was empowering.

We formed a loose network of people who were willing to do whatever was necessary to help these girls get out: Jay Beswick and Les Zitting, who had both been with me when I met with the DCFS about Ruby; Rowenna Erickson, who'd given birth to eight children in thirteen years, had been kicked out of her Salt Lake City sect for talking about how women and children were treated, and would soon co-found an organization called Tapestry Against Polygamy; Linda Walker, a Mormon antipolygamy activist who had recently started the Child Protection Project to get the word out about child abuse in polygamy; and Aunt Jenny, who was living in St. George and still working to ferry girls out of the twin towns.

We spread the word and got some news coverage. I did radio interviews and made TV appearances. People who had never heard of polygamy were appalled that this situation existed and that the legal system permitted it to flourish. Surely, I thought, someone out there would hear me and help me find my sister.

But even with so many people looking for Ruby, we had no luck. My baby sister seemed to have disappeared off the face of the earth, and Mom along with her.

So I kept trying to help the women and children who were now coming to me in ever increasing numbers. But I was finding out the hard way that saving them wasn't easy. They knew only what they'd been taught in the cult, and most of that was lies and damn lies. I and the people around me doing similar things had to start at the beginning with every one of these women and children, and what I describe here about the way things were then is still pretty much what we do today.

Each time I'd go to St. George or Colorado City to pick up a runaway girl or a mom and her kids, they brought a literal whiff of Colorado City with them. My childhood of living in cramped conditions with diaper pails overflowing came rushing back as if I'd never left. Most of these refugees—girls and boys alike—had never had a real soap shower in their lives. They wore the neck-to-ankle sacred garment and bathed the way I described back at the beginning of this book. They would keep on one leg of the garment, spray one side of their body with water, dry that part, put on half the clean garment, take the dirty leg side off, and spray that side. Soap? If you're forbidden to touch your own body, then soaping yourself in the shower could send you straight to hell.

They were completely unaware of the way they smelled, but everyone else knew they were coming a mile away. So the first thing I had to do was get them clean. The women and girls weren't too hard to convince—they balked, but they were used to taking orders. And once they learned the power of soap, they didn't look back. But the boys—who were raised to be little gods—kicked up a real fuss.

"You're taking us to hell!" they'd scream. "I'm gonna kill you!"

But they weren't dealing with their mothers anymore. I just put my hands on my hips and said, "Stand in line, honey; you're one of many. Either pick up a washcloth and soap your entire body, or I'm coming in with you!" One look at me and they knew I meant it. That threat was usually enough to get them clean.

The very next day after each of these women and kids arrived, we'd start the legal process. We'd file the papers for whatever court orders or processes were needed—divorce proceedings, custody hearings, restraining orders. Over and over, I had to convince grown women that they had legal rights. Many thought only men were permitted to have lawyers. It was pitiful.

Then it was time for a medical checkup. For most of these people, it was the first time in their lives they'd seen a doctor. The process—especially removing their clothes so a doctor could check them—was horrifying. Unless they'd been molested, they'd never exposed their bodies to another person since they had their diapers changed. In the FLDS, being seriously sick means you have evil demons. Usually, a priesthood elder would "cure" you with laying on of hands. If that doesn't work, the demons may win and you may die.

However, many of the kids we were seeing had problems that came simply from being dirty so much of the time. I've seen boys who had such severe skin infections that their skin would bleed if anything just touched it. The doctor would prescribe a medicated ointment, but getting them to rub it in every day would mean touching themselves. Every step in helping these children presented another hurdle to jump over.

Three sisters, ages seven, ten, and sixteen, all had terrible vaginal infections—not from sexual abuse but simply because they kept their underwear on continually and didn't use soap when they bathed. If the moms stayed out of the cult long enough to recover a sense of self, they usually began to feel terribly guilty about the way they'd been caring for their children. It was frustrating and also heartbreaking.

One of the most essential things was getting the kids into counseling so they could get some help in coping with the tremendous

changes they were having to deal with now that they were freed
from the FLDS. One of those changes was something most kids
take for granted—going to school. Getting these kids enrolled
in a real school presented a lot of problems. State law in Arizona
mandates age-appropriate classrooms. But these children had been
using textbooks written or at least approved by Warren Jeffs—
textbooks that taught them, among other things, that the theory
of evolution was a lie. We had to fight tooth and nail for a sen-
sible approach to schooling sixteen-year-old kids who test out at
fourth-grade levels. We fought to get them special programs, and
we fought to get them tutoring.

Then we had to deal with the almost inevitable psychological meltdowns. For many FLDS refugees—children and women
alike—it has been just too difficult to make the transition to the
real world. Counselors, unfamiliar with FLDS teachings and just
beginning to understand the range of abuses these people have
suffered, were often unable to offer adequate help. Many children
and women became quickly demoralized, just as I had at fourteen when I called Uncle Fred to come and get me so I could go
home, where everything was at least familiar and predictable, bad
as it was.

In Chery's case, she missed Salt Lake City and her friends and
wanted to go back there. I didn't want to let her go, but I had to.
Still, I didn't want to deliver her to her parents. Some good
friends of mine, Travis and his wife, Julie, had just moved up to
Salt Lake with their three boys. I asked if they'd take her, and
they jumped at an opportunity to help. They invited Chery to live
with them, and she accepted. We made sure she had an attorney,
and off she went.

When Warren Jeffs heard she was back, he instructed her family to get a gag order against me. No one was allowed to talk to
me about her, including Travis and Julie. This really scared me—
Travis and Julie had no idea about the kind of treachery the FLDS
would use in order to get her back.

Dear Mother, Father
Hi this is me Chery i Just wanted
to tell you that I am all right you
dont need to worry I am soory IF i ~~scared~~
scared you but you guys would not Let
me go so i went by my self i will call
when i fell safe that you wont try to
make me come home. I am sorry but
i do not wont that Kind of life i dont
Wont to get married that way i wish
you would of Just Let me go so i didon't
have to do this. I miss you all atote
but please stop traing because you
not going to find me and i am not
Coming home tell ~~everey~~ every body
hi and i mrss them give Levi and Lahen
a huge For me and i Love all you guys

Love
Chery

cheri Beth taylor
2001

Chery wrote this letter to her parents shortly after I rescued her from the FLDS.

I begged Travis and Julie to keep the channels of communication open. "Travis, please don't do this. You've got to keep me informed about what they're doing. I know I can't ask you to break the law, but for her sake, I'm begging you."

Travis and Julie were working hard to get full custody of Chery. They had started the court process, and they had been taking Chery to the DCFS offices in Salt Lake regularly to meet with social workers. They didn't know it, but some DCFS workers were bringing Chery's dad in through the back door to see her. These DCFS staff probably thought they were doing the right thing, but it meant a whole world of deceit was going on behind the backs of the people most concerned for Chery's welfare.

Warren had told the Taylors that they had to get this case out of the courts right now; media attention was not acceptable. Chery's dad told her that if she came home, and called off the court proceeding and the media, he would let her move out of the family home and would help to support her. Chery was about as naïve as they come, and she was raised to trust her dad. He was one of the priesthood and spoke for God. So she went back home. Travis and Julie were devastated, but there was nothing they could do.

Everything was fine for Chery for three or four days. Her dad gave her twenty dollars and told her to go out and have fun with her friends. She was thrilled. She went out and enjoyed herself for a few hours, and when she came back to the house, everything was gone. No furniture, no clothes, no people. Her family had just moved out and left her, and she had no idea where they'd gone. I guess they assumed she would collapse and perish without their help, and that must have been what they preferred to having her grow up with normal people who could help her survive in the real world. And they must have been right, because pretty soon she was on the street.

When I heard about it, I was furious. I drove up to Salt Lake City to look for her and finally found her living in an apartment with fifteen other kids, mostly FLDS lost boys, having sex with them to pay her share of the rent. I hauled her down to Planned Parenthood where we made sure she wasn't pregnant. I loaded up six bags with condoms and handed them out to the boys. But

I couldn't budge Chery. Not long after, she did get pregnant and finally married back into the FLDS. She had no skills—she'd barely learned to think. Where else would she go?

Chery was the first girl I saved, and the first girl I lost—mostly due to the dysfunctional legal system and social services. Over the next few years it would become a frustrating pattern. It was so damn hard to help these children fight and fight and to see them begin to shed years of conditioning only to have them give up and collapse back into the FLDS. But as many times as it happened, I had to keep trying to rescue them. All I could do was keep hoping and fighting.

Meanwhile, I was still searching for Ruby. Day after day I called the sheriff's office and the Utah DCFS to check on their progress, but they never had any answers for me. The folks in the twin towns had closed ranks, of course, shutting caseworkers and law enforcement out as effectively as they had always shut me out. Of course, I was used to being shunned by them, and I never stopped trying to break through those closed ranks.

I called Uncle Fred's house over and over again. Invariably one of Fred's wives would answer. And no matter which one it was, the conversation was always exactly the same.

"Where are Mom and Ruby?"

"We know where Ruby is, Flora," the sister-wife would reply. "She's fine. She's with family."

"Let me talk to her."

"Ruby does not want to talk to you. You just need to leave this alone."

"It's not going to happen. I want to speak to Ruby."

"Ruby does not want to talk to you."

"I'm warning you right now; I'm not going away. I want to see Ruby in person, face to face. I won't back off until she looks me in the eye and tells me she's happy, wherever she is. Until that happens, I'll fight for her."

Sometimes they'd try a subtle threat. "You don't want to go doing this, Flora. You're burning bridges that you don't want to burn."

"What bridges? Every bridge I have ever walked across coming out of that town blew up when I left fifteen years ago."

"Flora, you need to let it be. I'm done talking to you."

But I wasn't done. "Listen," I would say. "I need you to give Rulon Jeffs and Uncle Fred a message from me. You tell them that when the shit starts hitting the fans out there, it's coming from Flora Jessop. I'm committed and I'm not going away. I am going to do everything in my power to rescue Ruby and to stop the abuse of *all* the kids in Colorado City and Hildale." I hoped the sound of the phone slamming down hurt her ears really bad.

Finally, on June 26, after thirty-five days of silence, Gene Ashdown finally called.

"So," I said, "what happened to my sister?"

"Uhh, to put it in a word, nothing, zero, nada. . . . She said she was fine, gave no information of any concern, for anything. Period, that's it."

At long last she'd been brought to meet with DCFS workers in St. George. And naturally, they hadn't interviewed her alone—someone from the FLDS was always in the room. For legal reasons Gene couldn't tell me who it was. But it didn't matter—they were all intimidating. It was in this atmosphere that Ruby had said everything was "fine." What else could she say? End of interview.

I was furious. Some adult—one of her abductors—had brought her in, and watched her like a hawk the whole time. She knew what would happen to her if she didn't keep sweet.

I asked Gene if they'd done any medical tests to see whether or not Ruby, who was of course married but still underage, had had sex.

"We couldn't do a test on her," he said. "She has to give permission for that."

"So even though there were allegations of abuse . . ."

"There'd be no way to force a test."

So that was that. In the eyes of the state, even if the authorities suspected otherwise, there'd been no abuse.

"So now what? She just goes back and stays married?"

"Yep."

In fact it was no big deal for fourteen-year-olds to be married in the state of Utah. In 1996, a thousand children aged fourteen to seventeen had gotten married there—some of the girls to men in their thirties and forties. If they said they were doing it of their own free will, the state just didn't feel it could do anything.[2]

Ruby was saying that everything was fine, Gene said, so they didn't have a legal way into the case.

I pointed out that it was common for abused children to deny the abuse when they realized there might be harsh consequences for their abuser. He agreed, but his hands were tied.

"So if these kids are terrified to tell you . . ."

"Then they will stay there."

By the time they interviewed Ruby, she had been brainwashed and threatened. I wasn't really surprised at her response, but it saddened me. I got more and more frustrated, and kept pressing Ashdown for aggressive action. Finally, he hung up on me.

I even wondered if the girl who had gone in there *was* Ruby. So many of the FLDS kids—the offspring of sisters married to cousins—look alike. It was common knowledge that parents sometimes substituted siblings or cousins to fool the authorities. How would they know?

Screw it. If the agency wasn't going to act, I was. I called Gene Ashdown's boss, Abel Ortiz, in Salt Lake City. I asked him to confirm the department's policy on underage sexual abuse. He became very defensive and said he'd have to get back to me later. But he never did.

Much later I discovered where Ruby had been during those thirty-five days of silence. They'd taken her to Bountiful—a remote Canadian FLDS compound in British Columbia—and placed her in the custody of Winston Blackmore. Blackmore was the FLDS bishop of Canada, a friend of Warren Jeffs, and rich and powerful. He had more than twenty wives and over a hundred children. I shuddered to imagine what had happened to my sister in Canada during her "reindoctrination" program there.

My failure to get Ruby away from Haven Barlow was a bitter pill. I was determined not to give up though, and I kept her name posted on the Internet as someone who needed help. In the meantime, I started to get more cases, more runaway girls to find homes for. This was my work now.

This was a sad time for me. Ruby stayed married and in the FLDS. I have never again been able to speak to her. Through the grapevine I learned that Ruby had started having babies, and the last thing I heard was that she was the mother to five children. Being only twenty-one and having little education, it's no wonder Ruby now feels she has no option but to stay in the FLDS. How could she provide for all those kids otherwise?

I haven't spoken to my Mom since 2001, and no one will tell me where she is. I filed a missing person's report on her in 2004. I learned at one point that she had been sent to Warren Jeffs's compound outside Eldorado, Texas. She must have been thrilled to be so close to the Prophet. But when I heard later that she had been sent back to Colorado City because heart problems left her unable to work, I was terrified. I remembered what had happened to that old woman I met one day in the Colorado City clinic, left in her own waste.

I haven't gotten Mom and Ruby out—yet. But that fight has opened a door in my heart that has never closed. And it's the reason I'm still fighting to stop the abuse and free the FLDS girls and women to this day.

I'm still trying to keep my promise to Ruby.

16

Changes

By 2002, the media were really starting to get interested in polygamy. In March—just eight months after Ruby had been married—*Marie Claire* magazine ran a piece called "Rescuing America's Child Brides." It profiled three antipolygamy activists— I was the only one wearing a black leather jacket with rivets.[1]

But even though people were interested in learning more about what some were calling a homegrown Taliban, right in our own backyard, the state government was still dragging its feet when it came to enforcing its own laws. In 2000, Utah had announced it was going to start prosecuting polygamists. It was good timing: the Winter Olympics were set to begin in Salt Lake City in early 2002.

In May 2001, the state put together a bigamy case against a local independent fundamentalist polygamist, Tom Green, who lived just outside the city. After that, the state would also try him for the statutory rape of one of his wives—his thirteen-year-old stepdaughter. He'd married her when he was thirty-seven. Tom Green deserved to be prosecuted and found guilty and sent to prison—which eventually he was. But when that case was over, the excitement died down. Hildale—with thousands of known polygamists and many reported cases of abuse, incest, forced marriage, tax evasion, and welfare fraud—was still untouched.

In June, a fourteen-year-old girl named Elizabeth Smart was kidnapped from her bedroom in a middle-class neighborhood of Salt Lake City. When I heard that on the news, I felt sick to my stomach. My gut instincts told me she'd been taken to be someone's spiritual wife.

I just spat out, "Polygamists!"

Right away, I sent an e-mail to the authorities telling them that they should look for a polygamist as her kidnapper—some guy collecting spiritual wives. But they had other leads to follow. Nine months later they found her—wearing a gray wig, sunglasses, and a veil—with polygamist Brian David Mitchell and his wife, Wanda.

One reason polygamy has been so hard to prosecute in both Utah and Arizona is the political power of the LDS. A lot of powerful nonpolygamous Mormon families in both states come out of polygamous backgrounds. They have had a vested interest in keeping a lid on polygamy's dirty little secrets and have used their power to do it. Both states have defended their lack of action by calling the issues around polygamy "freedom of religion" issues.

Instead, they have gone after bigamy and child abuse issues, which in theory are easier to prosecute. But they have been slow to build even these cases. The Utah attorney general's office gave the same excuse they'd given me for not moving on Ruby's case—the crimes were hard to investigate. That was true; telling people that they will go straight to hell if they talk to the authorities is an effective way to keep secrets. The FLDS had plenty of practice in closing ranks and shutting out the outside world.

But I and other activists thought the state needed to try harder, so we gave it a kick in the pants. In August 2002, antipolygamy activists from Utah, Arizona, and Canada gathered to hold a press conference in Zion National Park. I spoke and so did a lot of others. We got good press—even the *Los Angeles Times* covered it—and we opened more eyes to what was going on. I reconnected with a lot of people, and Help the Child Brides got nonprofit status. And every time I spoke to the press, I told the reporters Ruby's story, always hoping for a miracle.

The next month, on September 8, 2002, Uncle Rulon died at the age of ninety-two. I heard through the grapevine that most people in the twin towns, including his wives, had expected him to live to be three hundred and fifty. Just like Uncle Roy, he didn't take the people with him. Instead of heaven, they got hell on earth: Rulon's creepy son, Warren Jeffs. Even though most people had expected Uncle Fred or one of the Barlows to take over after Rulon's death, Warren had spent years making power plays behind the scenes to ensure that wouldn't happen. He quickly declared himself the new Prophet and assumed control of the church's UEP trust—now worth an estimated $100 million. And Warren was young—just forty-nine. Given his family's longevity, he could be in power for decades.

Rulon had left behind more than seventy-five wives and sixty-five children. In order to consolidate his power and absolute control, Warren began marrying Rulon's wives in secret ceremonies—as Prophet, he was the only one who could conduct those ceremonies. Eventually, Warren married most of Uncle Rulon's wives—who were also Warren's mothers—effectively making himself his own stepfather.

I could still feel Warren's clammy hand on me as if it was yesterday. I knew my family and all the rest of the people of Colorado City and Hildale were being led by a tyrannical ruler who would be more oppressive than any other Prophet, and I suspected some of them knew it too. Everybody knew Warren.

On January 10, 2004, Warren announced that God had told him to expel many of the men from Hildale and Colorado City. He got rid of hundreds of teenage boys, as had been done by prophets before him, flooding the streets of Utah with more lost boys. Then he went a step further: he excommunicated some of his own brothers and even the mayor, Dan Barlow. Just like that, these formerly powerful men had to pack their bags and get out of town. Their wives and kids were left behind and assigned to other men. Warren let Uncle Fred stay though. Much loved by the community, he was the one man who could have threatened Warren's power. Maybe he thought that at ninety, Fred was just too old to

> **Please help me**
>
> Its just to damn late Ladell you have messed up everyone's life, you are a mass murderer you are just like a Hitler. You was not nobody's friend. You messed up Pete's entire company and Dave's also. Why didn't I die at birth at least I would have been saved. Now I can never ever be saved it is just impossible to ever become saved for me. You had no right to challenge god Ladell. Just what in the world was you thinking when you tried to challenge god. You have killed so damn many people. I should have never left the second time that I get baptized I had so damn many chances. I should just commit suicide right on the spot. I am damned for all eternity for ever and ever. Now Brety is going to commit suicide all because of your foolishness. You have caused problems for everyone Ladell and now you are totally damned you fool. You were supposed to become a god. Michael went to heaven you are going to hell Ladell. You have killed so damn many people I hope you are proud of yourself. I am fucked in the head, I am so damn stupid.

Ladell, a lost boy I rescued recently, wrote this letter to himself before leaving a rehab program I placed him in. It is evocative of the torment these children feel when they leave or are excommunicated from the cult.

cause trouble. But more likely, keeping him around gave Warren some added insurance and influence over his flock.

Warren began to take even more control over people's personal lives in a series of what he called "adjustments." He commanded those few who owned televisions and VCRs to get rid of them. Internet connections were banned, as were basketball games. Children's books—even those based on Bible stories and the Book of Mormon—were forbidden. Anything having to do with fantasy was not allowed. He canceled community celebrations, which were already few and far between. He banned red—red dresses, red shoes, red bedspreads, red trucks, red toys, red anything—first saying it was "the color of evil" and later saying it was the color Jesus would be wearing when he returned for the second coming.

He also adjusted people's private lives, increasing the strictures. He took the pulpit personally in order to explain the sex act to the congregation, telling them how it was supposed to be done: "If the female enjoys it," he said, "you are doing it wrong. Sex is for procreation only."

To reinforce this, he made ovulation tests mandatory before sex, and the clinic sold test kits for a dollar each. Households set up charts so everyone could keep track of the ovulating women and know when it was time for the sex act. Warren didn't have to worry too much about his wives' cycles. With dozens of wives, somebody was always ovulating at his house.

In July 2003, Jon Krakauer's book *Under the Banner of Heaven* was published. It soon became a best seller, and millions of Americans outside Utah and Arizona learned about, and were shocked and disgusted by, what was happening in the twin towns. Krakauer told many stories in that book, one of which was Ruby's. He quoted my friend, antipolygamy activist Lorna Craig, who compared the nationwide search for Elizabeth Smart with the nonsearch for Ruby. Both fourteen-year-old girls were kidnapped by polygamists. The difference?

"Elizabeth," Lorna told Krakauer, "was brainwashed for nine months," while Ruby had been brainwashed by polygamous fanatics "since birth."[2]

In August 2003, Rodney Holm—a Hildale cop and a powerful member of the God Squad—was convicted of felony bigamy and illegal sex with a minor, one of his three wives, whom he'd "married" when she was just sixteen and he was thirty-two. He was sentenced to a year in jail. His attorney took the case to the Utah Supreme Court. The verdict wouldn't come down for three years. When it did, it upheld his conviction.

Holms's conviction had a big effect on Warren Jeffs. This was a little too close to home for him, and he was starting to feel the breath on the back of his neck. Secretly, he started making plans to move the most faithful of his followers out of Utah and Arizona. He had one of his relatives, David S. Allred—Allred's sister was married to Warren's brother—purchase more than thirteen hundred acres of land near Eldorado, Texas.

I couldn't have been happier that Warren was starting to feel the heat. But what goes up comes down, too. In late 2003, I received a phone call from one of the women who had fled the FLDS and whom we had been supporting though Help the Child Brides. I started getting the feeling that something was wrong, and after spending several minutes talking with me, she broke down crying and told me something that made my blood boil.

"Bob Curran's been telling me that if I want help I have to have sex with him."

I wanted to throw my cell phone against the wall. That son of a bitch! I asked her if she had anything I could use as proof?

"Yes," she said, "I have some e-mails from him."

"Can you forward them to me?"

"I can, but I don't want to cause any problems," she said. "I just don't want this happening to anyone else."

I got hold of the other Save the Child Brides board members, and we discussed our options. I demanded that everything be kept quiet. There was quite a lot of opposition to that idea, but I insisted that the victim needed to be protected. We would deal with this internally.

Bob Curran had volunteered to start the St. George branch of Help the Child Brides. I'd trusted him. We all had. I drove up there burning rubber all the way, calling the office until he answered.

"Hello?"

"Get out of there, you son of a bitch. Get out right now. And you'd better pray to God I never find you!" I hung up, breathing hard.

By the time I got to St. George, he was gone. He'd disappeared, as I'd asked, but so did Help the Child Brides. We had to stop our activities, and the once-thriving organization lived on only as an informational Web site.

I was devastated. This was the organization that had been founded on trying to help Ruby. I spent some time crying on Tim's shoulder and feeling sorry for myself. I had known when I started this work that predators were going to be part of the package. I just didn't think I'd be fooled by them again.

My friend Linda Walker called from the Child Protection Project. I'd been working with her for a while, while keeping Help the Child Brides running at the same time.

"Flora?" she said. "I heard about the scumbag, Bob Curran. But I have an offer to make. Come on over here full time. I'd like you to be our executive director."

Linda was a lifesaver. I accepted her offer immediately, and shifted my activities completely to the Child Protection Project. Despite the demise of my organization, my work hadn't been affected. I had my hands full with the people I was trying to help

escape the FLDS grasp. I was also driving back and forth from court
to social services on a number of cases that had been going through
the system—some for years. And I still had my own family to think
about. Both Megan and Shauna were in school, and our home was
the hangout for their friends. The days when we had enough time
to take a family vacation to Lake Powell were long gone.

The runaways just kept coming. I was in contact with forty
or fifty people, some still living inside the twin towns and risking
their lives to help, as Trudy and Conell Bateman had once helped
me. Others who had already escaped, like Aunt Jenny, passed on
information, took in runaways, and drove them to the next stop
on their road to freedom. These frightened children were passed
hand to hand with great care. I still had rescued women and children crammed into my tiny home. I'd hear about the girl to be
rescued when my phone rang—and that was generally about two
o'clock in the morning.

The drill was always the same. I'd jump out of bed, pull on
my jeans and leather jacket—at five feet two and ninety-eight
pounds, I need to look and feel as imposing as I can. For good
measure I'd grab my bulletproof Kevlar vest. By this time I'd had
enough threats from the FLDS to make me jumpy. For insurance,
I'd pack my .38 caliber, 9 mm, and .22 caliber pistols. Tim kept
my guns cleaned, oiled, and ready to go. I'd never had to use them
except for target practice, but if I did, I knew I could count on
them to work.

I always took a video camera in case I needed to document
anything that went down. I would stuff the camera and a bottle of
water into a daypack and run out the door, hoping my four-wheel-
drive Suburban had enough gas in the tank to make the familiar
trip from Phoenix to Colorado City and back.

I had a system, of sorts, for what came next. If the girls were
still unmarried, I'd get them to the Utah Department of Child
and Family Services (the DCFS) and try to get them into a foster home. If they were fleeing a marriage, as I hoped Ruby might

one day, I sometimes had to go around the system, offering to hide them in safe houses until their cases could be resolved. I didn't feel I had a choice. For me, each girl was another Ruby, and I was pledged to save them all.

Dealing with the DCFS about Chery and Ruby had taught me a lot about how the system worked—or at least reinforced the cynical views I now had as a result of my own experiences and betrayals.

And the satisfactions were few and far between. So many of the girls ended up back in the sect, sent there by a state system that didn't know what it was doing. I got frustrated—a lot. I had let loose on more than one social services person: "Every kid that comes out of there screaming for help, you guys do nothing but turn them back over!"

As far as saving these children was concerned, it was becoming clear that I couldn't count on the government to back me up. I was sick and tired of going to court, getting injunctions, reporting to social workers—just to have kids legally sent back to abusive homes or polygamous husbands. I was going to have to work outside the system if I was going to get anything done. When I got a call about two runaway teenagers—both named Fawn—that's exactly what I did.

17

Rescuing the Fawns

I woke once again to the sound of the telephone at 7:30 in the morning, Sunday, January 10, 2004. For a second I lay under the covers, feeling my husband's body next to me, radiating warmth. *Maybe I should just let this one go to voice mail.* But then I remembered Warren Jeffs, ratcheting up control in Colorado City. I answered the phone before it could ring a second time.

"Flora? It's Rowenna Erickson." If Rowenna, a co-founder of Tapestry Against Polygamy was calling, I knew it was serious. "I've got a woman named Karen* in Hurricane, Utah, with two runaway girls from Colorado City who need your help bad." She sounded worried.

"OK, Rowenna," I said, reaching for a pen. "Give me her phone number and I'll call her right now."

Karen picked up the phone right away. "I've got the two girls right here," she said. "They're both sixteen, they're both named Fawn, and they want out of the FLDS."

I walked into my office and lit a cigarette. "Let me talk to them," I said. Those girls had probably left town on an adrenaline rush, without giving a lot of thought to what might lie ahead. But how could they have known? They had no idea what the outside world was like. By now, I knew that they'd have the best chance of making it if we *all* understood what we were getting into before we started.

"Hi . . . hi," said two young girls.

"My name is Flora," I said.

"We know who you are," said one of the girls.

*Not her real name.

"So you've run away from home, huh?"

"Yes."

"Well, that's good, but I need to make sure you girls understand what this means. You're cutting your ties with your families, at least for now. They're going to be worried and angry, and they're going to want you back. If you come with me, we're going to be on the run—and people are going to come after us."

I could hear them breathing, but that was all.

"You're going to have to talk to the authorities," I continued. "State social services and probably the police. They're going to ask you a lot of questions, and you are going to have to be real strong. You have to stand by what you feel and not back down—or they'll send you right back. Are you sure you're ready for all that?"

"Yes, we understand," said one of the Fawns. "We want out. We're not afraid. We'll do whatever you tell us."

You probably will, I thought, *after a lifetime taking orders*. But I heard something in their voices that made me believe they'd try as hard as they could. Still, I was hesitant. I'd heard that Warren Jeffs was preaching against me in church, saying that I took orders from Satan. I was worried that this might be a sting operation that he'd set up to nail me. If a child-bride-to-be screams that she's being kidnapped while she's in my car or in my house, I am in big trouble.

"OK," I said. I asked to talk to Karen again.

"Karen, I just need to know this is for real," I said.

"Flora," she said, "I can tell you these two girls mean business. Please come get them *now*. The God Squad's knocking on doors back where they came from right now, and I know they'll be here soon." She sounded scared. I believed her.

"OK, hang on, honey," I said. "We'll get them out of there."

It would take me hours to get there from Phoenix, so I hung up and dialed Aunt Jenny. Hurricane was just down the road from her place in St. George. "Jenny, can you go get those girls and move them somewhere safer?" She said she'd do it immediately and call me with the new location.

I was willing to do whatever it took to see these girls through their journey to the outside world. I'd break the law if I had to. But first, I wanted to make sure I did everything by the book. Calling the Utah DCFS was out of the question even if it hadn't been Sunday. But I had a cell phone number for Rick Cantrell, a member of the Utah attorney general's office, and caught him as he was leaving for church in Salt Lake City.

He said, "Flora, you go get those girls. Be safe and stay in touch. If anything happens, call me."

I had a contact in the Arizona attorney general's office too, but it was no use trying to call him now because I wanted assurance on a few things before permitting anyone else to meet with the girls.

Besides I did not want these girls put in a detention center, which is what the authorities usually did, and treated like criminals. I wasn't about to let that happen. In my experience, every time those young girls went to detention, they ended up being sent home to their parents—just as I had been. Not much had changed since the mid-1980s.

I swore I'd do everything I could to ensure that these two girls were given enough options to keep them safe from a betrayal by the system. If we let our guard down for one minute, the system would let them down, and they'd get sent right back home. Only now it would be worse. They'd be married and pregnant before they knew it.

I thought hard. What was I doing wrong? I had fought so hard for Ruby trying to do it *my way,* and I'd gotten exactly nowhere. I'd helped other girls get out of Colorado City, just to have the state authorities send too many of them back. *I have to turn this thing around.*

Please, please, I started saying in my mind. *I can't do this alone. Please protect these children. If they're supposed to be free, use me to free them. Please show me the way. I need your help.* Who was I talking to? Not the God who'd already damned me to hell, that was for sure. And not the God or Jesus from Carol's church, much as

I loved and respected Carol. I was talking to my own personal god, a good god who'd watch over me, like my Indian spirit, helping me and guiding me.

Suddenly I felt hopeful. Maybe this could work out after all. I couldn't trust the government to help me, and I couldn't even trust myself to always get it right. But at least in this moment, I had faith that whatever happened, *somebody* would be helping. How could I have survived all these years unless somebody was watching out for me?

But right now I needed more than a spirit guide: I needed a real, live witness to what I was about to do. And preferably one with cameras and sound equipment. So I got back on the cell phone and called a local reporter who'd been covering polygamy stories for years— Mike Watkiss, with Channel 3 News in Phoenix. When I couldn't get Mike on the phone, I turned to another reporter, Jim Osman, with Channel 15, the ABC affiliate, and he immediately called his boss to OK the trip. Then my phone rang, and it was Mike.

"Mike, I've got two runners and they're at a safe house. I'm going to pick 'em up. I'm leaving right away. You want to go?"

He said yes. Oh boy, now I had two reporters agreeing to go. Jim would ride along with me. Mike would meet us on the road, in Flagstaff.

I smiled with relief. If anything went wrong at least it would be documented.

By now it was past noon, and I was still on the phone, trying to line everything up. We'd need a safe house—someplace no one would ever think to look. I called my friend Candice Miracle, who lived right here in Phoenix. No one in the FLDS knew who she was, I was sure of that. When I explained what I needed, she agreed right away.

Then my husband, Tim, walked in. He'd driven off in my Suburban a while ago. Now, without a word to me, he walked into the bedroom and grabbed my pack. He checked my .38 caliber,

9 mm, and .22 caliber pistols and put them on the bed, alongside my Kevlar vest. Then he walked back into the kitchen, fixed me a fried egg sandwich, and handed it to me.

"Eat," he said.

I stuffed the sandwich in my mouth, grabbed my gear, and called Jim Osman.

"Get ready, Jim, I'm on my way."

Tim grabbed the phone from me. "Make her eat, Jim. When she's focused on something, she just keeps going until she gets there and she doesn't stop to eat." He grinned at me.

I dressed for action: Levis, cowboy boots, black leather jacket. I grabbed the Kevlar vest, picked up my guns, and went out to the car. My normally grimy white Suburban was shiny and clean. "It's all gassed up, too," said Tim.

"Bye, Mom!" said the girls, waving from the doorway. Just another day in the life of their outlaw mom. They understood what I had to do, and I was grateful. When they were younger, I know they resented it sometimes—the strangers I'd welcome into their house, the hours away from them trying to help other girls. But now, in their teens, they understood it—it's what I do. I know it hasn't been easy for them—they've sacrificed time with their mom, vacations, and privacy. But I also think it's taught them quite a bit about the dynamics of other people and how important it is to give something to other people when you can.

Tim gave me a kiss through the car window. "Be careful."

By the time Jim and I finally left Phoenix it was about four o'clock in the afternoon—more than eight hours since I had received Rowenna's call. Jim was excited to be on an "adventure." He began filming me as soon as we hit I-17.

"What are you thinking about right now?" he asked me.

I kept my eyes on the road. "I'm thinking that we're up against the clock," I said. "I fear for those girls."

Just off the road in Flagstaff, we pulled into a Denny's. We got coffee and a bite to eat while we waited for Mike. He showed up half an hour later. I was champing at the bit.

"All right," I said, "let's get back on the road."

We stood shivering in the parking lot, going over our route. By now it was pitch-black and bitterly cold. Mike grabbed the shoulders of my leather jacket and joked, "Flora, if they shoot me, promise right now you will call 911."

"Mike, if they shoot you, I promise I'll shoot back." He could see I was serious.

"What? You've got guns with you?"

"Oh yeah, I've got more than one. Do you want to borrow one?"

"Oh my God," said Mike. "What the hell did I get myself into?"

Jim and I jumped into the Suburban and Mike followed close behind. I love driving at night on those winding, two-lane highways, and I floored it. Jim was narrating the whole thing on tape. "The closer we got to Colorado City," he said, "the more tense the atmosphere surrounding this vehicle became."

He wasn't kidding. I had one hand on the wheel and the other around my cell phone. I learned Mike had called Steve Jackson, a TV reporter in Salt Lake City. Steve was feeling around in the area for any word of opposition and met us in Hurricane when we arrived. I didn't mind; I wanted as many lenses and eyes focused on the scene as I could muster up. Jim didn't seem to mind that I was inviting more media. He was too concerned for his own safety.

After you go through Flagstaff, Arizona, the highway splits. From there, you either go up to Page or over to Jacob Lake. I chose the Jacob Lake route—desolate country in the middle of nowhere— because there's a speed trap there. I wanted to contact local law enforcement before I hit Mohave County, where Colorado City was. Sure enough, when I flew through the Jacob Lake intersection doing 65 mph, a police officer flipped on his lights and siren.

"I'm glad to see you," I said, smiling at the cop as I handed him license and registration.

"You are, huh? Would you like to tell me what's going on?"

"I sure would. As you can see, my name is Flora Jessop, and I'm headed toward Colorado City. I just got a call from two underage girls who need rescuing, and I'm on my way to pick them up. I just wanted you guys to know what's going on, just in case."

"Yeah, I'm very aware of the situation up there," he said. "Look, here's my phone number." He handed me his card. "If you need backup, don't hesitate to call. Be safe. And good luck."

As we sailed down off the huge hill that winds down and around to Hurricane, I called Aunt Jenny to see where she'd taken the girls, and got the directions. Almost there. We were supposed to hook up with Steve Jackson at the town outskirts, and there he was. I was elated; now I had three reporters as witnesses. Mike parked his truck and climbed into the backseat of my Suburban, and Steve followed us.

Finally, more than twelve hours after the first phone call this morning, we pulled up to a little house at the end of a cul-de-sac. We knocked on the door and waited. The woman who answered took one look at the three men and their cameras and turned pale.

"Don't worry," I said, introducing them. "They're just here to make sure we all stay safe."

"Oh my God, you made it. Come in, come in. Oh, my hair's a mess! I didn't know you were bringing cameras. Girls?"

Two healthy, wholesome-looking young girls came to greet us.

"These guys are reporters," I said. "Is it OK if they film you?"

"Yeah, it's OK," said one of the girls. They didn't seem fazed by the cameras.

"Hi, I'm Fawn Holm," said one of the girls, smiling broadly.

"I'm Fawn Broadbent," said the other one, looking down at her feet.

Two Fawns—and they looked enough alike to be sisters. Both had long red hair and freckles, and both were dressed in standard plig garb—long skirts and long sleeves. But they had distinctly different personalities. Fawn Holm was outgoing and adventurous. It was clear that she meant to enjoy this experience to the fullest. Fawn Broadbent was quiet and more scared. I saw a lot of pain in her.

I took a deep breath. These girls were putting their trust in me, and it was a trust I knew I had to earn. I wanted them to feel comfortable with me, and not feel they were running off into the night with some zany woman.

"Let's get to know each other a little bit," I said. "Why did you girls run away?"

"I don't want to become some fifty-year-old man's wife or something like that," said Fawn Broadbent.

"I have thirty-two brothers and sisters," said Fawn Holm. "I don't want to be a polygamist! I want a normal life."

They both said they wanted to go back to school. Fawn Holm said she'd had to leave school in the fifth grade. It was obvious that they were smart girls. I thought of Shauna and Megan going off to school every morning, the most normal thing in the world.

As we talked the Fawns were sizing me up. They couldn't take their eyes off my leather jacket—leather is forbidden in the twin cities. One of the reporters asked the girls, "What did you think when you first saw Flora?"

Fawn Broadbent said she took one look at my leather jacket and thought, "Oh no, what am I getting myself into?"

But Fawn Holm said, "I looked at that leather jacket and I knew everything was going to be OK."

I told the two of them what I have told every girl I help, "I will not make any choices for you. I remember what it was like to have others make your decisions and I also know you will struggle with making those choices.

"What I promise you right now," I said, "is that I will help you start learning how to make choices, but each choice will have to be your own."

I also told them that I could make them no promises but that I would do everything in my power to ensure they were not sent back unless it was what they wanted. Both girls seemed to relax after that.

"Time to go, girls." I thanked the woman who had sheltered them that day for all she'd done. The Fawns said their good-byes too, and we all trooped outside and got in the vehicles. I quickly pulled onto I-15 and headed south, with Mike right behind. No one was following us but we would take a different route back to Phoenix anyway. I gave the girls my video camera. "Go ahead and tape what's happening," I said. "This is your show." I wanted them to feel they had a little control over their own lives for once.

By the time we'd been on the road an hour or so, the girls had really loosened up and were talking and laughing. Suddenly, I was dead tired. I knew I had to take a catnap and recharge before I passed out.

"Jim," I said, "can you take over for a while?"

"Of course," he said. We pulled over, and I climbed in the back. I was asleep in no time.

When I woke up, it was 2:00 A.M., and we were driving up the backside of the Strip—Las Vegas Boulevard—and the girls were riveted by the neon lights, just as I had been when I ran away at fourteen. Streams of white headlights and red taillights added to the moving light show on the four-mile-long Strip. They were awed. There was a lot of "Look at that!" and pointing, and the video camera never stopped rolling.

We stopped at a Denny's because I knew the girls were hungry. I was wide awake by now, and we were all laughing and cutting up. Then, out of nowhere, Fawn Holm looked at me earnestly and said, "We know who you are."

"Really? What do you know about me?"

"Well, we know that you go in and steal little girls out of their beds at gunpoint and make them go with you to hell."

"I do *what?*"

They both stared at me. "Yeah. Don't you do that?"

"No, honey, I don't do that." Now they were teaching these kids that I was the bogeyman. I didn't know whether to laugh or cry.

I looked right at Fawn Holm and said, deadpan, "Well, do you want to do it again?"

We all laughed, and now both girls said that I wasn't what everyone in Colorado City said I was. When we were back on the road I drove, keeping alert for anything dangerous while the three of them slept.

As we hit the outskirts of Phoenix, the sun was just coming up. It had been a hell of a long day, and now another had started.

I called Candice and told her we were on the way to her house, but I didn't want anyone to know exactly where we were going, so I took Jim to his TV station first. He did a quick interview with the two girls, and then we said good-bye. Over the next weeks and months, they'd do more news interviews than they could imagine.

Then I called Richard Travis, my contact in the Arizona attorney general's office. I told him that I had two FLDS runaways. "I'm taking these girls to a safe house," I told him. "We want to bring them to Arizona, but first I need some assurances from the state attorney general's office."

"Flora, you need to let us know where you're taking them and—"

"No, Richard, I'm going to tell *you* how it's going to be. I have three conditions. First, the girls have to stay at the safe house. They're not going into state custody, and they're not going to be locked in detention and treated like criminals."

Silence.

"Two, they have to stay together."

Silence.

"And three, you can't use criminal investigators to interview these girls. They're not criminals, they're kids."

I could just about hear him gnashing his teeth on the other end. I knew he didn't want to agree, but he had no choice. I was holding all the cards—the two girls.

It would take nearly a week of negotiating with Travis and enduring threats of FBI involvement and criminal charges being filed against me before the authorities finally understood that this time we would not let the system fail.

The Fawns had never seen anything like Candice Miracle. Divorced, with two boys, she's tiny and blonde—with hair extensions hanging nearly to her knees. She's pretty and bubbly and smart—and to top it off she plays stand-up bass in a bluegrass band. She made them feel at home, though they probably felt as though that home was on Mars.

I was drained and needed more sleep badly, but we had other things to do. The Fawns had only the clothes on their backs—we had to get them something to wear right away so they could start blending in. I made them both take a shower, and then we went to a big secondhand store and set them loose. But they just stood there like deer in the headlights, staring at the racks and racks of clothes in all styles and colors.

"What do you want us to get?" they asked.

"Remember I said I'd let you make your own decisions? Well, here's your first chance. You need to go pick out your clothes yourselves—I'm not the one who has to wear them."

Their voices got high and thin. "But we don't know what we're allowed to get!" They were freaking out. It reminded me of the time I asked Chery to pick up the living room. These girls weren't as damaged as she was, but they had the same learning to unlearn.

"I'll tell you what," I said, "you fill up this basket right here with whatever you want. Then we'll go through them together, and figure out what you can buy."

They just stood there looking at each other. It took forever to make them understand that they really could pick out anything they wanted. Finally, they took off. I just kicked back on a couch, almost slaphappy tired by this time, and watched those innocent girls laugh and laugh as they picked out silly things, holding them up to each other. They grabbed bright colored T-shirts, shorts, and pants—anything but dresses. They tried on loads of clothes, while I got on the phone with Richard Travis again, trying to negotiate a time and place for their state interview.

When we left the store, they looked like different girls. Dressed in jeans and T-shirts—one of them had picked out a Pittsburgh Pirates T-shirt, of all things—they had big smiles on their faces. Later we would take them shopping in the first mall they had ever seen. And—sin of all sins—they got their ears pierced. "Now you *really* can't go back," I said.

Fawn Holm wrote this letter to me in 2004 after running away from her parents and the FLDS.

The scare was like there was this great big hole with all these wild animals that would like to eat me and it was dark and dry, and someone was going to throw me in it. I have jumped into this hole and made friends with all the animals and learned to make light and let it rain. I have done it.

I have made out of this cult. I am free I have climbed out of the hole, and everyday the hand is realesing it's tight grip and the hand is softing. The hand is taking good care of my heart. Releasing a little at a time.

I have done this but not alone those animals turned out to be angels, at the right time too. These angels have cared for me like I am a fragile egg sitting on a high post. I have been chipped by none other than myself. Yes, I know have to help and do my part and help this egg hatch. I am almost out.

We were on our way back to Candice's when Rowenna called. "Flora," she said, "I've got the phone number for some guy named Carl Holm—he says he's Fawn Holm's brother, and he wants to know what he can do to help." My heart started beating a mile a minute. *Oh my god, who the hell is this Carl Holm?*

I turned to Fawn Holm. "Do you have a brother named Carl?"

"Yeah," she nodded, "I do. He lives in Salt Lake. My dad kicked him out a long time ago—he was gone before I was even born."

"Well, do you think he's sincere in wanting to help you?"

"I guess," she shrugged. "As far as I know . . . my dad hates him."

That was a pretty good recommendation. I figured we could use another ally. "Rowenna? Give me his number and I'll check him out myself."

Carl and his wife, Joni, both got on the phone. "How did you find out Fawn had run away?" I asked them.

"I saw her on the TV news," said Joni. Steve Jackson, the Salt Lake City reporter, hadn't wasted any time getting the story on the news. "I said, 'Carl, Carl! Your sister is on TV! She's run away!'"

Then Carl said, "Look, I want my sister to come live with us. What do we have to do?"

They both sounded sincere, but I'd earned the right to be suspicious. I said, "You do realize I have two girls, not one—and I'm not willing to separate them?"

By the end of the conversation, Carl and Joni had committed to taking them in, but we still had to go through legal channels to fully protect them. I figured we all needed some time to think.

In the meantime, I wanted the girls to call home. No matter what I thought of their upbringing, I knew their mothers would be worried sick about them. I drove them to my house to make the calls because my phone was set up to tape calls. I wanted a record of everything.

But Fawn Holm refused. "I am not calling my mother," she said, hugging herself with her arms.

Fawn Broadbent did call her mother. "Mom," she said, "I'm OK. I just want you to know that I'm fine. Please don't try to find me. I don't want to live there anymore. Please tell Fawn Holm's parents she's OK too." She hung up, on the edge of tears.

I drove them back to Candice's house and said good night. With my last ounce of energy, I drove back home. I crashed into bed next to Tim, right back where I'd started. Sleep would become very scarce over the next several months, but those girls were safe for now.

18

Running Away Again

It was the next morning that I learned Warren Jeffs had excommunicated twenty men, including Dan Barlow, the mayor of Colorado City. The newspapers were reporting that more and more young people were leaving town as a result.

And there was more good news: Carl and Joni called. "We talked about it," they said, "and we're willing to accept responsibility and custody for both girls—and we'll make sure they get into school. We'll be in Phoenix tomorrow." We agreed to meet in the parking lot of a large mall.

But things started to slide from there. When I let the Arizona attorney general's office know that the Holms wanted custody, a worker in that office called Carl and Joni, demanding to know where the girls were. "Flora is going to be arrested for this," the worker said. I'm sure Carl and Joni felt threatened and were beginning to worry about what they'd gotten into.

I didn't believe it for a minute, though, and I resented the attorney general's office trying to scare the Holms, who were just trying to help. Furious, I called Richard Travis. "What you're telling these poor people is bullshit. But I don't care. If you want me, come get me!"

"It's the FBI that wants to talk to you, Flora."

"Fine. You tell the FBI to come talk to me. If there really are federal investigators involved in this, just tell them to come get ahold of me."

The Fawns listened intently to all of this wrangling. Occasionally, they'd comment. They were terrified about being taken into state custody.

I looked them in the eyes. "I promise you—absolutely—I will not allow that to happen. You will not go into state custody; you will not be locked up."

After Steve ran his story in Salt Lake and Mike ran his in Phoenix, we were the center of a media circus. Not only was I still in negotiations with the attorney general's office but I was also fielding calls from the media nonstop. Everyone wanted to talk with the girls.

The next day we went to meet Carl and Joni. The girls ducked down in the backseat of Candice's boyfriend's truck, out of sight. Tim and I drove separately. We had agreed on a hand signal. I would talk to the Holms first. If Candice and her boyfriend saw me give the signal, they were to haul ass with those kids to another state.

I walked up to the Holms and introduced myself. Joni was Hispanic, and Carl was a big guy about forty, with a bit of red hair like his sister's. He was wearing sunglasses. "Take off your glasses so I can see your eyes," I said. Then I asked him straight up: "Is this a setup?"

"Absolutely not," he said. "I just want to protect my sister and her friend." We talked for a while, and I got a good feeling from them. Finally, after about a half hour, I called the girls over.

Fawn Broadbent was curious about everything; Fawn Holm looked shyly at the ground. Her brother was a stranger to her, but he gave her a hug. Joni tried to put her at ease by telling her that her own four daughters—the youngest, Megan, was eighteen, and the oldest was twenty-two—were all looking forward to meeting them. "I guess this is pretty scary stuff, huh?" she said. And with that, I just knew the Holms would do all they could to make sure these girls survived and thrived.

Now all I had to worry about was the government.

Upon discovering they could not coerce Carl and Joni into betraying the girls' location the Arizona attorney general's office relented and agreed to my terms. We agreed that a forensic interview would be done at Childhelp, a national nonprofit, nongovernmental organization with expertise in conducting child forensic interviews. Unlike criminal investigation interviews, these interviews are child centered—they are structured to find the truth rather than to assemble evidence for a court case. Childhelp is good organization, but I was still wary—I knew that in Phoenix Childhelp shared a facility with the stage agency Child Protective Services and with the police. And I didn't trust either of those organizations to keep their word.

Feeling uneasy, I made contact with someone I knew at Childhelp and was informed that criminal investigator Meg Pollard was there waiting for us. I was furious. When I had taken Chery Taylor to the attorney general's office, believing the staff's promises of help, they had interrogated Chery for hours about family connections. She was shown big books full of FLDS members' pictures and asked about who was married to whom and how many kids they had.

I learned a valuable lesson that day. The kids running away from the FLDS want to be free to make their own choices, but they do not want to see their parents in prison. Putting that burden on them along with everything else they had to deal with was crap, and I would have none of it. I had sworn that I would never allow another child to be used like that again, and I had also learned the difference between criminal investigators and civil or child protection investigators.

I called Richard Travis, told him I had found out about the criminal investigator waiting for us, and said I was done with the BS and to forget about everything we had agreed. I would just keep the girls underground, I said, and I hung up on him. In the weeks to come, the attorney general's office would continue to lie to us all and even told Carl and Joni that the office would represent them in trying to get custody of the two girls. None of us realized then that the attorney general's office also represented Child Protective Services (CPS)—which would present a real conflict of interest if CPS wanted to fight the Holms for custody.

A few minutes after I hung up on Travis, Meg Pollard called me, really pissed. "All right, bitch, I'm leaving," she said. "You can bring the girls in now."

"Thank you," I said. We loaded up and headed to Childhelp. Candice and the two girls rode in my Suburban, all of us rocking out to Pat Benatar and the Go-Go's. Carl and Joni followed in their own car.

The Childhelp office was a huge, rectangular room with a little waiting area on the left-hand side, in the front corner. The rest of the room was a big fantasy play area for kids—the floors were painted with yellow brick roads winding into the distance, and the painted pathways were lined with artificial trees. The whole thing was enclosed by a bulletproof wire-mesh and glass window wall, because the facility was designed for forensic interviews with severely abused children. Someone took the girls into the playroom and gave each of them a big stuffed animal. I wondered if they'd ever been given a gift before in their lives.

Then we were taken to an upstairs office where we waited for about twenty minutes before being met by Merritt Bingham from the attorney general's office and the two ladies who would be doing the interviews. Once again, I repeated my demand: "Now these girls will not be taken into state custody, will they?"

"No," Merritt assured me, "they are not going to be taken into state custody. They are going to leave with you tonight, but we must have someone from CPS check out the home they are in." That was what I wanted to hear.

Soon after Merritt left, the director of Childhelp arrived and spoke with us, telling the girls what to expect. He talked with us for quite a while and asked a lot of questions about the girls' health and well-being and our intentions for their future. We ordered a bunch of hamburgers and the girls seemed relaxed.

Then they took each girl separately for the forensic interview. Two people interviewed each girl, and each interview lasted about an hour and a half. Candice, Carl, Joni, and I waited, reading magazines, and feeling on pins and needles. We had been given assurances, but I was still waiting for the other shoe to fall and the betrayal to happen. It was going to be a very long night.

After a couple of hours, I got restless and went downstairs to walk around. Both girls were inside the glass-walled room. A woman was in there with them, and I could barely see their heads way in the back. They were watching something on TV. No interviews were going on. I finally got their attention and motioned them to come to me. They started walking up to the glass, but the woman walked right across and blocked them. The girls both turned around, looking back at me with expressions that said very clearly, "We don't know what is going on."

"Come here," I said again, motioning. But the woman stopped them again. By now Carl, Joni, and Candice were all downstairs too, and now I knew the betrayal was indeed going to happen.

I'd promised everyone that the girls would not be taken into custody, but it looked to me as if that was about to happen. "I have a really bad feeling," I said to the Holms and Candice.

Just then, a CPS worker came in. "I'm Germaine Abraham-Leveen." she said. She was African American and very short. She took Carl and Joni into a small conference room off the main room, and told them that Candice's home had not been approved, and CPS had decided to take the girls into state custody and place them in detention for the night.

"No," Carl insisted. "That's not what we were told, and that is not going to happen."

If I'd heard this conversation, I would have gone straight through the roof. As it was, I was going crazy with worry. It was almost nine o'clock at night, and the offices were officially closed. The building was secured by an alarm system. I looked at the glass wall and thought, *Son of a bitch. This wall is bulletproof, and it's got mesh wiring in between two plates of glass. The only way I am going to be able to get these kids out of here is to drive my friggin' truck through this building!*

Then Germaine opened the door to the glass room and spoke to the woman who was watching the girls. "I need to see Fawn Holm," she said. She cared only about Fawn Holm because Fawn Holm was the one related to Carl and Joni.

I looked at Fawn Broadbent. "Come over here," I said. She scooted right past Germaine and Fawn Holm and out of that room just as fast as she could, and sat down on the couch between Candice and me. A female cop walked in—a big, burly, white woman with the Phoenix city police department. She stood in front of the doorway that led to the outside, blocking it. OK, I thought, *this is not my imagination*. I was starting to feel very claustrophobic.

Meanwhile, Fawn Holm was in the little conference room with Carl and Joni. Germaine had left the door ajar, so I walked over and looked in. Fawn's eyes were huge. She was rising up out of her chair, saying, "No, that's not what we were told. No! I'm leaving here with my brother."

"No, you are not," Germaine said. "You are coming into state custody with me." Fawn looked at me, and I just shook my head no.

Then Germaine's cell phone rang, and she stepped outside the room to take the call. Joni ran over to me. "This is going south," she said, panicked. "They think they're taking these kids into custody."

"OK," I said. "Stay calm, but be ready. And tell Carl to be ready too."

I walked slowly over to Candice and tossed her my keys. "I want you to take Fawn Broadbent, the stuffed animals, and all of our stuff out to the Suburban," I said in a low voice. "Pull it up to the front doors with the nose pointing out of the parking lot."

I turned to Fawn Broadbent. "Fawn, I want you to climb into the backseat and get down on the floor." She nodded. I knew she was up for anything.

I turned back to Candice. "Leave the car running, and leave the driver's door open. Then you come back inside."

"Fawn," I said, "do *not* get out of that vehicle. Do you understand?"

"Yes."

Relaxed and easy, Candice and Fawn gathered everything up and walked toward the door. The cop moved to block them. "Oh, excuse me," Candice giggled, her arms full of stuffed animals. "We're just going to go put all this stuff in the car. It's so late, and we just want to get home to bed."

Candice had the cop so baffled with her bubbly blondness that she let Fawn scoot past her, right out the door. Candice followed Fawn out, smiling. Confused, the cop left her post to go talk to Germaine, probably to find out what she was supposed to do now that one of the girls was outside the facility.

I ran into the small conference room, grabbed Fawn Holm's hand, and we headed out the door and out of the building.

I jumped into the driver's seat. "Get in!" I said, but she didn't need any encouragement to get into the backseat next to her friend. "OK. Shut the door and put your seat belts on. We're out of here."

Then Candice opened the passenger's door to get in, I shook my head. "No, no way, darling. You're back inside."

"But I don't want to be arrested!"

"The only way you'll be arrested is if you climb in this truck. Because right now I'm committing felony flight. Get it? Go back inside. They can't touch you in there."

Candice got back inside just as Germaine and the cop returned.

"Where are Flora and the girls?" asked Germaine, looking around.

"They went for ice cream," said Candice. "They'll be back in a little while."

Meanwhile I was flooring it. It turned out that Candice had bought us just enough time to make a clean getaway. CPS staff didn't follow us, and the attorney general's office backed off. We would discover later that Germaine had been told the girls were to be released back to Candice but that she was to accompany them and do an initial inspection on the home. Germaine, not wanting to make the drive, decided to lock the girls up until she did her inspection. By taking the girls I had solved her problem, so she just closed her book, told Candice she would come by the house tomorrow, and left.

Maybe somebody really was looking out for me and the girls this time. Carl and Joni had to go back to Salt Lake City for a few days, and the girls went back to Candice's. On January 16, 2004, we went to juvenile court and got an emergency court order making both girls wards of the state, ordering CPS to conduct interviews with Fawn Holm's siblings in Colorado City, prohibiting contact with parents, and giving Candice temporary guardianship of both girls.

Two days later, I arrived at Candice's about 7.00 A.M. to take the girls to an appointment. I let myself in, automatically locking the door behind me. The girls were just getting up. Candice was still in her nightgown.

All of a sudden, *bang, bang, bang* on the door.

"They're here! They're going to take us!" cried the frightened teenagers. They made a dash for Candice's room and crawled into the back of the walk-in closet, behind the clothes and everything else. I could hear them crying in there.

I peeped out the window just about the time the doorknob started rattling. "Candice—911, right now," I whispered. "Call the cops." She dialed immediately. I flashed back to the time my brothers and sisters and I all hid from the Jehovah's Witnesses. Only this time the threat was real.

I took another peek through the curtain and saw two men and two women in plig garb whom I recognized, and they were doing their best to break into Candice's house. No doubt about it: the Fawns' parents had come to take their daughters home. *What bullshit! CPS finds out the address, and immediately these parents have it.* I was so damned pissed off.

I went into Candice's son's room and watched the parents through the window. They were walking around, writing down the license plate number of every vehicle outside the house. They checked all the windows and doors, looking for a way to get in. I thought, *Go for it. I have two babies in the closet, crying. You get in here and I'm going to shoot you.*

As I watched, I called the attorney general's office. "I have a court order giving us custody of these two children. Do you know that the Holms and Broadbents are out here *right now*, banging on Candice's door? How the hell do you guys expect me to trust you when you give out the damn address to the parents?"

Candice's 911 call brought four male city police officers within minutes. The Fawns' parents tried to force their way in behind them. "No way!" I screamed.

"We just want to see our girls and make sure they're OK. Can we just see them for a few minutes?"

"Hell no," I told the cops. "We have custody of these girls. You can't let them in here."

I would learn that day just how brazen the FLDS had become in legal matters. Those parents actually tried to enlist the aid of the four police officers in enforcing a bogus court order they had with them, one they had made themselves. Candice showed the cops the *real* court papers from Maricopa County, and the cops told the parents they'd have to arrest them if they didn't leave. In the end the only thing their visit accomplished was to upset the girls and make them even more determined to stay.

Candice was in constant contact with Germaine at CPS. I knew the lying that goes on and how words get twisted so I convinced Candice that she needed to record every conversation she had with Germaine or anybody else in regard to the girls. Thank goodness Candice listened, because the lies were only beginning.

Germaine had met with the Holms and Broadbents, and soon after issued a set of edicts that sounded as if they were straight out of Colorado City. The girls were not allowed to cut their hair. They were not allowed to meet anybody outside the FLDS community. They were not even allowed to go to the park. Candice's son was not allowed to have any friends over. Candice herself was not allowed to have anyone over unless he or she had been okayed by CPS.

"Where on earth did these rules come from?" I asked Germaine. Germaine couldn't give me a good answer, and I didn't really expect her to. I was disgusted. "The parents just want you to keep these kids as isolated as possible, so when they take them back to Colorado City, it'll be easier to force them back into the big brainwashed state of mind and CPS is helping them do it."

Not only was CPS in Maricopa County not going to protect these girls but CPS in Mohave County was also staying true to form. After closely watching to see if the Fawns were protected, another girl ran. Her first mistake was going to CPS and her last was believing they would help her escape the abuse. Even though she gave a statement detailing the severe physical abuse perpetrated upon herself and her brothers, often resulting in bruises and welts, she was put into juvenile detention for two weeks and then returned to her father.

This had a profound effect on Fawn Holm and Fawn Broadbent. They became even more afraid of CPS and especially the directives CPS was giving to Candice.

Fawn Holm's parents were strict FLDS members. While the girls were in state custody, they married off Fawn's fifteen-year-old sister in her place. And they certainly didn't want Carl getting anywhere near his sister—Carl's father had washed his hands of Carl long ago. "Your Honor," Carl's father told the judge, "I would rather see my daughter locked up in juvenile detention and punished every day from now until she's eighteen rather than live with that apostate Carl Holm."

Fawn Broadbent's parents were more open-minded, although they blamed me. I had several conversations with Fawn's mother,

Kathryn, trying to help her understand my role in her daughter's life. "If it was my daughter," I said, "I would damn well be appreciating someone who took her in and gave her a safe place to stay. You know your kid could have been out on the streets by now, being preyed upon by drug dealers and who knows who else."

A couple of weeks later, we were still waiting for Carl and Joni to get legal custody of the girls. Carl finally had to go back to Salt Lake to work, but Joni stayed behind to help. As we were all sitting down to pizza one day, Joni suddenly looked over at me and said, "Flora, I can't feel my arm."

I rushed her to the hospital. Incredibly, this young woman was having a stroke. Although she recovered quickly, it was frightening. Her speech, walk, and hand movement were affected for quite some time.

Carl left work immediately and returned to care for Joni. He was frustrated with everything going on with the Fawns and terrified about Joni nearly losing her life. But through everything, Carl and Joni stood by both girls. I couldn't believe I'd ever doubted their sincerity.

During Joni's long recovery, she and I met with Richard Travis and Merritt Bingham at the Arizona attorney general's office. They had been trying to nudge me out of the case, but I absolutely refused to abandon my promise to protect the girls. "If you can absolutely, positively, without a doubt guarantee that Fawn Holm and Fawn Broadbent will not be sent back to their parents, I will back out of this case, walk away, and never look back." It was a direct challenge, and they were floored. They wanted me out of it desperately—I was making it hell for them. But they couldn't do it.

"We can't promise you that, Flora," they said.

"Then I'm done with you," I said. I walked out of that meeting more determined than ever to protect those girls and help them live whatever lives they chose to live.

Concerned with the tactics being used by the attorney general's office and CPS, I was glad to hear of someone who might help us ensure that the girls remained safe. I loaded Candice, Joni, Megan, and the two Fawns into the car, and we went to find out. We walked into a small, central Phoenix office at 4:55 P.M. on February 6.

"Can I help you?" asked the woman at the door.

"I was told you help children when the system fails to protect them," I said, "and I need attorneys for everyone here immediately."

Very calmly this lady looked back at me. "You can all fill out an intake form if you like, but I should tell you my first concern is for those two right there," she said as she pointed to Fawn and Fawn.

I grinned. I liked the way this lady thought.

"OK," I said, "let's get this done."

When we walked out of the Defenders of Children office two hours later, everyone had an attorney except me. I was offered one and it was suggested that I might be in the greatest need of one, after the girls of course, but I refuse to take resources for myself when there are so many children in need. I can take care of myself, so I was willing to wait on my needs and to use everything within reach for the kids.

That was the beginning of a relationship that would help secure the freedom of many women fleeing polygamy. With Defenders of Children I had finally found an organization that believed more in protecting children than in the political agenda.

By this time, the girls were famous, featured in newspapers and TV news stories across the country. Most of these reports tied the girls' story to another story that was gathering steam: Warren Jeffs's rise to power in Colorado City. On January 27, 2004, Nick Madigan wrote a story in the *New York Times* that said in part:

> A power struggle between members of a fundamental-
> ist Mormon sect has exposed deep fissures in the largest
> polygamous community in North America, a town in
> which most men have several wives and sometimes doz-
> ens of children. . . .

The rebellion was put in motion this month when
Mr. Jeffs expelled more than 20 men from the church,
separating them from their wives and children and forcing them from their houses, over which the church claims
ownership through a land trust controlled by Mr. Jeffs. . . .

"I knew at 13 that I didn't want to live like that," said
Fawn Louise Broadbent, 16, one of the teenagers who
fled recently. . . . "I want to go to a real school, not a
church school. And I want to be a clothing designer,
not somebody's 15th wife."[1]

A producer from ABC's *Primetime* came down to Phoenix. He
wanted to do a story with the Fawns, but CPS and the attorney
general's office said the girls were not allowed to talk to anybody,
including the media. They threatened the network with a lawsuit
if they aired any footage of those two girls. But the *Primetime* people didn't believe in being gagged any more than I did. "Bring it
on," they said.

Years ago—so long ago that it seemed like another life—I'd
hung up on Patti Hassler when she called to ask me to appear on
60 Minutes. Now, I understood that when the media turned a spot-
light on polygamy, the FLDS had nowhere to hide. I embrace media
coverage as a way to get the message out that we need help, aware-
ness, and understanding to free the child brides and the abused
wives and children of polygamy. So when *Primetime* asked me to be
part of a feature on the Fawns' rescue and said the program would
tie into what was going on in Colorado City, I said, "Absolutely."

Primetime's John Quiñones and I drove into Colorado City.
I disguised my appearance with a blond wig, sunglasses, and a
baseball cap—the last time I'd been there, FLDS goons had beaten
me up. I showed John the house I had grown up in, still unfinished, and told him about my twenty-seven brothers and sisters.
I told him about "bleeding the beast" and all the welfare scams.
The camera crew rode in a car in front of us, filming everything.

We finally reached Uncle Fred's house, where my mom was living. We hadn't been there long when we were challenged by Willie Jessop, a well known God-Squad member and bodyguard for the Prophet. Soon we had five or six Colorado City and Hildale police vehicles converging on us.

Helaman Barlow, Colorado City Town Marshal, pulled directly up to the camera crew, "You are trespassing on private property," he said.

While Helaman was demanding we leave, Willie Jessop walked up.

"Can I shake your hand?" John asked.

"No," said Willie, "you can leave." He grabbed for the camera, snapping off the microphone.

I noticed a vehicle start to move forward and that was when I realized that Sam Roundy, the Colorado City Chief of Police, had been sitting in his vehicle watching the entire confrontation. Sam motioned to Willie to get into his truck, where then he sat in stony silence.

John got out and talked to Roundy, asking him why they were so hostile and asking him about the church policy of holding girls against their will and forcing them into marriages.

Roundy said, "We are just living our religion."

"Is Warren Jeffs your boss?" John asked.

"My boss?" Roundy exclaimed. "I have a religion and I have a job. You have a religion and you have a job, and we just want to be left alone to live our religion."

When John got back to the car, he said, "They want to arrest you, Flora."

"They don't want to arrest me," I replied. "They want me dead."

"Why?"

"Because I take their biggest asset—their daughters."

The funny part was, Roundy hadn't even recognized me.

Joni went home to Salt Lake briefly to tend to her family. To help us with the Fawns, she sent her eighteen-year-old daughter, Megan, in her place. At eighteen, Megan was adventurous and outspoken.

She was also an insulin-dependent diabetic, but she didn't let that stop her from enjoying life. The three girls got along great.

We were all worried about the upcoming custody case, and we needed a break. When a friend offered his weekend place in Tonopah, Arizona, about thirty-five miles west of Phoenix—complete with horses and quad ATVs—four-wheeled all-terrain vehicles—to ride. It sounded like the perfect prescription for our ailing souls.

On February 15, Megan, the Fawns, and I drove up and settled into the ranch house. We were making plans for the day when Linda Walker called from the Child Protection Project to say that the organization was having an emergency meeting in Phoenix about an ongoing case. Linda picked me up, and she and I went back to Phoenix for our meeting. I left the girls back at the ranch, wrongly figuring that at eighteen and sixteen, they could take care of themselves for a few hours.

As Linda and I were driving back to Tonopah, I got a frantic phone call. "Flora? It's Joni."

"What's wrong?" She was on the verge of hysteria.

"Megan's in the hospital in Phoenix."

"I'm on my way."

The girls had taken the quads for a ride, and Megan had rolled hers. A neighboring woman had driven her to the hospital and stayed with her. The woman had told Joni that Megan had broken her collarbone, a leg, her neck, her back, a rib, and an arm and had gone into shock and a diabetic coma.

I thought, *Oh my God, she is going to die. This is my fault. I should never have left them out there by themselves.*

When we got to the hospital, the Fawns were sitting there scared nearly to death. Fortunately, the neighbor had exaggerated—a lot. Megan was pretty banged up, especially her leg, but she had no broken bones. She had gone into insulin shock, but quick treatment had put her back to normal. She wouldn't even have to stay in the hospital overnight. We breathed an enormous sigh of relief and called Joni to put her mind at ease.

We were all exhausted. But the day was far from over. As we waited for Megan to be patched up and released, Candice called. Her voice was tense. "I need the kids back here," she said. "I need them back right away."

Something in Candice's voice put me on the alert. Instead of asking what the problem was, I said. "Sorry. These girls are on a vacation, and their friend is pretty banged up. And we're way out of town," I lied. "I just can't come back this minute. I'll be back Sunday night."

I didn't know what was going on, and I didn't want her to have to lie to me about it. I wasn't about to bring those girls back just to have them end up in custody, and I didn't want Candice to have to lie to the authorities about anything. Because Megan's pain medication was wearing off and she needed to rest, we decided to get a motel room close to the hospital. As soon as we got there, the girls wanted to use the swimming pool.

Linda and I sat down on the bed. But we didn't even have a chance to catch our breath before the phone rang again. It was Joni. "The court issued an order allowing the parents to get the girls," she said. "The girls are not allowed to have any contact with me or Carl and especially not with you, Flora. What are we going to do?"

My phone started beeping, and it was Tim.

"Hey, babe," I said. "What's up?"

"I was just served court papers prohibiting you from having contact with Fawn Holm," Tim said. "They were signed on the twelfth."

"What about Broadbent?" I asked.

"Nothing about her, this is only for Fawn Holm and the only thing her dad was asking the court for," Tim replied. "The court denied everything else but dad's demand that you not be allowed around his daughter."

"OK, I'll call you in a bit," I said.

The court must have ordered Candice to turn the girls over to state authorities immediately. I was glad she didn't know where they were. She wouldn't have to lie about anything.

I got back to Joni. "Hang in there, Joni. We'll figure this out. Just hold on."

Just then the girls returned, dripping wet. I hung up and started telling Linda what was going on. Linda looked at the girls and said, "Let's go outside and finish talking about this."

"No," I said. "Absolutely not. I promised these girls I would never make a decision without letting them participate in the process. This is their lives. It's something they have a right to decide." I looked at them, and they sat down to listen.

"This is exactly what is going on," I said. "The court issued an order that allows your parents to come take you back home. So you basically have two choices. You can go back to Candice's and wait for your parents to show up, or you can both take off right now and run away. I will drive you to another safe house until we can work this out. You won't be on the streets. But if you choose to run, and you're caught, you'll be treated as runaways."

"We don't want to go back!" The Fawns were terrified. "We'll run away again before we do that."

Megan, half-crippled and in pain, proved to be a rock. She stood by her new friends. "You guys aren't going anywhere without me coming along to take care of you," she said. "You can't survive out there by yourselves."

The Fawns looked at each other and then at Megan. "Well, get ready, because we aren't going back," said one of them. "We're running."

"OK," I said, "that's your decision. I'll do what I can. Get dressed and get ready."

I knew I had to stay put in Phoenix—I couldn't risk being charged with transporting these girls across state lines. So I called someone in the network we had built up for helping the runaways, explained the situation, and asked him if he was willing to make the drive.

"No problem, Flora." I told him how to find us and hung up.

Then I turned back to the Fawns. "You have to leave some type of letter stating that you're running away. You can figure out the words." They attacked the project with enthusiasm, writing letters that slammed the state of Arizona for not doing its job. Fawn Broadbent wrote, "I do not want to go back because I will be locked up and even married." Fawn Holm wrote, "All [the state of Arizona] seemed to want to do is to send us back to like prison (back to Colorado City). Well I won't go back so I guess I'm going to be running until I'm 18." Both of them said it was their own idea to run away, and they both signed their letters.

The volunteer showed up with a motor home. I gave him my credit card for expenses, and told him to take the girls to Colorado to a place where I knew they would be safe. They took off, while Linda and I drove back to Phoenix. On the way, we called Joni in Salt Lake City.

"Joni, the girls are fine. They're with friends, and Megan is with them. We're flying you down here to Phoenix immediately. You and I must be ready for what's coming, and we are in this together."

After I got home and the girls were well on their way out of Arizona, I called Richard Travis and lit into him. "All right, you son of a bitch. You issued orders for these kids to be turned over to their damn parents, and now they've run away. What the hell are you going to do now?"

On February 17, Joni and I held a press conference in front of the CPS offices. We both spoke our minds. I was so proud of Joni. In part, her statement said:

> I do not appreciate the way this was handled and want to let the public know some of the problems we are encountering as we try to keep Carl's sister and her friend safe. These girls want their story told so that others will not suffer as they are. They would like also to assert their right to freedom of speech, something they have never had. They also want the right to freely associate, determine their destiny, and return to school. CPS is hindering these simple goals.

I am disappointed and upset by these events and hope that in the end justice is served. To this end we are no longer relying on the State of Arizona to do the right thing by us and these girls. We have contacted Defenders of Children, a nonprofit group that assists people dealing with a state system in widespread failure. The State of Arizona does not help girls escape polygamy and abuse. They are returned to their abusers.

Now here is the good news. Last night we had brief contact with my daughter and we heard the girls were safe. She refused to tell me where they are, but all are safe.

By the next day, the story of the Fawns' second run for freedom was in all the papers. In a TV news interview, Carl Holm said, "I think they need to be in some schools and I think they need to be around family. . . . They need to be around people who understand what they've been through and what they're gonna be going through."

I was served with another court order on February 23, demanding that both girls be returned immediately to CPS and threatening criminal action for noncompliance. The next thing I knew, I had investigators from CPS and the police knocking at my door. At first, they were polite. "Come on, Flora. We know you know where those kids are. Just tell us where they are, and we'll get out of your hair."

"I don't know where those kids are," I shrugged. Technically, I didn't—because they were still on the road. "You guys are the ones who lost them. You go find them. We have two teenage girls and a diabetic teenager with a messed-up leg from an accident, and they're out here on the streets somewhere. What are you gonna do about it?"

They were livid! One big ol' pot-bellied cop gave me a big smile, trying to charm me. "Flora," he said, "just tell us where those girls are at. Let us make a phone call to them. Let us make contact with them. It's not that big of a deal. We'll make all of the arrangements and nothing will happen."

"Dude, I don't know where the hell these kids are, and if I did I would not tell you so you can betray them like the dozens of other children betrayed from Colorado City."

Finally, they got tired of playing nice and started threatening me. "You tell us where these kids are at, or we're going to hand-cuff you and take you to jail."

"Fine, handcuff me. Don't threaten me, cuff me." I held out my wrists.

"You mean you're actually willing to go to jail for these kids?" The cop was still trying to convince me to come clean. "It's not worth it, Flora."

"You don't get it yet, do you?" I stared straight into his eyes. "I'm actually willing to lay my life down to protect these kids. How far would *you* go to protect kids?"

Now they were getting nasty with me, and I finally lost it. "You people seem to be under the impression that CPS stands for Child Protective Services," I said. "But you know what I think? I think it actually stands for Can't Protect Shit!

"Get out of my house," I ordered.

They stormed out of my house. Two weeks later, a woman from CPS yanked my daughters Shauna and Megan out of school and questioned them. Did they feel safe living with me? Did I have a bunch of people coming in and out? How did they feel about "weird people" coming and living in my home? Were there drugs or alcohol at home? Were there weapons in the home? Did I abuse them?

My kids thought the questions were crazy. They just shook their heads and said, "Are you serious?"

"If you ever feel threatened you can call me," the woman said, handing them each a business card. She also left a card on my door.

When the girls came home from school, they couldn't wait to tell me. "Guess what happened today?"

I was furious. I picked up the phone, pounded out the woman's number, and started on her as soon as she answered. "OK, now that you're done harassing my kids, how about you come and have a chat with me?"

She showed up at my house the next day, but she wasn't what I expected. She was a nice woman and a bit confused. "I don't even know what I'm doing here," she confessed. "I deal with group homes, and this is not a group home." She was one of only two investigators in Arizona who investigated group homes, and they'd sent her to my house to investigate the Fawns' case.

"Where did the phone call come from to even open this case?" I asked.

"That's classified," she said. "We aren't allowed to—"

"Listen," I said. "I can tell you where the damn phone call came from. You check your records—I'll guarantee it came from inside your office."

"Why do you think that happened?"

"Do you have a couple of hours? Let me show you something." I sat her down in front of the TV and started playing videotapes of news coverage of the Fawns' case. By the time I was done, she was amazed. "Oh my God," she said. "I had no idea this is what we were dealing with." Then she got up and left. We never heard from her again.

On March 4, 2004, ABC's *Primetime* aired its feature on the Fawns' rescue. They called it "Daring Rescue from Arizona Religious Sect." They used some of the footage Jim Osman shot the night of the rescue, and John Quiñones interviewed the Fawns.

"Do you know who George Bush is?"

"No," said Fawn Broadbent.

Fawn Holm said, "I think he's the president, but I don't know what he looks like. I have never seen him. We are told Warren Jeffs is the president."

I could relate to their ignorance. Shortly after I escaped, some-one asked me if I knew who Ronald Reagan was. I had no clue that he was the president of the United States.

Megan and the two Fawns stayed on the run for a couple of weeks. Finally, I drove Joni back to Salt Lake City. On the way, we detoured into Colorado and picked up the Fawns and hauled them back to Salt Lake with us. It was months before anyone outside my family and the Holms knew they were there.

19

Laurene

I wish I could say that life settled down for me after the Fawns had escaped and been hidden. But all I can really say is that my life went back to normal—an unending round of midnight calls, rides through the desert, news conferences and court dates, moments of wild hope and deep despair—all punctuated by a brief and precious moment of peace with my husband and daughters. But even then, not a day went by that I didn't think of my sister Ruby.

Shortly after the girls went to live with the Holm family, Joni got a phone call in the middle of the night.

Terrified that someone was hurt, she picked up the phone. It was a woman from the FLDS who used to live in Salt Lake City and who knew Joni. She was concerned for her former friend and was calling in a warning. "If you are in any way, shape, or form involved with Flora Jessop," she said, "you better get away from her. Because it is going to be *very dangerous* to be around her."

"What do you mean by that?" Joni snapped.

"You could get hurt."

By this time, Joni had learned not to be threatened by these people. "You know what Flora wants," she said. "So just *give* her what she wants."

"What do you mean?"

"Her sister. She just wants her sister Ruby. Give her sister to her and she will go away."

"Well, now, I know Ruby, and she is very happy right where she is."

"Well, then, let Ruby tell Flora that herself. Flora will back off if you just let her sister tell her that's where she wants to be."

"Ruby isn't strong enough to tell her sister that yet," said the woman. She hung up.

Joni called right away to tell me about the conversation. She was very concerned about the implications. But far from frightening me off, it made me want to fight harder. The language she used—"Ruby isn't strong enough to tell her sister that"—told me that Ruby was still fighting. She hadn't been brainwashed completely yet.

During the last week of May 2004—three months after the Fawns had gone into hiding—I was in Salt Lake City to introduce an attorney to Brent Jeffs (Warren's nephew) and other FLDS abuse victims, hoping a civil case could be filed. I was staying downtown at a big hotel, and invited Joni and the two Fawns out for the day to have lunch with me and Debbie Palmer, who had come down from Canada to meet with the attorney. We had just ordered when Sam Barlow—Mr. God Squad himself—walked in. If Sam spotted us, that would be it. Nobody was supposed to know where the two Fawns were—especially not me and Joni. Before he got any closer, the two Fawns slipped quietly out of the restaurant and went back to my room. I wasn't sure whether he saw us—he sure didn't come to our table to say hi. It turned out that Sam was meeting none other than Rodney Parker, a longtime FLDS attorney, who was just as suspect as some FLDS leaders, and Merrill Jessop. When they finally left, we all breathed a sigh of relief.

A couple of days later, Joni got a call from Esther Holm, Fawn Holm's mother. "What the hell is this I hear about you being seen with my daughter and that damn bitch Flora Jessop having lunch up there in Salt Lake?"

Joni was shocked, but she held her own. "Well now, Esther, you'd want me to see Fawn while she was in town, wouldn't you? To make sure she was doing OK?" Esther interpreted this statement as meaning that I'd brought Fawn to lunch with me. That, it seems, was intolerable. So, simply to prevent me from getting my hands on her daughter—after all this time and all our battles—she and Fawn's dad signed their power of attorney over to Carl and Joni. The fight was over.

I laughed like hell when I heard. This was a real victory: the first time we'd managed to keep runaways from going into the system and being sent back to Colorado City. These girls were in a real home now, with a real family who cared about them and would do everything they could to make sure the girls had all the support they needed to recover from what the FLDS had done to their lives, and to move forward. What they decided to do with their lives, for better or worse, was up to the girls themselves—and that, of course, was as it should be.

I was overjoyed for Fawn Holm and Fawn Broadbent. But I was laughing for a different reason: this was another nail in the coffin for Warren Jeffs. I would not allow the public and the press to forget the terrible things he was doing to people in the name of God.

At about this time I was also involved in trying to stop yet another frightening and abusive FLDS practice. In May 2004 I had a call from Richard Allen Cook, a lost boy who thirty years ago had managed to survive being beaten and left for dead in the desert. He'd first gotten in touch with me a few months back, after he heard about me through the news stories about Fawn Holm and Fawn Broadbent. I'd encouraged him to reunite with his brothers and sisters. I'd even helped him get information on a daughter he had never seen. So the man had a soft spot for me, and he knew I'd help people if I could. I knew he was serious and wouldn't call if he didn't have a good reason.

"Hey, Richard," I said. "What's going on?"

He didn't mince words. "Flora," he said, "my sister Laurene's in trouble. Can you help?"

Laurene was my cousin, another victim of the Jessop clan's devotion to the laws and abusive traditions of polygamous doctrines. I'd been trying to track her down for quite a while after

I learned she had been put in a mental institution by the FLDS Priesthood, but until now I had had no luck.

"Just tell me where to go. I'm already in my car."

My cousin Laurene was a sweetheart who had been married as the second wife to the man who had also married her half-sister, Marie. Her husband, Val Jessop, had repeatedly had her committed to a mental hospital to punish her for speaking her mind and for trying to protect her children from Marie's abuses. So I was really excited to think that maybe I could find out where she was and try to help her escape from this bondage.

I picked up Richard, and we went to Flagstaff to get Laurene, meeting her, her three daughters, and her friend Bob Coody at a restaurant there. Her two sons were still in Colorado City with Val and Marie. A friend of Richard's took the girls out for a ride while we all talked.

I was so happy to finally see Laurene again after all these years. But Richard hadn't told Laurene he was bringing me with him, and Laurene was upset when she saw me. She knew my reputation as a rebel within the FLDS, and church leaders had warned the people never to have anything to do with me. However, she did tell what had been happening to her recently, and she sat and listened to me as I laid out her options.

She'd been living in Flagstaff for the last five years, after refusing to return to Colorado City because of the abuse. After she had been locked away in the institution for the fourth time, one of the hospital workers had helped her find a job in Flagstaff after her release and she had stayed. Val had been allowing Laurene to see her children (against church rules), although usually only one or two at a time, but now things were about to change for the worse.

With her red hair and freckles, dark circles under her eyes, and worn out look, Laurene could easily be any young mother. But I knew her experience was dramatically different from the way most moms in this country live.

"What happened?"

"Warren kicked Val out of the church, and Val is going to give our children to Warren to buy his priesthood back," she said. "I didn't know what to do."

"Don't worry," I said. "We'll figure this out. First thing we're going to do is get you an attorney, then—"

She got right in my face and started screaming. "You're a damn liar! You don't want to help me. Get out!"

"Whoa, sit down, honey. Why would I lie about that?" She was looking at me like I had lost my mind.

"Flora, you know damn well that only men can have lawyers. Women don't have that right."

Laurene had left home, I thought, but she'd brought a heavy load of FLDS baggage with her. At that moment, I just hoped I could keep her from going back to Val long enough for her to understand that the freedom she'd always longed for was now within her reach. All she had to do was take it.

After more discussion, Laurene agreed to come to Phoenix and meet with an attorney. Pretty soon Richard's friend returned with his family and Laurene's girls, and it was agreed that the girls would go home with his family while Laurene tried to get the initial protective order from the courts.

As hard as it is for young girls to get out of the FLDS and stay out, it's even more difficult for their moms. Born into the cult, married off as teenagers, they start having babies when they're babies themselves. By age thirty, many of these women already have eight or more children. When they finally decide they're ready to leave behind everything they've ever known, they're poorly equipped to make a new life. It's hard enough for a single mother who is capable of going out and getting a job. It's nearly impossible for an undereducated, wrung-out young woman who doesn't even know she has the basic human rights America guarantees everyone.

I've seen many women go back to the FLDS, defeated. Trying to make a life on their own—even with the support of others who have left—is just too much for them. And the loneliness eats away at them. Most normal men wouldn't touch a relationship with a troubled woman who has a lot of kids and an angry husband. Many men who do seek out these women are predators who are mainly interested in getting close to the children.

Sometimes the women go back because the teachings they were raised on are just too strong. "I'm nothing without a man," they tell me, in tears. "I'm never getting into heaven without a man!"

They can't wrap their minds around the idea that women have rights, just like men. I try to educate them, but I have to get through a lot of conditioning. Eventually, I tell them all the same thing.

"You've got to believe in yourself, honey."

But for many of them, it's just too late to do even that, especially without help and support. That's why runaway moms left to their own devices often turn around and go straight back "home," often to situations worse than the ones they left.

I feel fortunate to have had the kind of success with runaway moms that I've had. Even though we're still in the middle of some court battles that have been going on for seven years and counting, I've been able to offer enough support to convince all but one mother to fight it out until she had absolute custody over her kids.

The one woman I had lost before trying to help Laurene was convinced she'd be jailed if she didn't bring her kids back to her husband. She did bring them back, and she's now lost them again, probably for good. But I don't consider the time she spent outside the cult as wasted. For the time I was able to work with her, she received something precious: a window on the outside world. Nobody can ever completely shut that window. I was determined that Laurene would have that window too.

I thought I knew everything there was to know about how evil the FLDS can be, especially to kids. But in 2004, when Laurene and her kids came to stay with me, I saw how that abuse can continue right on into marriage.

Laurene, like so many others, was a victim of systemic sexual abuse as a child. Then, when Laurene was nineteen, she was told she was going to marry Val Jessop the next day. But she wasn't rescued by this marriage. Not at all.

A lot of folks watch that HBO television series *Big Love* and get the idea that once you're married into a large polygamist family as a first, second, or third wife, it's all hunky-dory and life is one extended love fest. But I hope everyone who's been reading this book and has heard my story up to this point realizes that *Big Love* is completely a Hollywood story. I hope everyone who's been reading this book understands the reality of the competition for painfully limited resources—food, clothing, any free time, the love of the all-powerful man—not to mention the horrible incestuous abuse, brutal rapes, and child sexual molestation.

What's been good about the *Big Love* show is getting everyday Americans to understand at least something about how organizations like the FLDS work, and to begin to take the issue of polygamy seriously. Nevertheless Laurene's experience in plural marriage is far more typical of the way most women live in polygamy than anything you'll ever see in *Big Love*. And it isn't pretty.

The stories Laurene told me about being Val Jessop's second wife were harrowing. His first wife, Marie, was jealous of Laurene from the beginning. Laurene and Val's honeymoon night was spent at home, in bed—with Marie hanging onto Val's back during the sex act.

Val had allowed Marie to interfere with a situation that should have been sacred and private, and that gave Marie a power over Laurene that would become more extreme with every passing day. Even worse was the way Marie manipulated everyone around her into participating in the abuse against her sister-wife and half-sister, including Val.

She made Laurene's life miserable in any number of petty ways. Once, Val and his two wives went for a drive in a canyon five or six miles from their home. Marie whispered to Val, "She's not riding in my car on the way home!" So Val left Laurene by the side of the road and made her walk all the way back.

Val had been trying to get his wives pregnant for years with no success. Finally, he went to the doctor and discovered a problem that made it impossible for him to have children. After a lengthy process of application, the Prophet finally gave him permission to have a medical procedure to fix the problem.

In the meantime, devastated by her childless state, Marie had turned to pets for comfort. In short order she had amassed fifteen cats and dogs. She let them wander around the house, more or less untrained.

Then, for Marie, the worst happened: After Val's surgery, Laurene got pregnant first. In polygamy, pregnancy is celestial math: the number of children you give your husband to build his kingdom determines your worth. Naturally, relations between the sister-wives (or in this case, as my daughter Shauna once joked, "sister-sister wives-wives") deteriorated.

Moreover, Laurene had tolerated the pets until her children were born, but like a lot of children in Colorado City, Laurene's first infant, a girl, had a birth defect—she was born without an esophagus. Lots of babies are born with worse problems in Colorado City. For example, as I mentioned earlier, owing to inbreeding, Colorado City and Hildale have the world's highest incidence of fumarase deficiency. Babies with this genetic condition are born severely mentally retarded, have oddly shaped facial features, and are prone to epilepsy.

Laurene's baby was in and out of the hospital for operations, and was sent home with a gastric feeding tube in her belly.

"The doctors told me I had to keep it clean," Laurene told me, "or she'd get infected. They specifically told me to keep animals away from her." She shook her head, still angry at the memory. "But Marie didn't care. Those cats would jump up into her crib. I'd keep finding them licking around the tube." Her baby kept getting sick. "I begged both of them, please, just keep the animals confined to a different part of the house! They can't be near my baby. But that bitch would just open the door and allow the animals into the baby's room."

Despite repeated infections, the little girl survived—she was now the teenager sleeping in my living room as Laurene told me this harrowing tale.

Then Laurene learned that she was pregnant again and that Marie was pregnant for the first time. They delivered within ten days of each other. This time, Laurene had a little boy, and Marie had a girl. When the boy was old enough to crawl, Laurene caught him eating cat feces off the floor—Marie had never trained her cats to use a cat box.

"He got salmonella poisoning so bad I couldn't put a diaper on him for four months," Laurene told me. "He had terrible blisters from the infection. Val didn't do anything about the animals. Finally, I just couldn't take any more of it. Marie flat out refused to keep her cats and dogs away from my kids, so I loaded them into my car and drove them to my brother's place in the country." She grinned at the memory.

"What happened?"

"Marie called the police. She told them I was trying to kill her animals and she was afraid I'd kill my kids." The police—all members of the priesthood of course—didn't try to find out the real story. They just handcuffed Laurene and had her committed to a mental institution—standard procedure in the FLDS for disobedient wives. This left her babies at the mercy of Marie. Laurene returned home, chastened—at least for a while.

Eventually, Laurene had five children, three girls and two boys. Marie had three, and she abused all the children in the household. When Laurene's fourth child was only nine months old, Marie would snatch the baby while Laurene was doing the dishes and hide her—often in the bathroom. Laurene would go crazy hunting for her baby. Later, Laurene's oldest daughter was routinely held down in a chair and beaten while Marie screamed, "You're just like your mother and I'm going to beat it out of you!"

"What did Val do?" I asked.

"What do you think? I had tried to tell him about it when it first started, but he always sided with Marie. She was his first wife. It didn't matter how many kids I had. If I told him how Marie was treating me and my kids, he'd just punish me for causing discord in the home." I knew that the priesthood taught men not to take sides or listen to complaints of wives about sister-wives—doing that might create an atmosphere where wives can take advantage of husbands.

Laurene was trapped and desperate. Keeping sweet hadn't gotten her anywhere; and acting out had landed her in a mental institution. Val felt desperate too because he didn't know how to cope with her. One day Val took Laurene to the deputy sheriff's house. He left her in the truck, complaining loudly that she was an out-of-control wife.

"What are we supposed to do with her?" he ranted at the sheriff. "How the hell can you help somebody like this?"

Laurene was furious. Couldn't they see she was right there? She tried to get their attention, but they just ignored her. Then she just snapped. She took a pair of scissors off the dash and snipped a small hole in her dress over her abdomen, revealing her sacred garment. She waited for the men to look at her and react, but they just kept talking.

She got out of the truck and cut a bigger hole, but they still didn't notice. Before long, she had cut through her dress, slips, bra, garment, and panties. Finally, Laurene was standing next to the truck—completely naked. That got their attention.

"Oh heck," yelled Val. "What the hell happened to your clothes?"

"I am flesh and blood!" Laurene shouted. "Do you guys understand this? Can you talk to *me*? I am a person too, damn it!"

Val wrapped his wife in a blanket. The deputy covered his eyes and arrested her for destroying her husband's property—her dress. And once more, she was hauled to the mental institution. At least she got to rest. Far from being chastened, she felt the embarrassment she had caused Val to be a sweet measure of revenge.

Now that I had Laurene and the three girls at my house, where I could keep track of them, I was working to get the oldest girl to look at me. All the girls had been taught early on that looking adults in the eye is a sign of disrespect. I'd sit on the floor with her, telling her I'd wait for as long as it took. It seemed like a really important milestone—to make eye contact with another human being and not be afraid.

Laurene won temporary custody of her five children, and then we worked hard to get her housing transferred to Phoenix. Soon she and the girls were living in a nice four-bedroom house, close enough that I could be there quickly if needed. When we tried to sign Laurene up for food stamps, we learned that Marie was collecting welfare for Laurene's kids and that agency records said Marie was their mother. We had to prove that Laurene was their mother to receive services, and even then Arizona never charged Marie with the welfare fraud it should have.

The girls were excited about everything in their new lives, but the two boys—both old enough to be privileged priesthood holders—were angry. We fought over everything Laurene or I told them to do—from taking showers to visiting the doctor. I was used to that from boys, but I soon found out these two had much worse in them.

One day Laurene confided to me that she was becoming afraid of her boys and that they had been hitting her. I explained to them that beating their mother was unacceptable behavior. Period.

They just laughed at me.

"If it happens again," I told them, "you *will* go to jail."

"Everybody knows boys don't go to jail," the oldest one said. "Only girls go to jail. We can do what we want."

"Try me," I said. "Just go ahead and try me."

If anything, they got worse. They both wanted to go back to Colorado City and the Prophet, but Laurene had gotten custody—that made absolutely no sense to them. How could their mom have any power over them? The older boy was threatening to burn the house down to kill his mother and siblings to save them from hell.

One day I was at the community college, taking a course, when I got a call from Laurene. "The police are here," she said.

The place was in chaos when I got there. Apparently, the boys had been hitting their mother again.

"Flora, are they going to arrest me?" Laurene was shaking so hard she could barely talk.

"No, Laurene. Why would they do that? You didn't do anything." I explained the situation to the cops as best I could while they took the boys into custody.

The boys were dumbstruck. They absolutely could not understand why they were being arrested.

The strip search was traumatic for them, with their long underwear and all. They knew it was wicked to be naked in front of anyone; they didn't want anyone looking at them; they didn't want to be touched. The cops could see right away that this was not a normal situation. They were afraid to lock them up with other kids because the boys—angry as they were—were also as naïve as could be.

The judge ordered competency hearings for them. Each boy was evaluated by three doctors, who found the boys to be "incompetent" and "unredeemable." Incompetent, in this case, meant they did not have the ability to defend themselves in a legal proceeding. Unredeemable meant they could not even be *taught* how to defend themselves in the future.

But I refused to believe they were beyond saving. The oldest was put under house arrest and had to report to a probation officer, but I feel the experience taught him more acceptance and respect for not only his mom but also the law. The entire family was in psychological counseling. I stuck with them all the way. And I had to educate the counselors, too.

I sat in on many counseling sessions, acting as both advocate and interpreter. I spent every day for two years helping them cope, teaching them common sense, just helping them learn how they thought. It seemed impossible at times, but these boys did turn around. The oldest had once threatened to blow up his school. By the time the family left Phoenix, he'd actually made friends.

In the end, Laurene was granted custody of all five of her children and Val was to have only supervised visits. Val had refused to cooperate with most of the court orders, and protection had to be given to the judge due to threats against him. Val even sent Laurene wacky papers saying he was suing her for forty million dollars for holding his kids hostage, which really scared her.

In spite of all Val had done, he eventually breached the protective barrier around Laurene and was able to erode the confidence she had fought so hard to build. It would seem her original indoctrination was so deep it took little for him to sway her.

With Laurene and the kids gone, Val had suffered. Warren had by now kicked him out of the FLDS, and Marie and their three children were taken away from him. Laurene heard he was despondent. People told her he'd changed. He begged her to come back.

Laurene had found an amazing partner in her friend Bob Coody, a man who had spent two years supporting and protecting her and the children. Even with this incredible man who was willing to accept all the FLDS baggage she carried, the doctrines and fear were too much for Laurene.

Eventually, Laurene buckled to the belief that the children belong to the priesthood and their father. And the kids missed their dad. She went to see Val and discovered that he'd "mellowed," as she put it. Finally, she told him she'd go back to him on two conditions: they would never go back to live in the FLDS community, and he would never take another wife.

When Laurene told me she was going back I was devastated but I told her it was her choice and I respected that. The family reunited and lived outside Colorado City for a while. I really hoped things would work for them, but then the rumors started, and I soon got a call from one of my brothers after the older boy had gone to him asking how to reach me. I learned Val was mixed up with some nut case who had convinced him I had teamed up with the government and was coming to kill him. Then I was told Val thought there were snipers on a hill five miles from the house who were trying to kill him, and I was supposed to be the one who had hired them.

Wow! Snipers who could make a five-mile shot? Were these people crazy? Not long after that the whole family disappeared, and the police started asking me questions. They said Val had been buying weapons and was planning some type of confrontation with the authorities. Rumors circulated that the family was moving through Colorado, Utah, and Arizona, eventually landing in Idaho. Val has teamed up with some white militia group and Laurene has recorded a document in Maricopa County that states "No government owns her" and that she renounces all governmental powers over her, including her social security number and driver's license.

Working with the Fawns and with Laurene and her children was only one of the things going on in my life in 2004 and the years following.

By March 2004, Warren Jeffs had started putting up buildings on his Texas property near the town of Eldorado. And it was in March that I was on ABC's *Primetime* after journalist John Quiñones went with me to Colorado City. A lot of people saw that show—including people in Eldorado, Texas, who were beginning to get worried about exactly what these people from Utah had in mind.

I was no longer fearful of the media. I'd learned that they could help me get my message out there. Right away, I started contacting people in Texas, including newspaper editors and other journalists. I made a trip out to Eldorado to try to warn people about what was coming. The local papers starting interviewing me for a series of stories they were writing on the FLDS compound. The reporters told me that David S. Allred, the man who had purchased the land, had said he wanted it for a hunting retreat. I laughed my head off.

"I'm not wrong," I warned them. "This has all the signs. People need to be aware."

In April, I held a news conference in Eldorado. It was attended by government and law enforcement officials from Texas and Arizona—including Mohave County, Arizona, supervisor Buster Johnson, whose district included Colorado City. And it was covered not only by media in the Southwest but also by the *New York Times* and ABC's *Primetime*.

I told them my story. I told them about sexual abuse, forced marriages, child abuse, tax evasion, welfare fraud, and child labor. I told them exactly who had purchased the land that Warren was now calling YFZ, LLC, a limited liability corporation. YFZ stood for Yearn for Zion. The FLDS members believed that Zion would be their place of refuge when the sins of the wicked destroyed the world. The name chilled me to the bone. I wondered what Warren might be planning.

20

No Sympathy for the Devil

In July 2004, twenty-one-year-old Brent Jeffs filed charges against three of his uncles—Warren and his brothers Blaine and Leslie—for molesting him when he was a child. They'd told him it would make him a man. In his suit, Brent said that his uncles also told him "that it was 'God's will' that he never disclose the abuses to anyone, and if he did, it would be upon pain of eternal damnation."

I was overjoyed by the lawsuit. Even Utah Attorney General Mark Shurtleff was saying that he would "follow up on any potential criminal charges." I told the press, "I'm hoping, with what Brent has had the courage to do, it will bring more victims forward to stop the cycle. Our complete support is with Brent and his family, and we just pray that he can heal from it and live a normal, healthy life."

Finally, things were breaking badly for Warren Jeffs. I could only hope they would get worse. A lot worse.

In October 2004, I went to Kingman, Arizona, to meet with Mohave County attorney Matt Smith and newly appointed Mohave County investigator Gary Engles about a case we were working on. Matt Smith told me he had just seen Sam Roundy, the Colorado City police chief, who was also there on a case. *Uh-oh.* Roundy hated me. He'd told John Quiñones outright that he wanted to arrest me. I definitely felt threatened by him. *I'm going to have problems going home,* I thought.

After the meeting, I checked my SUV to make sure it was OK—just to be on the safe side. Those FLDS guys love to disappear people in traffic "accidents." If he'd known which vehicle was mine—though I was pretty sure he didn't—I figured he would've either loosened the steering wheel or taken the lug nuts off the tire rims.

Why would Roundy want to see me dead? Because I was rescuing his women and threatening his world. Besides, he was convinced I was working for Satan. Warren himself had said so, from the pulpit. I was a prime candidate for blood atonement—holy murder—an ongoing theme in Short Creek.[1]

When I was a kid, people disappeared every once in a while. We called them "poofers." One day you're here, and the next day, poof! You're gone. Some of the poofers have turned up over the years—a lot of lost boys have resurfaced, as have girls who had been sent to another compound and married off. But there have been some people who have just poofed and were never seen or heard from again.

Rulon Jeffs published a series of sermons in 1997 in which he addressed the issue of blood atonement: "[Blood atonement] is loving our neighbor as ourselves; if he needs help, help him; and if he wants salvation and it is necessary to spill his blood on the earth in order that he may be saved, spill it."

After Uncle Rulon died and Warren seized power, he continued touting blood atonement in his sermons. In one well-publicized case, Warren Jeffs ordered the blood atonement of Vanessa Rohbock, a teenage girl who was married to Jeffs's younger brother. Vanessa hated him and fought the marriage from the beginning. Like Ruby, she was in love with a boy her own age. When Jeffs ordered her to marry his brother, she told him she wanted to marry her boyfriend. Warren, of course, considered her defiance an act of disobedience and adultery. The simple act of "taking a boyfriend," whether having sex or not, is considered adultery, an offense worthy of blood atonement.

Vanessa ran away to the Bountiful compound, in British Columbia, with her boyfriend. One of her sisters was married to Winston Blackmore, the leader of the Canadian branch of the

FLDS, and Vanessa asked Blackmore to protect her. Jeffs demanded that Blackmore return Vanessa to his custody. Vanessa's father, Ron Rohbock, was one of Warren and Rulon Jeffs's top lieutenants. Warren ordered him to travel to Bountiful to bring Vanessa back to Colorado City. He went, but Vanessa refused to return with him. Warren ordered Rohbock back to Canada several times to attempt to retrieve his daughter, but each time she refused. Finally, Warren had enough. He ordered Vanessa blood atoned.

Vanessa asked Blackmore to rebaptize her. He complied, and soon after Vanessa asked permission to marry her boyfriend. The news infuriated Jeffs. The official publication of the Bountiful FLDS, *The North Star*, quotes Warren Jeffs as saying to Blackmore, "There it is. I told her father, if you let this girl get re-baptized then the next thing she will want to do is get re-married, and there it is. Her baptism did not work, she shall not be re-married. There is nothing left for her to do but to come and have her blood shed for the remission of her sins. You are instructed to tell her to gather up her things and to go away. You and Ron are instructed to pray night and day for the Lord to destroy her from off the face of the earth."

Blackmore went to the priesthood members in Canada and asked for a vote. "Do we protect her or do we turn her over for blood atonement?" The entire community of Bountiful could have been adversely affected by refusing Warren Jeffs's order, but the counsel voted unanimously to protect her. One counsel member, however, told Warren Jeffs where Vanessa was staying.

When we got word at the Child Protection Project that Warren had picked up Vanessa and was on his way back to the United States with her to perform blood atonement, the story became personal.

The situation was very tense—I believe Warren Jeffs is absolutely capable of executing blood atonement. I called the Mohave County sheriff's office and spoke to an investigator, Jace Zack. I told him our suspicions, and asked him to do a welfare check on Vanessa in Colorado City. I trusted Zack to do the right thing, and he did. He asked for photos, fingerprints from a soda can, DNA from a hairbrush—anything that would positively identify her. He knew that when record checks had been done in the past, the families would often just swap one kid for another. As I've pointed out before, most kids in an FLDS family will look nearly identical because the bloodlines are so close.

Right away, the Mohave County sheriff went into Colorado City asking questions about Vanessa—"Where is she? What is going on? We want to see her. We want to make sure she's OK." Then we contacted the media and made them aware of the situation. A few days later, they found her safe and sound in Colorado City and made it perfectly clear that if anyone around her harmed a hair of her head, he or she would be prosecuted to the full extent of the law. As Winston Blackmore said, "I think she was the safest girl in the nation by the time that she went back to Colorado City."[2]

Our involvement and the calls we made saved a young girl's life. We stopped a blood atonement. We blocked a murder.

But it was close. I fully believe that without our intervention she would have been killed, and people in the outside world might never have known. Why would they? It would have been almost impossible to trace the fact. A traffic accident or a supposed suicide would easily cover up a murder.

Even the Utah attorney general's office was convinced. "Warren wanted Vanessa blood atoned," said Ron Barton, a criminal investigator in Utah Attorney General Mark Shurtleff's office. The attorney general's office considered prosecuting Jeffs for conspiracy to commit murder but finally decided the evidence was not substantial enough to win a conviction.

So, as I checked my Suburban for tampering that evening, I knew that Warren was riled up and that I was definitely on his radar. Finally, I was convinced my Suburban was OK, but I was still nervous as a cat when I started the long drive home. The sun had gone down, and I had to drive the winding two-lane stretch

Thursday, August 25, 2005

Dear Brother Holland:

I am involved in the rescue of women, children, and young men who are escaping the abusive polygamous lifestyle inherent in the FLDS. My efforts and small successes have been the subject of many news and television shows, including Primetime Thursday and Dr. Phil this year.

The leader of this group, Warren Jeffs, who makes a mockery of the word Prophet, is now on the FBI's Most Wanted List. For years I have endeavored to bring these criminals to justice both through the use of the media and by cooperating with law enforcement to the fullest of my ability. The LDS Church could be instrumental in helping former polygamists exit this massive human and civil rights nightmare. However, it has come to my attention that when these women and children seek the help of the LDS Church, primarily in Southern Utah, the Bishops and Stake Presidents withdraw their support. I am seeking answers about why this would be so.

The Mormons in public relations efforts claim they have nothing to do with polygamy. However, you and I both know that some members within each and every extensive ancestral polygamous family line did not stop practicing polygamy because of the manifesto. Consequently, this is a continuing problem that affects us all adversely, a problem that no matter how difficult to honestly face, must be faced.

I am planning to start a transition center to help former polygamists to live in the outside world. I would like to meet with you at your first available opportunity to discuss how you can become a part of the solution to this massive problem Utah and sadly the LDS Church has so long ignored. A press statement denying responsibility is woefully inadequate considering the routine crimes we have uncovered inside polygamy in the Intermountain West. I am certain you have wanted to help and am now offering you an opportunity to do so.

Please let me know when we can meet to discuss these issues. Thank you for your consideration.

All the best,

Flora Jessop
P O Box 71038
Phoenix, Arizona 85050
602-373-0793

cc: Joseph B. Wirthlin

I wrote this letter in an effort to seek help from the Church of Jesus Christ of Latter-day Saints. Brother Jeffrey Holland agreed to meet with me but did not take any further action, saying, "As a church we . . . do not endorse or become directly involved in private ventures."

of highway between Wickenburg and I-40. It was no comfort to remember that locals call it Death Highway because so many people have been killed there.

It was pitch-black dark and raining like crazy, and I had to go slowly. As I topped a hill, I got a good look, despite the rain, at what was coming around the next four curves. In the distance I saw a gas tanker truck approaching the last curve. At the same moment, I realized someone was tailing me, real close. And I was pretty sure I knew who it was. *Damn.*

All I could do was keep driving. Going down the hill, I was driving blind. But I knew the tanker was coming. *Son of a bitch! When is he going to do it? I know he's going to pull something.* The next thing I knew, the car behind me pulled out, as though the driver was trying to pass. But instead of passing, he just slowed down and drove right next to me for several seconds.

I looked straight ahead, trying not to run head-on into the tanker or get sideswiped by this lunatic. Suddenly, I saw a flash out of the corner of my eye and heard a loud pop. Then another flash and another pop, and my back left tire blew out. *You son of a bitch!* As my SUV swerved into the next lane, I knew the tanker couldn't see me. I struggled to get my fishtailing vehicle back into its own lane. At the last second, the tanker blew past me with a rush of air and a tremendous blast from his horn. I wasn't dead.

Shaking, I kept driving straight down the hill. I didn't want to get stuck on this blind curve. My SUV went *bump, bump, bump* on the flat tire. No way was I getting home tonight.

The shooter slowed, did a U-turn, and sped away.

If he was just trying to scare me, he did a damn good job.

I rolled to a stop on the muddy shoulder, shaking. I just sat there for a while with the rain pouring down and the windshield wipers going back and forth. I must have smoked half a pack of Camels trying to calm down. I was way out of cell phone range here. Finally, I got out to check the damage. The flat tire was demolished from my driving on it to a safe pull-out place.

Exhausted, I got my tools out of the back and tried to change the tire. But one of the lug nuts just wouldn't budge, at least for me.

I was soaked and muddy. Most people were not as crazy as I was—they weren't traveling on a mountain road at night during a driving storm—and the road was deserted. I figured I'd have to wait until sunrise to flag someone down, so I climbed in my SUV, turned the emergency flashers on, and went to sleep. Three hours later a young couple drove by and stopped to see if I needed help. Together we managed to break the lug nut loose and change the tire.

As I drove on down the hill, all I could think was that I wanted to get home. When I finally got cell service, I called Tim.

"What the hell happened? Are you OK?" My family was freaking out. All they knew was that I had left Kingman hours ago, and hadn't shown up at home.

"Yeah, I'm fine. I just blew a tire. I'll be home soon." It was a couple years before I told Tim that someone shot at me that night. He was already worried enough about me.

Roundy didn't come after me again. Even if he had, no one could stop me from speaking out about Warren Jeffs. By the beginning of 2005, Eldorado, Texas, was really beginning to worry about what Jeffs was planning at his nearby YFZ Ranch. According to Richard Holm, whom Warren had excommunicated the year before, millions of dollars had been pouring in to finish the building. "They call it the Holy City," he said, "and everybody who is worthy can go to Zion, either to visit or to live."[3]

All through the first half of that year, we kept Warren's name in the news. The true story of the FLDS and its abuses was finally getting out to the public. I guess we had Warren to thank for that.

In March 2005, Uncle Fred died, alone and neglected, in a Colorado hospital, at age ninety-four. He'd been missing for over a year, since December 2003. All that time, rumors had circulated about where he might be. Some insisted he was on a mission; but I and other concerned family members had gone so far as to file a missing persons report on him. I was pretty sure Warren had made some compromise between getting rid of him altogether and keeping him alive—just in case. But at the time of his death, he was still the much-loved Uncle Fred. Some estimates put attendance at his funeral at more than 3,000—a substantial portion of the population of the twin towns. The funeral lasted more than three hours, and the hymns included a song with the refrain "perfect priesthood man."

I was still friends with Trudy and Conell Bateman, who'd driven me out of Colorado City almost twenty years ago, at the risk of their own lives. The Batemans, along with others whose Colorado City homes were owned by the United Effort Plan trust, had never given up their battle to break the trust and own their own home. In May, a Utah judge removed Warren Jeffs and the rest of the priesthood as trustees of the $100 million UEP trust, in a response to allegations of misconduct. Other would-be trustees stepped up to be nominated, including Winston Blackmore. In June, the Child Protection Project filed its own petition for a new set of trustees to sit on the board. Most of us were women who'd left the FLDS: myself; my cousin Laurene Jessop, who was still working with me and living in Phoenix at that point; Janet Johanson, who so long ago had convinced me to go on 60 *Minutes;* Pam Black; and Fawn's brother, Carl Holm. We also had two politicians—Arizona State Senator Linda Binder; and Buster Johnson, the Mohave County supervisor who'd gone with me to that first press conference in Eldorado.

I couldn't have put our reasoning any better than Linda Binder did: "You have to cut off the head of the snake," she said. "And that's the money. . . . I'd love to see the victims get that money to educate and relocate the women and children, give them a fresh start in life." Polygamy, she said, is "the biggest con game going. The men up there are fat and happy, smiling. They've got all the women they want, all the sex, and the government pays for their children."[4]

In the end, citing possible conflict of interest, the judge decided to give the trust's management over to a neutral party—a special fiduciary, Bruce Wisan, and an advisory panel. Wisan has landed a cash cow and he has exploited the trust almost more than Warren Jeffs ever thought of. In just two years of overseeing the trust, Wisan has paid himself over two million dollars and paid his attorney another two million. Because the trust was left with no cash assets, Wisan sold some of the prime real estate and has done more to take property from the rightful beneficiaries to cut cushy deals with corrupt and powerful FLDS priesthood leaders who remain loyal to Warren Jeffs. Just two years later, plans were under way to privatize property in Colorado City and Hildale and Wisan began selling land to outsiders. The FLDS would no longer have absolute dominion over the twin towns and their inhabitants and the people who worked there all their lives are once again losing.

The noose was slowly tightening around Warren's neck. The last time he'd been seen in public was on January 1, 2005, at the dedication of the YFZ temple site in Eldorado. Author Jon Krakauer, who never stopped following news about Jeffs, even after his book about the FLDS became a best seller, was one of many who came to observe. He told the *Eldorado Success*, "Schleicher County is clearly the new world headquarters of Warren Jeffs's enterprises. After seeing Warren himself conducting what appeared to be a consecration of the temple foundation on January 1, and considering the incredible pace of new construction on the YFZ property, there can no longer be any doubt."[5]

In June, the state of Arizona charged Warren Jeffs with sexual assault on a minor and conspiracy to commit sexual misconduct with a minor for arranging the marriage of a fourteen-year-old girl to a young man who was already married—and who was also her first cousin. She alleged that her cousin had raped her on her wedding night. The girl, known as Jane Doe in court records, played out Ruby's terrible story for me once again.

So Warren was finally going to be tried for something. But there was a catch: he'd dropped out of sight right after the YFZ dedication.

In August 2005, the Colorado City school district was about to be forced into bankruptcy by the state of Arizona. In a real understatement, Arizona Attorney General Terry Goddard said the reason was "a very serious story of mismanagement." In 2000, Warren Jeffs had ordered all the children in Colorado City to be pulled out of school. A few were home schooled after that; for most, that was just the end of their education. But Warren didn't let the buildings go to waste. Among other things, the district had used the public school buildings for a private FLDS school, racked up $1.8 million of debt, and bought a private airplane.

Through the Child Protection Project, we were also making headway on another mystery that had haunted me for more than twenty years: trying to learn who all those children were that were buried behind Aunt Lydia's clinic, and finding out how they died.

Linda Walker and I went out to the two cemeteries in the twin towns—one was called Babyland, because it was just for babies. In those two graveyards we found 324 marked graves for children under eighteen years of age. Fifty-eight babies were buried in unmarked graves. We videotaped all the evidence.

Then we marched that tape down to the Utah attorney general's office and talked to a Washington County prosecutor named Brock Belnap. I explained that over the years I'd lived in Colorado City, I'd heard of many children who had died in mysterious yet uninvestigated circumstances. And I'd seen Aunt Lydia bury plenty more. In a letter we asked the office to see whether death certificates and causes of death had been recorded for all the children buried in the FLDS cemeteries. If not, we asked, "shouldn't criminal charges be filed for improper disposal of remains? And if some of the babies died from abuse or neglect, shouldn't that also be a criminal matter?"

Finally, we gave them a list of seventy-four sect members—some children—whom we knew had died and also eight stillbirths, none of whom were buried under headstones in either of the two cemeteries.

Belnap was sympathetic, and horrified, as he should be. But he didn't know what he could do. "The statute of limitations on homicide never runs out," he said. "If you have direct evidence, bring it to us."

"Look," I said, "you know and I know that the Mohave County coroner signed off on most of these deaths without even seeing the bodies." I hammered away at him. "What are you going to do about this? You know I'm not going to stop asking that question."

Finally, he promised us that his office would investigate the deaths. He kept his promise, and so did I—I didn't stop talking about it. By 2006, so many people knew about the nameless babies that I was asked to talk about it on Anderson Cooper's 360 Degrees on CNN. On that show, Arizona State Representative David Lujan said, "I would be interested in looking to see if we can change the law to look at the death certificates for the children in Colorado City to see what was the cause of death in these instances."

Finally, late in 2005, the FBI put Warren Jeffs, Prophet of the Fundamentalist Latter Day Saints, on its most wanted fugitives list. Seeing his face on a wanted poster warmed my heart. And now he was not only fleeing his nephew Brent's charges, he was facing new charges: unlawful flight to avoid prosecution.

I knew Warren would be caught now. It was just a matter of when it would happen. But I remembered those guns stockpiled in the cavern in Hildale, and I knew by heart the tale of Short Creek. I couldn't help but remember Waco and Ruby Ridge as well. I was worried what would happen to my family, and all the families in the compounds, if Warren declared the coming of Armageddon.

Part Four

No More Pain

It's amusing how many people now want to take credit for
the fall of Warren Jeffs. It's a seductive story. Everybody
wants to be seen as the hero. . . .

But Flora Jessop—well, she's the real McCoy—one of
the original warriors and genuine heroes. In fact, in many
ways, Flora Jessop and a childhood friend of hers from
Colorado City are truly Arizona's Founding Mothers of this
hard-fought, human rights revolution. A campaign that had
to overcome more than a half-century of institutionalized
neglect and indifference on the part of Utah and Arizona
officials before a man like Warren Jeffs could finally be
brought to justice.

There are people who might dispute that claim—but
I would argue that they are people who either don't really
know the story or are lying to cover their own asses.
—Mike Watkiss[1]

21

Fighting On

On August 29, 2006, the law finally caught up with Warren Jeffs on Interstate 15, just north of Las Vegas. After a routine traffic stop for a registration check, he was quietly arrested on a federal charge of unlawful flight to avoid prosecution, sexual misconduct, and two felony counts of rape as an accomplice. He was traveling with one of his wives, Naomi Jessop Jeffs, and his brother Isaac. He had $54,000 in cash, gift cards totaling $10,000, numerous cell phones, women's wigs, four laptop computers, a Global Positioning System device, a police scanner, and countless unopened envelopes containing more cash.

He was riding as a passenger in a 2007 Cadillac Escalade—and it was red, Satan's own color.

I was relieved that no blood had been shed capturing him, but I was also on high alert. First thing, I called the relatives in Colorado City who would still speak to me to see how they were taking it. "It's so tense here, Flora," one of my sisters told me. "We don't know what's going to happen."

As soon as the news broke, my phone was ringing off the hook with reporters trying to get a quote—everyone from MSNBC to the local newspapers. "I'd sure as hell would like to shake the hand of the officers who picked this son of a bitch up," I told the reporter from the *Las Vegas Review-Journal*, "because if it wouldn't have been for good law enforcement work on the local level, I don't think he ever would have been caught."

I had feared that Warren would be found in Colorado City and that many people—including some of my own family—would be killed in a fierce gun battle. In recorded sermons, Warren talked of a looming showdown with law enforcement, and I figured he was courting violence. But in the end he was taken into custody without incident as the wimpy little sexual predator he is.

Still, I was worried about what the people would do without a leader. As I explained to Fox News the day after the arrest, "With Warren Jeffs being on the run, there was a buffer between the members of this group and the potential for violence. Now that he is in custody, that buffer is removed and so any one of the members who is a potential witness against Warren is under great threat right now." I was also worried that one of two men I feared would be bad leaders—Wendell Neilson or Merrill Jessop—would take control.

As the date for Warren's trial grew closer, I could hardly wait. I planned to be sitting in the courtroom every day, making as much noise as I could and watching that worm squirm. Meanwhile, I had my cases to keep me busy. As well known as I am there, it's not easy to get into Colorado City, meet with families and children, and get out of town without being discovered. One day though, I immediately ran into my sister Maryett at the grocery store. She was loading groceries into her truck, and she had a bunch of her kids around her truck—kids I should have known. But I didn't have a clue if they were my nephews and nieces or neighbor kids.

Without thinking twice, I walked up to her and said, "Hey, Maryett, how you doing?"

She almost dropped her bags on the asphalt. "What are you doing here?" she snapped. "I don't want to talk to you."

"Why is that?" I asked.

"Because I believe in Heavenly Father, and I believe that Warren Jeffs is Heavenly Father's Prophet, and you are fighting against the Prophet, and therefore Heavenly Father doesn't want me to talk to you."

It made me tired and sad to hear that kind of mindless talk. I said, "I believe in Heavenly Father too, Maryett. But the Heavenly Father I believe in doesn't say, 'Throw your family away because they don't believe the same way I do.'"

She just kept her eyes down and shoved groceries into her truck. "I don't want to talk to you. Get away from me."

I kept pushing, even though I knew it was pointless. "Maryett, I support your right to believe that Warren is a prophet. Why can't you support my right to believe that he's not?"

She was really mad now. "Don't talk to me about this! I just want you to go away. I never want to see you again. I wish you were dead!"

"I am really sorry you feel that way, Maryett. I think you need to reconsider. Go back and read your books. I guarantee you, God doesn't say, 'Throw your family away like trash.'"

"Well, then, quit acting like trash!"

Just then, five or six men came running out of the store, surrounding us, as if I was going to attack her. But I was a big girl now, and they no longer frightened me. I stood my ground and looked each one of those guys in the eye. Then I turned and spoke to Maryett. "I want to tell you something. I love you. You are my sister. You'll always be my sister, and nothing will ever change that. I want you to know that I will respect your wishes and I won't come around you again. But I also want you to know that I will always be here for you—no matter if we believe the same things or not."

"Do I need to call the police and have you arrested for harassing me?" Maryett was almost in tears at this point she was so angry.

"If you feel you need to call the police, go ahead. I forgive you for that now."

"Just get away from me! I never want to see you again." The men closed their circle a little tighter.

"OK, I will. But I really do love you." I looked deep into her eyes. "I hope you know that."

I waited, but she never said she loved me back.

I turned and walked away.

I replayed that argument in my mind for weeks. I had always thought I'd be strong enough to deal with a confrontation like that, but I didn't realize her scorn would cut so deep. I thought I'd dealt with all this—I thought that working with people like Laurene and the Fawns was my therapy, that I was healing through them. But I wasn't as healed as I thought I was. I felt that I might be crumbling a little around the edges, and that was scary for me.

To make matters worse, a cousin of mine and her six kids—including seven-year-old triplets—were living with me at the time. My cousin Laurice and her husband had been living a monogamous life outside the FLDS for some time; but recently, her husband had decided to return to polygamy—and of course he wanted the kids. Laurice's mom, my Aunt Noreen, asked me to help Laurice, so I took her in. We put her kids in public school, which made Laurice's husband even angrier.

Laurice had found work in Phoenix, the kids were in school, everything was fine. And then one day she just started freaking out. She asked me if she could borrow my truck to go up to Utah, because a friend of hers was going to cosign on a vehicle for her. I said, "Yeah, fine." So she loaded the kids up and went up to Utah.

She came back late Sunday night and said, "I need to talk to you."

"Where are the kids?"

"They're in Utah."

"What's going on?"

"The kids heard you and Tim talking about how you didn't want us to be here. That you are tired of us."

"What the hell are you talking about?" I was floored.

"Are you saying that my kids are lying?"

"No, Laurice. I just don't know what you're talking about, because I have never said that. Trust me, if I didn't want you in my house you wouldn't be here." I really couldn't imagine what conversation her kids had twisted up to get that meaning out of it.

"Well, I just think we need to go," she said adamantly. "It's been six months. I'll gather my things and be gone soon."

"Laurice, please don't do this," I begged. "You're going to end up losing the kids if you do this."

"Well, that's just something I have to do."

"All right," I said in disgust. "Do what you want."

She took her kids and went back up to her mother's. Later, she called to tell me she had lost custody of her kids. Could I help?

"There's nothing I can do to help you now, Laurice," I explained. "The court has reverted custody to your husband. Until he screws up, there's nothing we can do to get those kids back. It's that simple."

I hadn't seen any of this coming. I was still nursing a deep wound from Maryett's words, and I was devastated. I couldn't seem to bounce back the way I usually did. Worse, I was beginning to lost faith in my ability to truly help people. All I could think was, *Damnit! If they don't want my help then why in the hell am I trying to help them? If I'm not helping anybody, then why am I doing this?*

A black cloud enveloped me. I'm usually a fireball. Now I had no energy, no drive, nothing. I decided it was time for some soul searching and self-examination. I had to ask myself some tough questions that all boiled down to one: *Why am I doing this?*

I probably should have gotten counseling, but I've always done things my own way. I told Tim and the girls I had to take a "sabbatical." I know they were worried about me, but I had to leave— the ringing phones in the middle of the night, the long car drives through the mountains and desert, the cell phone that by now was pretty much glued to my ear, and the burden of responsibility I felt—all of them were just too much to handle right now. I chose to go into hiding and to spend time with my family. We all went to Mexico for a week while I struggled to sort it all through. Many times I said to myself, *That's it. I'm not doing this anymore. I'm done.*

When we came back to Phoenix, I still wasn't back to myself. I met with my friend Donnalee Sarda, who runs Defenders of

Children, an organization that helps abused children. I told her what had happened and why I hadn't been around for a while.

"How are you now?" she asked.

"I think I'm really depressed."

She thought for a minute. "No," she said, "you haven't been depressed. You've been sad. There's a big difference."

She was right. I had been sad. Sad that my family hated me so much they didn't want to speak to me. Sad that no matter what I did, even as successful as I'd been, even with Warren Jeffs publicly humiliated and facing trial, children were still being abused by parents who should have been protecting them and girls were still being married off to polygamous abusers to breed more children. I was sad.

"You have every right to be sad, Flora, don't you think?"

"I guess I do," I said. And right then, I started feeling better.

I went back to work. I hadn't completely snapped out of it—once the sadness comes up, it doesn't just go away in a minute—but I had some of my old energy back. Slowly, I began to feel my way back into the various cases I had been involved with before I left. And of course new ones were coming in all the time. I realized that I didn't have to be angry twenty-four seven to have enough drive to do my work. Feeling sad sometimes was all right too.

On September 7, 2005, jury selection began for Warren Jeffs's trial in St. George, Utah. Before I ran off to Mexico, my plan had been to lead a group of picketers outside the courthouse, demanding justice for all of Jeffs's victims. But I just couldn't muster up the intensity that would drive that kind of action.

I had also planned to sit in on every day of the trial. But the courtrooms in St. George are small, and half the seats had been set aside for Warren's followers. There were only about five seats allotted to the public, which is the classification I would have fallen under. I also knew that every media outlet around the world would be represented there, and they'd all want a sound bite from me. I was tired of giving so many interviews.

If I wanted to see the trial, I could watch most of it on TV, like everybody else. For once in my life, I just tried to stay away from all the hoopla.

The only reason I would have wanted to be in the courtroom now would have been to support Elissa Wall, one of my three hundred plus stepsiblings, and the victim in the case, who was to testify that she had been forced into marriage by Warren Jeffs. Elissa turned out to be an amazing and affecting witness. She said she had been fourteen years old. She had had no idea what sex was or how babies were made. She had known she didn't want to be married. She had begged Uncle Rulon, the Prophet, to get her out of this marriage. But he told her that she "didn't know her own heart," and she was then "forcefully married" to her first cousin, Allen Steed, in a marriage officiated by Warren Jeffs.

Elissa testified about the wedding in a quiet voice shaking with emotion. "[Warren] turned to me and he asked me, Do I take Allen? And I just sat there, with my head hanging."

"Were you crying?" asked the prosecutor. "What kind of tears were they?"

"Fear," said Elissa, with barely controlled emotion, putting long pauses between her words. "The room was completely quiet. And I couldn't say anything. I could not agree to this. Warren looks at me, and he repeated himself. 'Do you take . . . Allen . . .' Excuse me . . . can we take a break?"

As this once-composed twenty-one-year-old woman dissolved into tears, the courtroom was stunned and silent. Later she testified about being raped on her wedding night, when her cousin told her she had to do her duty to him.

"I was sobbing," she said. "And my whole entire body was just shaking, because I was so, so scared. And he didn't say anything. He just laid me on the bed." Afterward, she hemorrhaged for hours.

I was sick to my stomach. I knew this story so well: it was also Ruby's story, almost to the last detail. In fact Elissa and Ruby had been forcibly married to their first cousins at the same age and on the same day. I was so proud of Elissa and what she had been able to do here. I hoped the message would reach inside the walls of lies that surrounded Ruby. I hoped she could hear—and have hope.

A couple of days into the trial, I had a meeting with Brock Belnap, one of the prosecuting attorneys in Warren's trial. We were meeting concerning one of my ongoing cases, but neither of us could get our minds off Warren. I was still feeling emotionally fragile and also so grateful for everything Brock had done. He was the first investigator who ever said to me, "I don't know if I have what's necessary to do this, but I'm going to give it my best shot." Now, I just wanted to tell him how much his effort meant to me personally.

"Brock," I said, "I don't know which way this trial will go—I hope Warren is found guilty. But however it turns out, I just want to say thank you. You're the only one who had the balls to go ahead with this. You've given validation to every single child who's come out of there. Thank you so much for everything you're doing—for trying."

My feelings were raw—that tough exterior I'd worked so hard on over the years was gone. It was a struggle to keep control of myself especially when I looked up at Brock; he had tears in his eyes too.

"Flora," he said, "I want to thank you. If you didn't keep kickin' the crap out of everybody involved in this, we wouldn't be sitting here!"

I had to laugh at that. It was true. I kept pushing and pushing, annoying the hell out of everyone. I just didn't want Warren to get away with this anymore.

Belnap laughed too, but then he got serious. "If it wasn't for you—and everybody being so damn afraid of what you would do to them if they didn't do their jobs—we wouldn't be sitting here having this conversation. I'm telling you, if it wasn't for you, Warren Jeffs would not be here right now."

Those words were powerful. They meant everything to me. It was like sunlight breaking through the clouds. OK, I thought, feeling the sadness lift for the first time in a long time. Maybe I am doing all right after all.

As the trial went on, I steeled myself for the possibility that Warren might be found not guilty. I didn't want to set myself up for disappointment. When the case finally went to the jury, Channel 3 in Phoenix asked me to come down to the station and do a live shoot as soon as the verdict came down. I got the call sooner than I expected. "Flora, they're back. Come on down!"

The jury had deliberated for only sixteen hours over three days. I had exactly forty-five minutes to get down to Channel 3. I hopped in my car and sped to the station. I was sitting in the Channel 3 studios watching what was happening in the court-room on their monitors. When the verdict came back—guilty on both counts of rape—I burst into tears.

I was stunned. I suddenly felt so light that I thought my body would float right across the room. And I felt validated—for myself, for every one of Warren's victims, and for every person who has fled that cult just to face a law enforcement officer or child welfare official who refused to believe the stories of rape, abuse, and forced marriage. With that verdict, every single person who has ever told his or her story of the horrors of polygamy was validated.

After it was all over, Elissa Wall said, "This trial has not been about religion or vendetta. It was simply about child abuse and preventing abuse. The easy thing would have been to do nothing, but I have followed my heart and spoken the truth."

Allen Steed, Elissa's ex-husband, has now been charged with rape. Warren is still facing federal charges, Mohave County charges, and charges from Texas, where photos have surfaced of Warren kissing a girl of twelve on their "wedding" day. He will probably never get out of jail—not alive, anyway. He's told people that he's going to be martyred, just like Joseph Smith. To make sure he stays alive to face further trials, he's being held separately from the general prison population.

Afterward I was filled with the kind of energy I hadn't felt in years. I felt renewed and refreshed, ready to keep fighting for the victims of polygamy. Since then I've had a permanent adrenalin rush. And I've already begun to see how Warren Jeffs's conviction is affecting the lives of the women and children who flee polygamy.

Not too long after the trial was over, I was working to help an ex-wife of William Black. Black grew up in the FLDS and, like Warren Jeffs, became a self-proclaimed prophet. He considers himself an archangel who communicates directly with God. He started his own sect, and a few people from Colorado City followed him to Mexico, where he fled as a fugitive from the law. One of his followers even gave William his wife and children, and it is believed that William has since taken some of those stepdaughters as wives when they were very, very young.

While talking to a sergeant from the St. George Police Department about another case, he mentioned that he had spoken with Black's ex-wife. She had told him that someone was coming to her apartment and peeking through her windows. He said, "Before Warren Jeffs's conviction, I would have dismissed her as another loony. But my instincts told me that I needed to listen to her. That she wasn't crazy."

I said, "I'm going to tell you right now, if she says somebody is peeking into her windows, then somebody is peeking into her windows. She's fragile because of the psychological crap she's been through, but she is not paranoid. You know that William Black was seen around there a couple of months ago . . . I guarantee you, if she thinks somebody's snooping around, he's back up there."

Jeffs's conviction not only saved more women from being taken and passed around like chips in a poker game, it also stopped more children from becoming victims of his twisted sexual abuse. And now I know that it performed another real miracle: it caused a police officer to take a cult refugee seriously.

Just as this book was going into production the biggest polygamy story yet exploded, with the Texas Department of Family and

Protective Services (DFPS) getting an order for a raid on the FLDS compound near Eldorado, Texas, and taking 468 children into protective custody. It is suspected that the call alleging sexual abuse of an underage girl that prompted the raid was actually a hoax, possibly carried out by a thirty-three-year-old African American woman in Colorado named Rosita Swinton.

Perhaps not coincidentally, about a week before the raid I had started getting calls from someone who sounded like a very young girl and who said she was locked in a basement in Colorado City, Arizona. I was working with several members of law enforcement to try to find this girl when the Texas raid occurred. After that raid, the Texas Rangers met with me in Arizona and by maintaining my phone connection with Swinton, they were able to trace the calls and locate the caller. When I was informed by the Rangers that I had been speaking with a black woman in her thirties I was stunned. It did not seem possible.

Two months after the children had been taken into custody, the Texas court of Appeals ruled that the Child Protective Services (CPS) of the DFPS had no jurisdiction to remove the children and ordered that they all be returned, regardless of the rampant sexual abuse discovered in the compound. The CPS appealed, but in a stunning decision the Texas Supreme Court upheld the lower court and returned every child, no matter the evidence of numerous girls as young as thirteen who either were pregnant or had given birth.

The full story of what has happened in Texas will have to be written later, but this decision has done untold damage to the fight for children's civil rights in America. Because of this action, the FLDS has made new friends with many other dangerous hate groups and renewed death threats now abound against any victim with the courage to fight back.

All I can say is we have all suffered worse than the words now being thrown at us. So I ask, "Do you want to dance?"

Epilogue

People always ask me, "After all you've been through, do you believe in God?" Sometimes I tell them this story.

A couple of years ago, I ran into my dad. I suddenly said, "Dad, I want to thank you for molesting me." Of course he just stared at me as if I'd finally lost it completely. But I wasn't thanking him for all the years of being molested, locked up, shunned, and beaten, or for my years of running away, doing drugs, and coming clean. No child should ever have to experience any of that.

I looked him right in the eye. "You educated me about exactly what I need to know to help all these little girls and women who are still being abused in this godforsaken town."

He started to walk away. "Dad, if I didn't understand in my heart and in my gut what these children have been through, and what they were fighting for, I couldn't help them get out and stay out."

"Damn you, Flora," he said.

But I haven't been damned. I haven't been forsaken. Maybe God really has been watching out for me after all.

But if He has, He's sure not the God I grew up with.

So here's how I answer that question about God. Yes, I do believe in a just, loving power. And I know that I'm not afraid to die—and I'm pretty sure now that I'm not going to hell, at least not for running away from Colorado City.

Am I perfect? No. Is anybody? No one I've met! I just know that people—whoever they are, whatever they've suffered, and whatever they've done—need to believe in themselves, in who and what they are, and know that they have the right to be safe and secure and happy.

Pain, abuse, and fear are not a part of *my* God's world.

Notes

Part One

1. *FLDS Priesthood History for 5th–8th Grade Students, Taught by Warren Jeffs, Alta Academy (Sandy, Utah)*, Tape #2, October 31, 1995, Subject: Work for the Dead. Retrieved February 13, 2008, from http://www.childpro.org.

Part Two

1. *FLDS Priesthood History for 3rd–8th Grade Students, Taught by Warren Jeffs, Alta Academy (Sandy, Utah)*, Tape #36, April 2, 1996, Subject: Reasons for the Apostasy. Retrieved February 13, 2008, from http://www.childpro.org.

Chapter Fifteen

1. Tom Zoellner, "Rulon Jeffs: Patriarch, President, Prophet for Polygamy," *Salt Lake City Tribune*, June 28, 1998.
2. Greg Burton, "Utah Remains Haven for Older Men Seeking Teen Brides," *Salt Lake City Tribune*. December 14, 1997, p. A1.

Chapter Sixteen

1. Helen, Thorpe, "Rescuing America's Child Brides," *Marie Claire*, March 1, 2002, pp. 149–154.

2. Jon Krakauer, *Under the Banner of Heaven* (New York: Doubleday, 2003), p. 50.

Chapter Eighteen

1. Nick Madigan, "Leader of Polygamous Sect Faces Rebellion," *New York Times*, January 27, 2004.

Chapter Twenty

1. The belief in blood atonement doctrine has been handed down through generations and was openly preached through the years. Joseph Fielding Smith, the tenth Mormon prophet and president, wrote, "Man may commit certain grievous sins—according to his light and knowledge—that will place him beyond the reach of the atoning blood of Christ. If then he would be saved, he must make sacrifice of his own life to atone—so far as the power lies—for that sin, for the blood of Christ alone under certain circumstances will not avail. . . ." Joseph Smith taught that there were certain sins so grievous that man may commit, that they will place the transgressors beyond the power of the atonement of Christ. If these offenses are committed, then the blood of Christ will not cleanse them from their sins even though they repent. Therefore their only hope is to have their own blood shed to atone, as far as possible, in their behalf. Joseph Fielding Smith, *Doctrines of Salvation*, Vol. 1. (Salt Lake City, Utah: Bookcraft, n.d.), pp. 135–138.

2. John Dougherty, "Double Exposure," *Phoenix New Times*, December 25, 2003, retrieved March 25, 2008, from http://www.phoenixnew times.com/2003–12–25/news/double-exposure.

3. John MacCormack, "Some Fear Polygamists' Story Will End in Eldorado," *San Antonio Express-News*, USA, February 2, 2005.

4. Judy Nichols, "Wives Suing to Bring End to Abuse Under Polygamy," *Arizona Republic*, October 15, 2003.

5. "Jeffs Dedicates FLDS Temple Site at YFZ Ranch, Jon Krakauer Watches Ceremony from Overhead," *The Eldorado Success*, January 6, 2005, retrieved August 8, 2008, from http://www.myeldorado.net/ YFZ%20Pages/YFZ010605.html.

Part Four

1. Mike Watkiss, "Confessions of an Ambulance Chaser—The Flora and the Fauna of an Insurgency—Women of the Revolution," November 11, 2007, retrieved March 23, 2008, from http://www.azfamily. beloblog.com/3tvTalks/2007/11/confessions_of_an_ambulance_ch_ 11.html#more.

About the Authors

Flora Jessop, often called the Martin Luther King of the anti-polygamy movement, was born into the Fundamentalist Church of Jesus Christ of Latter Day Saints (FLDS) in Colorado City, Arizona. At the age of sixteen, she escaped the oppressive cult after being forced to marry her older cousin.

Flora now lives in Phoenix with her second husband and their two daughters and is a relentless crusader for rights of the victims of polygamy. She has devoted her life and resources to helping others escape the tyrannical grasp of the FLDS.

Paul T. Brown is a best-selling author and nationally acclaimed wildlife photographer. Other books by Paul Brown include *Escape in Iraq: The Thomas Hamill Story, Conserving Wild America, Paul Brown's Wild Visions,* and *Freedom Matters.*

To learn more about Paul's work, visit http://www.trueexposures.com or call 800-323-3398.

Index